THE ART OF
RAISING
A PUPPY

Also by the Monks of New Skete

THE MONKS OF NEW SKETE

THE ART OF

RAISING

A PUPPY

COMPLETELY REVISED AND UPDATED

Little, Brown and Company

NEW YORK   BOSTON   LONDON

Little, Brown and Company
Hachette Book Group
1290 Avenue of the Americas, New York, NY 10104
www.hachettebookgroup.com

First edition published by Little, Brown and Company, March 1991
Second edition, June 2011

Photographs by The Monks of New Skete

Excerpts from "East Coker" and "Little Gidding" in *Four Quartets,* copyright 1943 by T. S. Eliot and renewed 1971 by Esmé Valerie Eliot. Reprinted by permission of Houghton Mifflin Harcourt.

Little, Brown and Company is a division of Hachette Book Group, Inc. The Little, Brown name and logo are trademarks of Hachette Book Group, Inc.

The publisher is not responsible for websites (or their content) that are not owned by the publisher.

Library of Congress Cataloging-in-Publication Data

Monks of New Skete.
 The art of raising a puppy / the Monks of New Skete. — 2nd ed.
  p. cm.
 ISBN 978-0-316-08327-0
 1. Puppies. 2. Puppies — Training. I. Title.
 SF426.M65 2011
 636.7'07 — dc22   2011002744

10 9

RRD-C

Printed in the United States of America

The loneliness and solitude of man can be dispersed by spiritual inter-course, but man is of the earth too, and Nature lives in him and holds him fast. She is his mother, and just as in all young things that stray from home there is a yearning after associations which recall the color and the atmosphere of the old home now lost, so does the solitary man seek Nature, a life in Nature, Nature's answer, the animal that understands his voice and can respond to it.

         —*F. J. J. Buytendijk*, The Mind of the Dog

There is a word from the time of the cathedrals: agape, *an expression of intense spiritual affinity with the mystery that is "to be sharing life with another life." Agape is love, and it can mean "the love of another for the sake of God." More broadly and essentially it is a humble, impassioned embrace of something outside the self, in the name of that which we refer to as* God, *but which also includes the self and* is God. *We are clearly indebted as a species to the play of our intelligence; we trust our future to it; but we do not know whether intelligence is reason or whether intelligence is this desire to embrace and be embraced in the pattern that both theologians and physicists call God. Whether intelligence, in other words, is love.*

         —*Barry Lopez*, Arctic Dreams: Imagination
             and Desire in a Northern Landscape

Abba Xanthias said, "A dog is better than I am, for he has love and does not judge."

         —The Sayings of the Desert Fathers

Contents

THE ART OF
RAISING
A PUPPY

Introduction

Monasteries are not as otherworldly as you might imagine. If they appear secluded and removed from the mainstream of society's activity, it is only because they attempt to create a climate that fosters an authentic engagement with life at its most profound and human level, something often lost amid the noise and distraction of today's world. When we are quiet enough, freed from all our inner noise and chatter, we can see with new respect the natural beauty and wisdom of the world around us and appreciate our ties to it. Such perceptive silence opens up our lives to healthy reverence and awe for all things; it creates a capacity for acceptance that is both humanizing and life-giving.

So what does all of this have to do with raising a puppy? A great deal, we believe. Our monastery is set in a quiet, rural area in upper New York State. For more than forty years, as part of an effort to support ourselves, we have been actively involved in the breeding and raising of German shepherd dogs. We have also operated a training program that is open to dogs of all breeds. During this time we have worked closely with numerous professional breeders, trainers, and veterinarians to deepen our understanding of all facets of canine care.

We have learned that our monastic environment offers us a unique perspective. Here we are forced to reexamine our attitudes about everything, including dogs. We are constantly challenged to become more open to the language dogs use to communicate with us. This experience confirms our deepest intuitions about the relationship of human beings not only with their dogs but with every aspect of the world in which they live.

In our book *How to Be Your Dog's Best Friend*, we took what we had learned about dog behavior and training and made it available to other people and their dogs in the varied and diverse environments in which they live. We hoped to foster in our readers a more realistic understanding of their dogs and an increased awareness of the benefits of canine companionship. Drawing on our own experience here at New Skete, we described how dog training actually goes far beyond the elementary instruction of basic obedience commands; it must encompass a whole new attitude and lifestyle with your dog. It must touch on the levels of a dog's own life that have often been ignored. This is why we explored the broader issue of companionship itself.

We still firmly believe in this approach, and the years since the publication of our first book have deepened our understanding and commitment to the principles we discussed there. We continue to be energetically involved in the breeding of healthier, sounder German shepherds, as well as in working with owners of many breeds on a training basis. These are demanding tasks, and the fact that we are a close-knit community permits us to pay careful attention to these concerns and learn from them.

But we still see that, elsewhere, ignorance on a vast scale continues to make dogs the victims of human thoughtlessness and abuse. As anyone seriously involved in the field knows, working with dogs and their owners is a bittersweet experience. It regularly forces us to witness the collision of philosophy with reality. The remarkable little puppy so filled with the capacity for life and companionship one week can easily become an incontinent, destructive, and hyperactive annoyance the next. We have seen this happen repeatedly. Poor management all too often leads to irritating or even dangerous behavior problems that quickly sever the human-dog bond before it ever has the chance to develop. While most of the dogs we deal with are intelligent, happy, and well-adjusted, some are not. Every day we encounter dogs who have serious behavior problems and for whom obedience training has been described as the "last chance." Usually they clearly manifest signs of a bad start in life: poor breeding, limited handling and socialization as puppies, and lack of owner understanding concerning the importance of proper diet, exercise, discipline, and obedience training. As we work with these cases, we cannot help being convinced that most of these dogs, had they been treated more carefully and intelligently as puppies, would never have developed the problems that now beset them and their owners.

If we look honestly at the way many people manage their dogs today, we are faced with a staggering reflection of irresponsibility and lack of compassion. It is difficult to refer to a dog as "man's best friend" when more than six million unwanted adult dogs and puppies are euthanized every year. We are not speaking here of the humane killing of animals done out of a sense of responsible stewardship but of the massive human negligence that leads to euthanasia.

For those who doubt the serious implications of this situation, a trip to the local animal shelter can be a real eye-opener. We recall one client who dismissed our advice about spaying her female shepherd, explaining she felt it was important for her children to have the experience of seeing puppies born. When we asked her how she intended to care for and give homes to the puppies, she responded that she really had not thought about it at all and that she would probably leave them at the local humane society when it was time for them to be weaned. We then asked her what value such an experience would have if the principal lesson her children would learn is that puppies are cute little playthings who, when sufficiently used, may then be conveniently disposed of. Fortunately, our questioning convinced her of her faulty thinking, and she left with a new respect for the implications of bringing puppies into the world.

In our view, the dog is not a possession, a personal commodity to be used solely for our own amusement or ego gratification. Rather, he is a living, autonomous yet highly social pack-oriented creature who has an amazing capacity for companionship and love. Your role in determining your connection with your own dog is a vital one. Capacity is precisely that — a natural potential. A good relationship with your dog can be established only if there is an enlightened commitment to working with his proven needs, instincts, behavior patterns, and, yes, capacities.

We know numerous trainers and animal behaviorists whose dedication and talents have helped many problem dogs change their behavior, enabling them to live happy and safe lives with their owners. Often in such cases owners find themselves changed as well. Nevertheless, it makes sense to avert behavioral problems before they begin. We have found that untangling these issues is a long and difficult process, requiring lots of time and energy and often a large financial investment. When faced with this prospect, many owners choose simply to give up their dog or else take the risk of trying to control the problem without precise and intensive retraining. Fortunate indeed is the problem dog whose owner goes the extra mile in trying to solve his particular issues.

The key to developing a healthy, rewarding relationship with your dog lies in getting off to a good start in puppyhood. There is an art to raising a puppy that is not solely the domain of the naturally gifted. It can be acquired by any responsible owner; what is needed is a desire for true companionship, an openness to learning, and a willingness to invest time and energy in caring for and training the puppy. The more informed you are on the background, development, and training of your pup, the more you will approach him with the patience and understanding necessary for an enjoyable and rewarding relationship.

That is why we originally wrote this book and why we are grateful for the opportunity to bring out this new twentieth-anniversary edition. We remain passionate about puppy-rearing issues, and while there have been positive strides made over the past two decades, there is still plenty of ignorance. Puppy mills continue to be big business, and often new dog owners have very romantic notions of what adopting a puppy involves. Happily, within the dog-training profession there have been new insights that we believe will make raising and training a puppy a more successful and enjoyable experience. We have continued to learn over the years, and we feel privileged to share with our readers the ways in which our understanding has grown. Our hope is to provide an even clearer guide to raising a puppy that will sensitize and educate owners to the many possibilities present with their new or expected companion. We have found that when owners adopt their new puppy, they are rarely aware of just how much development and growth has already taken place in his life. They have only the most general idea of where he came from and lack a context from which to appreciate his true uniqueness. When owners begin to understand the early developmental stages of a puppy's life, they cultivate a sense of responsibility that is more clearly in keeping with the nature of a human-dog relationship. Relating in a healthy way with their pup, owners will change as their puppy changes; they will grow as their puppy grows. The bond becomes enriching and genuinely transforming.

In this book we will bring you into our world here at New Skete, using our experience as the lens through which you may broaden your understanding of your pup. By taking you through the birthing process and the critical early stages of a puppy's development, we will show you how scientific knowledge is an integral part of the practical world of breeding and caring for a puppy. This background will help you understand the experiences your pup has had before arriving in your home. Later we will look at the practical aspects of adopting a puppy, including how to evaluate your own needs, choose the right breed, and prepare and train your pup. The stage will then be set for a balanced, lasting relationship between you and your best friend.

I

Monk as Midwife

We are going on a walk with one of the monks and his monastery shepherd, a daily, routine occurrence here that now has special significance. It is the fifty-ninth day of Anka's pregnancy. On this crystal clear March afternoon, the sun lights up the ordinarily dark woods surrounding the monastery. Anka has been restless all day. Taking her into the woods for a brief walk provides a promise of marvels to come, the first link in an intricate chain of events leading up to her labor. Now nature conspires to display signs hinting that gestation is nearing full term. It is important for the monk to notice these, for although the average span of gestation is sixty-three days, it is not unusual for a shepherd to begin labor as early as the fifty-eighth day after her first breeding. Throughout this time, Anka's body has been talking to her in new and different ways, and on this walk, its natural eloquence becomes an open invitation for us to witness the first promptings of new life.

As she runs along the trail, her swollen abdomen gently sways from side to side, and her wagging tail allows us a glimpse of an overly enlarged vulva. From a few feet ahead of us on the path, she repeatedly looks back as if for reassurance, carefully avoiding the remnant patches of snow that have not yet thawed. The woods are as restless as Anka. The wind sweeps through the trees, gently ushering her back and forth along the trail. Her quick, clipped panting is absorbed in the quiet commotion. Even the trees sense something is up.

Usually on such walks Anka is beside herself with curiosity. From the time she leaves with her monk-guardian, she immerses herself in a feast of scents, darting from moss-covered tree stumps to low-lying wild junipers to old stone hedgerows, through which heaven knows

Anka leads us into the woods on the fifty-ninth day of her pregnancy.

how many animals of the woods have passed. She stops frequently to listen, then quietly moves forward and glides over the leaves that cover the path, occasionally startling a group of pheasants or wild turkeys, which then take to the air in a blaze of chaos. With intense delight she pursues, leaping in short bursts of energy.

Nevertheless, at the voice of her guardian, she quickly gives up the chase. This comes from plenty of training and a quality of bonding that overrides her prey instinct. A simple utterance of her name draws her back to the trail, and she is soon preoccupied with wrestling a stick from a dead tree, eagerly providing herself with something to play with for the remainder of the walk.

Today, however, is different.

Anka seems to be lost in herself in a very unusual way. Today, she lacks any of the casual playfulness so naturally present on ordinary walks. She displays impatience, constant circular pacing, rounded eyes, and a nervous, panting tongue. She stops only to mark, a frequent need now that there is constant uterine pressure on her bladder. As she reaches a spring-fed pond, she pauses momentarily to drink and then is off again, glancing quickly at the small shrubs that line the path.

Anka looks for a nesting place under the cover of a pine tree.

Something clicks.

Suddenly bolting ahead, she disappears around a group of pines. As we near the trees, we hear frantic pawing beneath a large, low-hanging evergreen. The branches move slightly, and dead leaves, pine needles, and dirt come flying out from beneath the tree, where Anka is improvising a nest. In her instinctively maternal way, she is preparing a natural den, a kind of cave. What makes this behavior remarkable is that none of it has been taught. Anka is a maiden bitch, only two years of age the week before. She is simply responding to a deep, instinctual knowing.

Were this den in the wild, it would have been more carefully planned. In studies of wolves, researchers have often found excavated dens in elevated areas such as cut banks or vacated caves — sites that provide a clear frontal view of the surrounding area. In fact, it is not uncommon for wolves to remodel vacant fox dens or even abandoned beaver lodges. The preferred soil is dry and sandy. Most dens are located near rivers, lakes, springs, or other sources of water, owing to the mother's constant need for hydration. Usually the entrance hole is one to two feet in diameter and linked to an inner chamber by an upwardly sloping tunnel, up to ten feet in length. Often the female wolf will stay close to the site a full three weeks before she is due.

All of this is evoked by Anka's digging.

As we pause to observe her for some time, she finally settles comfortably on her side in what is now a smooth, slightly depressed circle. Barely visible from where we stand, she peeks out from beneath the branches. Her look, alert and expectant, indicates that she is rather pleased with herself. It is clear, however, that all of this is merely preliminary, for there have been no uterine contractions, no intense licking of the vaginal folds, no rapid lowering of her body temperature — the sure signs of the onset of labor. Nonetheless, it is obvious that the process is moving irrevocably toward the final stages of gestation and birth. Just before the walk, her temperature had fallen to 100.5°F, a sign that labor is still a little while away. At the beginning of labor, her body temperature will drop at least another full degree, to between 98 and 99.5, though the temperature can fluctuate up and down several days prior to the actual birth. Still, paying attention to Anka's state of mind gives us solid clues that labor is near. We can see that she is aware of the mystery that is occurring within her. Responding to all sorts of natural cues, Anka is consenting to it, allowing it to culminate in its own time. Now she is ready to go back to the puppy kennel.

Here at New Skete, we have reserved a separate building for the whelping and raising of litters. There are six individual whelping rooms — this helps us to maintain a controlled environment that is clean, dry, and protected. Over the past week, Anka has been left for short periods each day in her ten-foot-square whelping room, allowing her to become familiar and relaxed within it. It is important that she feel at ease and secure in the room, enabling her to focus entirely on the whelping. At New Skete, we use a plastic wading pool for the nest because it is durable and easy to clean, and has high sides that keep the pups safely confined.

Returning from the walk, Anka drinks more water and then climbs into the whelping nest and relaxes atop several layers of newspaper. Panting heavily and stretching out so that her abdomen is exposed, she manages to rest for a time. Then we offer her a bowl of food.

Ordinarily, from twelve to twenty-four hours prior to whelping, dogs are not inclined to eat. Anka, however, has never been known to spurn a meal, even early on in pregnancy when this would have been

Anka rests on the cool ground behind some shrubs.

expected. She still has a voracious appetite and gulps down the food without hesitation.

It is now late at night. As is our practice here in the monastery, Anka spends the evening in the room of the monk responsible for her. Before lights-out, her temperature was 99.4, and her panting was becoming increasingly labored. We spread old bedsheets on the floor in case she began to whelp while her guardian was still asleep.

When a monk is expecting the whelping to start in the middle of the night, he sets his alarm at regular intervals to check for the beginning of labor. This time it is hard to sleep anyway because of Anka's increased restlessness. By 1:30 a.m. her breathing has become a wildfire panting, her body tied rhythmically to this breathing, and she is quivering incessantly as if she is chilled. Now she licks her vulva ever more frequently, methodically preparing the birth canal by cleansing it. Getting up, she paws at the sheets she is lying on and pulls them into a nest. Then, quite suddenly, her face becomes rigid and her breathing stops. She announces her first contraction with a slight moan, her tail arching out behind her. As her breathing begins again, a second contraction follows momentarily, and then a third. Panting now resumes with its previous intensity as Anka takes a slight rest.

Over the years, we have found that whelping often develops like this, in the middle of the night, so when it is obvious that labor has finally begun, the monk simply takes the hour in stride as he goes about the last-minute preparations. Anka is understandably restless during this brief wait, pacing around as if she has to use the kennel run. This behavior is quite common, for the sensation of a puppy entering the birth canal seems very similar to that of a bowel movement. When offered the chance to use the run, however, Anka makes it immediately clear that this is not what she wants. All she wants is to have her puppies. She has no sympathy for the fact that it is 1:30 in the morning.

On the short walk from the monastery to the puppy kennel, the only light comes from the stars, but Anka leads the way. With a certain resoluteness, she knows what to do, even though she is a maiden bitch. Once in her room she makes a beeline for the whelping nest and begins pawing at the papers in short, reflexive spasms of energy, the beginning of the birth ritual. Holding the newspaper on the floor of the nest with her paws, she starts to shred it violently with her mouth and then to moan and circle. Finally settling down, Anka once again begins to lick her vulva. Four sustained contractions quickly follow. As she pushes, her lips purse and her ears are erect and held back ever so slightly, as if she is listening to her body. She then turns her head down to her tail and begins licking the paper. There, beneath her tail, is the final sign: a puddle of liquid. She has broken her water—that is, discharged her uterine liquid. Now the vigil begins in earnest, and the first pup can be expected within the hour. Anka is still lying against the side of the whelping nest but pants more gently and almost fully closes her eyes. It is as if she is gearing herself up for the final thrust.

Here at the monastery it is typically our practice to have the mother's guardian be the attending monk, a presence intended to quietly reassure and assist her during the whelping. His responsibility is to be on hand, to watch as the whelping takes place, aiding where needed, and to see that things run as smoothly as possible. Should complications

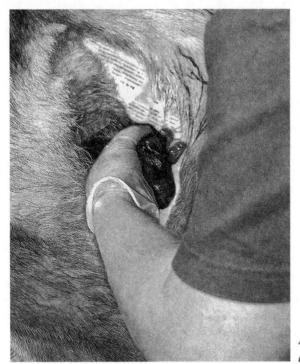

Anka gives birth to a puppy.

develop, his immediate response may be very important in determining whether a puppy will live.

After resting a half hour, Anka finally stirs and starts scratching at the newsprint abruptly; her back humps and her tail arches, causing her to squat low in the nest as if she is pressing herself together. A long, drawn-out contraction follows, and suddenly the amniotic sac begins to push through the vulva. As the sac emerges gradually, like a gigantic blob of ink, the light from the heat lamp above the whelping nest allows a glimpse of two silhouetted front paws reaching forward within the sac. As Anka pushes courageously, she lets out a scream that can be described only as primordial, her eyes like saucers as she is initiated mercilessly into motherhood.

She quickly begins to lick her vulva as if to help the rest of the sac out. As she does so, the amniotic membrane surrounding the pup is ruptured, and with it a stream of fluid and blood drains to the floor. In the midst of this is a dark, wriggling puppy. Anka immediately consumes the placenta and begins to lick the puppy, tentatively at first, but then quickly and vigorously. While she does this, the attending monk

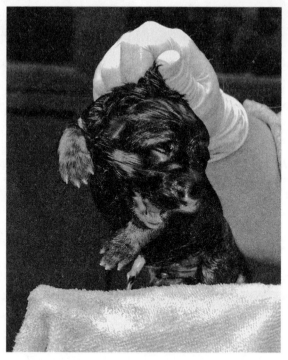

*The newborn pup lets
out a loud squeal.*

cuts the umbilical cord and then uses a rubber bulb syringe to draw
fluid from the puppy's throat. A few quick squeezes clear the breathing
passage, and the pup lets out his first gasps and wails, struggling as if
annoyed by the gentle toweling that removes the amniotic fluid from
his warm body. The scene reveals a natural harmony and coordination:
Anka fully trusting her helper, and the monk respectful of Anka's
duties as well.

As soon as the pup is dried off, he is weighed on a scale—he writhes
back and forth on the cool surface. Anka's first puppy is a large male by
our standards, a pound and a half, and when he is placed on the floor of
the nest, he lifts his head up, waving it from side to side, and immediately crawls toward Anka, who is lying on the opposite end of the nest.
She encourages him by licking him and nudging him forward. There is
no hesitation in the pup's movement as he stubbornly and insistently
heads for the middle of Anka's body, somehow unmistakably aware of
where the nipples are. This first pup has a remarkable determination to
reach the teat. When puppies are born they are unable to see or hear,
senses that will develop in the first weeks of life; the fact that smell and

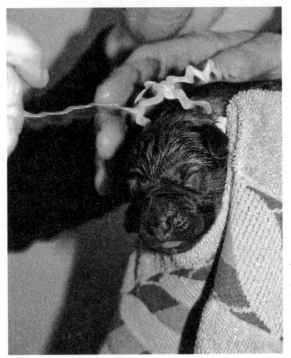

*After the newborn
pup is dried off with a
towel, we tie a string
of colored rickrack
around his neck to
identify him.*

touch are their only tools at birth makes the movement all the more amazing.

Continuing on, the pup forges straight to the rear teats — those with the most ample supply of milk — and he fastens himself on to one of them. The head bobs back and forth rhythmically as the pup pushes his paws against the teat in harmony with his suckling, a kneading motion that stimulates the flow of milk. His rear legs simultaneously thrust against the floor as if to propel him deeper into the breast. Anka continues to clean the pup periodically, then relaxes with a deep sigh, grateful that the ordeal is over.

She soon learns that it has only just begun.

Some forty minutes after the birth of the first male, a resting Anka is suddenly roused and begins turning in the nest and scratching the floor again. Her pup, now with a bright-orange rickrack collar around his neck, is a sheen of black as he sleeps quietly. For the puppy's safety during the next delivery, the attending monk places him in a small cardboard box with a heating pad that is wrapped in a towel. It is necessary to keep the puppy very warm, for when he is apart from the mother, he has no capacity to regulate his own body temperature. At birth neonates have a body temperature of 94 to 96°F. This climbs to a normal 101 to 102 over the next two weeks. For the time being, the heating pad will keep him warm and content while Anka delivers her next pup.

As she passes through a similar chain of events for this second puppy, there is already a marked difference in Anka. It is clear that she now understands what is happening. There is very little moaning, only at the end of contractions, and as her face sets, her look of determination is sober and resolute. Proper exercise during her pregnancy has given her good muscle tone, and the steady contractions are strong and sure. Quickly, with a final quivering that ripples through the length of her body, she passes the second puppy while lying down. This one comes out gently, with the placenta attached to the umbilical cord. As the amniotic sac containing the puppy lies momentarily on the floor, we clearly see the pup floating inside and moving his paws in a vigorous, thrashing motion. Anka quickly bursts the sac and cleans the pup off while he squirms around on the newspaper. After biting down on the umbilicus until it is only about an inch and a half long, Anka picks up the puppy in her mouth and begins to parade around the nest in a circular motion. This precipitates a loud, high wail from the puppy, which seems to satisfy Anka. As she places him gently back on the floor, he twists and turns, and she continues to lick him off. A bit smaller than the first, the puppy instinctively knows where to go, but his movement is slower, and it takes Anka more licking and nuzzling to encourage him along. The first pup is now placed back in the whelping nest to join his newborn brother, and both nurse contentedly on a fatigued mother. For several moments Anka scrupulously cleans the puppies off, then finally heaves a long sigh and relaxes for the next episode.

Night passes into dawn. In the ensuing deliveries, Anka follows the same pattern, with one exception. It is this exception that brings a sobering edge to the night of wonder. Anka has a difficult time passing the fourth pup; for a long while her numerous contractions yield nothing. Finally, when the pup does come out, all attempts to revive her are without effect. She is stillborn — completely developed but with lungs full of fluid. As seconds pass, we try not to lose hope; it is not unknown for a pup to begin breathing after several minutes. We repeatedly aspi-

Anka continues licking and cleaning the newborn pups.

rate fluid from her lungs and manipulate her back and forth in our hands. Dopram, a stimulant helpful in reviving slow-starting puppies, is then given under the tongue. Finally air is blown down the lungs, but in vain. The pup does not move. Anka looks on at the attempts with grave concern, clearly aware that something is wrong. Whimpering as the pup is kept away from her, she paces back and forth impatiently in the nest, demanding something that cannot be given. Quickly the pup is taken from the room, and Anka retreats back to the remaining three, burying her disappointment in scrupulous attention to their needs. We hope that this reaction is linked to a quick forgetting.

Meanwhile, holding a cold and lifeless pup outside the room, we are vividly confronted with the radical difference between life and death. The body is inert and limp. A white tongue sticks out the side of her mouth. There is no potential, no vibrancy, nothing. It is a sad note amid a joyful chorus of life.

As the hours slide by, Anka takes her time delivering the final pups. There will be two more—alive, happily. The long pauses between puppies invariably become valuable moments of reflection, important if we seek to appreciate the beauty of what is happening. During the actual birth, events take place so quickly that we cannot fully fathom the mystery that is occurring. Instead, we gain an in-depth understanding of this night through the whelping experience as a whole. Unlike in human birth, which usually provides us with only a single delivery, here we watch birth occur again and again, giving us the opportunity to absorb the incredible marvel of it. Similarly we become aware in equal measure of the drastic change that has taken place in Anka, one that is as real as the pups who nurse at her side. It, too, is a birth of sorts, a birth into motherhood, and the event is written all over her. As the puppies nurse, Anka is radiant; her clear eyes glow, and she grins in quiet fulfillment. Mother and pups bring to one another a completion beyond shallow sentimentality.

By 10:30 a.m. Anka is resting quietly in her nest with five healthy puppies close by her side. Each pup has a different colored rickrack collar for identification purposes. By using wide rickrack for male puppies and narrow for females, we can quickly recognize pups at a glance. This will be particularly important later on, when we begin making behavioral and structural notes about the litter. As the puppies sleep, we can see quite clearly that there are three males and two females. Huddled close together, they sleep very restlessly; they twitch and jerk continually. This normal phenomenon is known as *activated sleep*, which is linked to the development of the pups' neuromuscular systems. Healthy pups are never still for an extended time while they rest.

After her sixth puppy arrived, at 8:30 a.m., we knew that Anka had finished. The previous week our veterinarian had x-rayed her to determine how many puppies she was carrying, and the six fetuses were clearly visible. Still, just to be sure, we thoroughly palpated her uterus to confirm that she was now empty. Anka's breathing was relaxed as she stretched out on her side, exhausted, to allow the pups to nurse. When we see that whelping is finished, we usually give the mother an injection of oxytocin, a hormone that stimulates passage of any retained afterbirth. We then disinfect the whelping area and place fresh papers in the nest, after which we clean the mother by rinsing her off in a tub of warm water. She is then thoroughly dried and offered a bowl of food, which, in this case, Anka devoured.

Anka nurses her full litter at the end of whelping.

The conclusion of the whelping is quiet — a peaceful aftermath to the whole process of birth. The only sound is the occasional mewing of the pups. After the remaining chores are complete, Anka is left alone with her litter. Her guardian, a tired midwife, retires for some much-needed sleep. Others will check in on Anka periodically throughout the morning and afternoon to make sure that all is well.

2

The Mystery of Development

We do justice to a relationship with a dog when we honor it as it is—a dog, a creature who, for all we may understand about it, is still fraught with mystery.

—I & Dog

A puppy's life clearly displays what characterizes the whole of life: the mystery of development. The entire universe, it seems, is in a continuous process of growth that extends from before the first moments of each individual existence to the end of life and beyond. Nothing is excluded from this movement, though our own consciousness of its breadth can be dulled by the chaotic pace of modern living. Too often we take this journey for granted, carelessly letting it pass unacknowledged. With our busy lives, we can easily grow insensitive to the basic wonder of life, leaving us spiritually impoverished and unhappy. This is perhaps why animals (particularly our dogs) are so important to us and why we benefit from their companionship: they root us in life.

Part of the joy in raising a puppy is the very concrete way it puts us in touch with the process of existence and the natural world around us. Watching the pup grow takes us outside ourselves and helps reestablish our own capacity for appreciation and wonder. But even more than this, we believe that paying attention to how a puppy matures is important for his health and vitality. Studies have shown conclusively that the first sixteen weeks of a dog's life are significant in determining his later behavior as an adult. Negligence by a breeder or new owner during this time can scar a puppy for life. Thus, if you hope to raise a puppy who will be a trusted companion and friend for the next ten to fifteen years, the best foundation you can lay for yourself and your dog is to understand thoroughly how he grows during this time of early change and development. In this way you will be able to provide every available aid to help him grow to his potential.

A Miniature Adult?

A while ago we were speaking with a gentleman who had come to us for help with his rambunctious three-and-a-half-month-old golden retriever puppy. As we sat talking about his difficulties in adjusting to his new pup, the conversation kept returning to his former golden, a calm, well-trained dog who had died several months earlier at the age of twelve. The man's eyes filled with tears as he recalled this dog, explaining how he had obtained her at seven months and how quickly she had picked up house-training, learned her obedience exercises, and adapted to the rhythm of his daily routine. Then he pointed to his new pup, Argus, now wildly jumping up for attention at his side and nipping at his hands. Without trying to hide his frustration, he launched into a detailed account of the trials of the first month and a half, the disappointments and irritations he had experienced, and his growing fear that Argus was simply a deficient representative of the breed. He was ready to give up.

As we listened to the man, it became clear that he was overlooking a very important point. All of the problems that he was having with Argus were being measured against the stability and maturity of his first dog, one he had obtained after a good deal of her development had already taken place. In fact, the pup who was now giving him so much trouble appeared to us to be a normal, energetic dog who was simply being mismanaged and misunderstood. When we asked the owner about the circumstances in which he obtained the first dog, he replied that she was sold to him by a man whose sudden job transfer had required that he and his family move to Europe. Regrettably, they were unable to take the puppy with them. But from our client's description it was clear that the family had been very conscientious in raising their puppy, providing a sound basis for the relationship that had then developed with this man. When we pointed this out, he was surprised. He had assumed that she was simply a "good dog." Not having shared with this first golden retriever the initial months of growth so critical to adult behavior, he did not appreciate how dynamic an organism a young puppy is. As a result, he was now transferring a mistaken set of expectations onto Argus based on what would be normal for an older, properly socialized dog. He was treating Argus as a miniature adult instead of as a fourteen-week-old puppy.

The Development of Individuality

It is not uncommon for puppy owners to have misconceptions about early growth. Because they have not had a breeder's experience in observing young puppies' development, they usually have only a vague grasp of how the process occurs, which can lead to the type of misunderstanding displayed by Argus's owner. To help prepare yourself for the proper reception and intelligent raising of a new puppy, you must take the time to examine the growth process in detail, thus gaining some necessary insight into an otherwise obscure period.

The birth of a litter signals a new opportunity to observe ever more deeply a remarkable series of events — those moments that mark the passage of a totally dependent puppy into a fully mature dog, capable of true companionship. If you have the good fortune of such companionship, you will no doubt understand how life-enhancing it is. What you may not realize, however, is that the seeds of your dog's capacity for relationship are planted very early in his life, well before he has been placed in your home. The development of a puppy is not an automatic process that occurs precisely the same way in each dog. Rather, it is a dynamic unfolding of life that, while following general patterns, reflects the subtle and ultimately mysterious interaction of three factors: type of breed, genetic makeup, and environmental influences. The results of this blending produce a wide variety of canine personalities. This is why raising puppies defies routine: each puppy is unique; each is an individual.

This insight is at the heart of what has become one of the most authoritative studies on dog behavior, *Genetics and the Social Behavior of the Dog,* by John L. Fuller and John Paul Scott. When these men began their research in Bar Harbor, Maine, on the effects of heredity on human behavior, they chose the dog as the subject of their work precisely because, like human beings, dogs show a high level of individuality. The researchers believed that by studying the parallel development of dogs they could make valuable observations for child rearing, thus allowing for psychologically better-adjusted, healthier members of society. Their study helped distinguish the important relationships among genetics, early experience, and adult behavior. In the process, it illuminated how a dog becomes an individual, unique creature, and provided a more comprehensive and accurate view of canine behavior than had existed previously.

The complete results of the research, exhaustive and quite technical, go well beyond the scope of this book. Yet one finding in particular is important to single out because of its profound effect on our understanding of development and on the way conscientious breeders raise their puppies. It also provides a helpful framework in understanding how a pup grows. Over the course of the seventeen-year study, Scott and Fuller followed in detail the development of litter after litter of pups. In analyzing their data, they discovered that puppies pass through four clearly identifiable stages on the way to their full adult personalities. Each of these periods begins with natural changes in the pups' social relationships, identified by the way the puppies relate to their environment. Taking into account the slight variations present from individual to individual, Scott and Fuller noted the following stages: the *neonatal period*, from birth until the opening of the eyes at about thirteen days; the *transitional period*, from the time the eyes open until the opening of the ears at twenty days; the *socialization period*, which extends from approximately three to twelve weeks; and the *juvenile period*, lasting from this point until sexual maturity, which may occur from six months to a year or more.

In addition, in trying to determine why some dogs matured into happy, sociable pets while others did not, the researchers found that the timing of early experiences played a vital role in the development and shaping of behavior. Events that occurred at a certain stage of a puppy's life affected his development more than if the same incidents had happened at other times. This suggested to Scott and Fuller the presence of critical periods—special times when "a small amount of experience will produce a great effect on later behavior." Though somewhat ambiguous as to precisely how many of these periods there are, the researchers singled out the period between three and twelve weeks as the most important, the "critical period of socialization," when a puppy has certain experiences that exert the maximum influence on his future personality and temperament. Through correct socializing at the critical period, puppies could be conditioned naturally to behave as friendly, people-oriented pets.

This sable-coated litter shows off its robust vitality.

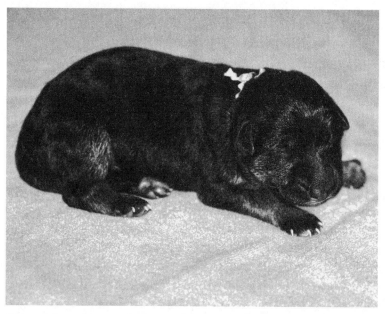

Kairos is just about ready to open his eyes at thirteen days.

During their fourth week, the pups can be coaxed out of their pen.

The maturing puppy needs to experience supervised play with a pack of adults.

While most acknowledge the overall value of Scott and Fuller's study, not everyone is comfortable with the term *critical period*. Critics argue that it is too absolute and seems to rule out the possibility of rehabilitating the animal who is the unfortunate victim of abuse and neglect during infancy. Instead, they prefer the term *sensitive period* as a clearer expression of reality. If we look at it this way, we see that timing and quality of experience, though undoubtedly important factors in influencing behavior, are not straitjackets that frustrate any future attempts to modify behavior. Development is much more complex than that. These periods simply approximate the time when a pup is most naturally susceptible to socializing influences.

This does not change the main point: early experience plays an important role in the development of personality. So if you are serious about purchasing a puppy, you should try to get as clear an idea as possible of the sort of background he comes from. The more you can learn about a puppy's early experiences, the genetic heritage he carries, and the general characteristics proper to his breed, the better prepared you will be to understand your pup and help him develop to his potential. Nevertheless, keep in mind that this knowledge will still not completely solve the riddle of your dog's individuality. There are limits to what science can teach us about our dogs. Ultimately, we must leave room for mystery.

In discerning the way a dog develops, we must recognize that our knowledge reflects general patterns and not absolute rules. We can never understand fully why a dog is the way he is. In fact, "the dog" does not exist, only individual dogs and the unique way each develops. Thus, in every stage, though the process of growth is basically the same, the particular way it manifests itself varies from pup to pup. This is why littermates raised under the same conditions develop differently. The very nature and chaos of life disposes them to behave and grow in individual ways.

This diversity is not without purpose. The dog, like his chief ancestor, the wolf, is a pack animal. While each dog has his own individual personality, he also has a pack identity that is manifest at a very young age, while he is still within the litter. These personality differences are important, for they highlight the fact that a pack is dependent upon mutual cooperation for its survival. Each member has his own role and importance; each is worthy of respect.

This is seen most clearly with wolves. Were a wolf pack made up entirely of alpha, or leader, personalities, then the members' ability to stick together would be pressed beyond the pack's limits. Continual infighting and challenging for control would make pack unity impossible. Conversely, were all members submissive types, the pack would lack the leadership necessary for effective hunting. In both cases, survival would be jeopardized. What gives the pack its strength are the different personalities that exist within it. These individual traits are linked directly with the experience of puppyhood. It is the diversity of developing personalities within the litter that forms the basis of an efficient, coordinated pack wherein each member's strengths and abilities are used to serve the whole while benefiting each.

This insight is vital to understanding the domestic dog. As we return to Anka and her puppies, we now have a general framework for discussing puppy growth and various related issues. Yet it is important to remember here that we are dealing with a litter of German shepherd pups. In addition to a particular dog's individuality, the size and breed of a puppy can affect his rate of physical and behavioral growth. For example, toy breeds such as the Chihuahua tend to mature sexually at around six months and reach adulthood at about a year. Larger, more slowly developing breeds such as the Irish wolfhound and mastiff do not reach sexual maturity until about a year and a half and reach adulthood from two to three years. Every breed has a natural growth rate you should be aware of when you obtain your puppy. The purpose of following Anka's litter is not to make a standard of their growth rates, nor to chronicle every detail of their growth. Rather, it is to provide a real-life background for our discussion and to help you better understand the early development of your own pup.

Ordinarily, it is not our practice to give proper names to nursing puppies, but we have done so here for the sake of clarity. We named the first two males Sunny and Kairos, the two females Oka and Yola, and the last male, who at birth was the smallest puppy in the litter, Kipper.

3

More Than Meets the Eye

NEONATAL PERIOD: 1–13 DAYS

We are now standing next to Anka's nest, pausing a moment from kennel chores to observe her nursing her pups. They are two days old. A heat lamp glares down over Anka, ensuring that the room temperature is kept warm and constant. She is lying with her underside fully exposed, and the puppies are lined up next to one another in an orderly fashion, each on a teat, each kneading gently with his or her paws to stimulate the milk flow. They look like little sausages attached to her side, their smooth black coats giving off a sheen under the light. Anka pants heavily as they suckle; she is unconcerned by our presence, her gaze fixed on a solid white wall that borders the nest.

Minutes pass.

Finally the calm is broken as Anka shifts herself and stands up. As the pups lose their hold on her teats, they roll off to the side, helplessly landing on their backs, squealing at the sudden disruption. This lasts for only a moment. Quickly they right themselves, and after a few seconds of crawling, they fall fast asleep next to one another. Anka, meanwhile, lies down on the opposite end of the nest and looks up at us.

After the excitement of her whelping only two days before, the quietness of the following days might easily lull us into overlooking the critical importance of this time, when the principal activity of the litter is the alternating rhythm of sleep and nursing. In this quiet, however, a great deal occurs that will provide the essential foundation for the future development of the litter.

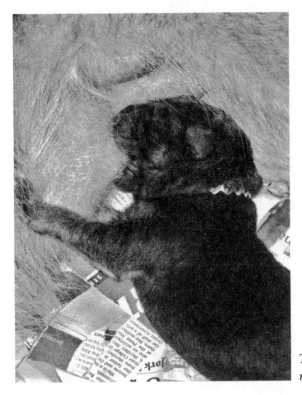

*Three-day-old Oka
nurses.*

Vulnerability

Entering a world they can neither see nor hear, newborn pups exist in a
sensory desert, necessarily well insulated from harsh disturbances.
They are entirely dependent on their mother; without her (or the equivalent care by humans) the pups will die. Anka knows this. During the
first days she is continuously in the nest, leaving it only to eliminate. As
mother, she is a portrait of concentrated, faithful attention to every
detail of the puppies' lives, reflecting her profound awareness of just
how vulnerable they are at this stage. It is a vulnerability that she is prepared to defend with her life.

An example: While the puppies are asleep, Anka remains awake in
the nest, occupying herself with a rawhide bone. Suddenly her ears
stand erect and she begins to growl tentatively. Strange voices drift into
the kennel from outside. At once, she is out of the nest and flying
through the kennel hatch into her outdoor pen, ferociously barking out

her alarm. As she paces back and forth, her hackles are fully raised and her tail stands straight up. She appears, through this natural illusion, substantially larger-than-life to the strangers, tourists who have inadvertently wandered too close to the kennel building. Quickly they hurry off in the other direction, convinced of her seriousness. Anka, however, continues the warning, her bark echoing throughout the monastery grounds for several minutes. It is only when she is satisfied that the danger has passed that she returns to the nest and the sleeping pups huddled in the corner, oblivious to all the commotion.

The fact that the puppies lie clustered together should not be interpreted as evidence of neonatal sociability. It is simply a way to conserve heat. Newborn pups have poor control over their body temperature, so they tend to gravitate to the warmest area of the nest. As soon as the first pup, Sunny, awakes, he begins a restless search for a nipple by inconsiderately piling over the others, ignoring their presence. His stirring causes a chain reaction of mad maneuvering, each pup struggling to reach one of Anka's teats. The scene confirms that the pups have no direct awareness of one another; their behavior is confined largely to reflex actions that they have been equipped with at birth, such as sucking, crawling, attraction to warmth, and distress vocalizations arising from pain, hunger, or cold.

Development

Conventional wisdom, reflected most authoritatively by Scott and Fuller, portrays the newborn as an essentially tactile creature, incapable of any real learning, and relying exclusively on the sense of touch for getting nourishment. Other astute observers, however, such as author and veterinarian Michael Fox, have demonstrated that this view needs to be broadened in several respects. First, it has been shown that a newborn puppy also possesses a well-developed sense of smell. In a cleverly conceived experiment, Fox coated a nursing mother's teats with aniseed oil, a rather unpleasant-smelling substance, and then let the newborn pups nurse. Twenty-four hours later these pups would crawl toward a Q-tip dipped in aniseed oil and held close to their noses. Other pups who had not received this previous exposure while nursing recoiled sharply from the odor.

In addition, neonatal behavior reveals a capacity for the simple learning necessary for survival. A newborn puppy will instinctively begin a burrowing motion with her muzzle when she first contacts something warm. This helps her find her mother's teat, which can sometimes be hidden beneath her hair. In watching Yola behave this way shortly after she was born, and then again several days later, we see that there is quite a difference. While at first she was awkward and clumsy, after three days she is quite adept at it. Proficiency clearly improves with time.

Over several days she also develops strength and assurance in nursing. It is interesting to feel the difference in sucking ability of a pup shortly after birth and then again after many days. We did this with Yola by letting her nurse briefly on our fingers. Initially, after birth, the pressure was a little weak, unsure. When we repeated the exercise a few days later, the pressure was surprisingly strong and forceful. This is evidence of an elementary learning that will form the basis for later, more complex learning.

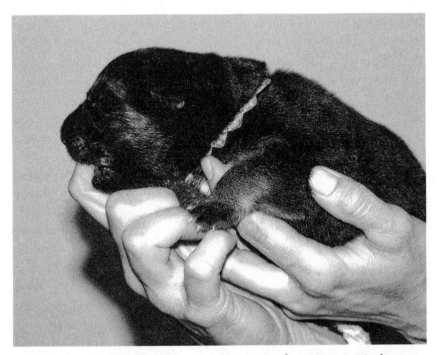

The pressure of a four-day-old pup nursing on your finger is surprisingly strong.

Immaturity

Regardless of how one interprets infant behavior and what constitutes true learning, the fact remains that the pups' brain, motor, and sensory capacities are all immature during this period. The pups exist in a naturally protected environment where they possess only the basic abilities necessary for their survival. None of the behavior we most commonly associate with dogs is present: no barking, tail wagging, walking, or playing. In fact, the most dominant impression we receive of newborn pups is their need for sleep. During the neonatal period puppies spend about 90 percent of their time sleeping, waking only to nurse or to be cleansed by their mother.

This abundance of sleep is an absolute requirement. It is vital to the development of the central nervous system and the brain. When measured with an electroencephalograph (EEG) during the first three weeks of life, a pup's brain waves will be the same whether the pup is awake or asleep. This indicates how immature the brain is at this period. In particular, the reticular formation—the section of the brain that controls sleep and wakefulness—has not yet developed sufficiently to keep the puppy awake for any significant amount of time. It is only after the third week that a marked change begins to register on the EEG, showing a clear differentiation between wakefulness and sleep, and only after four weeks that pups are able to stay awake for any sustained period. Early in this initial phase, it is the quietness of sleep, combined with regular nourishment, warmth, and elementary movement, that establishes the proper climate wherein the brain and central nervous system may mature.

"Gross immaturity" characterizes what newborn puppies call to mind; they have an appearance entirely unique to this time in their lives. The shepherd pups born to Anka bear no resemblance at all to the familiar image we possess of a noble German shepherd. At six to eight inches from their pug noses to the tips of their tails, they have rounded, oversize heads, barrel-shaped chests, and short, stumpy legs. Their ears are quite small and seem stuck to the sides of their heads. Their eyes are closed tight. If you did not know better, you could easily mistake them for members of a different species!

Even the ability to eliminate is a reflex completely controlled by the mother, since newborn pups are unable to urinate or defecate on their

Handling a four-day-old puppy.

own. During the first three weeks of life, they require the regular stimulation of their anal and genital areas by the mother's tongue to eliminate bodily waste, which the mother licks up immediately. This keeps
the nest completely clean and guards against the serious health risk of
waste buildup. Such behavior may have another important function.
Wildlife biologist L. David Mech, in his study on the wolf, points out
that this activity may also establish the postural and psychological
beginnings of submission in a pup. Although Mech was speaking specifically of the wolf, we have observed the importance of this in our
own shepherds. Living as they do in a semi–pack environment, younger,
more submissive dogs often assume the identical posture of a pup
when submitting to an older, more dominant pack member. They roll
over on their backs and expose their undersides while the other dog
proceeds to investigate and sniff the anal-genital region. This posture
defuses the threat perceived by the submissive dog and establishes pack
hierarchy.

Individuality

All of these details form the background for the later growth of each pup. Overall, we can now see that a pup's early development lays the foundation for the future, despite the obvious immaturity of a puppy at this stage. It is a simple fact: life is growth. And even now, so early in life, the individuality we spoke of begins to show through. In keeping daily records of weight gain, we notice that Sunny and Oka are putting on the most weight and appear to nurse the most vigorously. In the nest they are the two who consistently manage to nose out the others when competing for a teat. These are preliminary signs of dominance that we will pay attention to throughout their puppyhood. Also, because of the growth differences within the litter, sometimes we find it necessary to place the slower-growing puppies on the mother's teats for longer periods without the presence of the more dominant pups. It is a gentle way of trying to level the playing field a bit.

Daily weighing also gives us a chance to note which puppies are more reactive and more vocal when being handled. Anka's second female, Yola, for example, seems quite sensitive to touch and squirms vigorously

Yawning and starting to investigate one another in the latter part of the neonatal period.

when held. When we place her on the cold scale, she cries more loudly than the other pups, who are not so alarmed by this experience.

Benefits of Stress

The presence of this type of behavior in Yola raises an important issue about puppy development. Though some breeders and scientists claim that physical handling has no effect on a puppy during the first three weeks of life, our experience suggests otherwise. Over the years we have found it beneficial to introduce the pups to moderate amounts of human handling throughout the course of puppyhood, not simply during the period of socialization. This handling is actually a mildly stressful experience, though it in no way reaches traumatic levels. Contrary to what might be expected, mild amounts of stress are beneficial to the development of puppies, provided the exposure is not excessive. Whereas toxic stress in the form of prolonged isolation and lack of handling can have a profound effect on puppy development, moderate stress can be helpful. Not only have several scientific studies confirmed this but the U.S. military even developed a program based on this premise during the 1970s called "Bio Sensor" or the "Super Dog" program, which was designed to enhance the performance of dogs used in various capacities by the military. The basic idea of the program was that early neurological stimulation of pups from the third to the sixteenth day of their lives positively influenced neurological growth and development and set up the pups for success when they were older.*

Puppies exposed to mildly stressful experiences from a very early age (one to six weeks) usually develop into mature dogs possessing superior problem-solving ability, with less emotional imbalance than their counterparts raised without such stimulation. In the young pup, stress, in addition to raising the heart rate, causes an involuntary hormonal reaction in the pituitary-adrenal system. This helps in resisting disease and handling stress. The overall effect is to prime the entire system, building it up and making it more resilient to emotionally challenging experiences later in life. We find that at each particular stage of growth, specific types of handling enhance the development of pups

---

* A very thorough and clear discussion of this can be found in the article "Early Neurological Stimulation" by Dr. Carmen L. Battaglia at www.breedingbetterdogs.com/articles/early_neurological_stimulation_en.php.

and orient them in a positive manner to adulthood. When puppies receive consistent, nontraumatic handling, they become more outgoing and friendly and show less inclination to be fearful once they are older. When the time comes to welcome a new puppy into your home, you may want to ask your breeder what type of early handling your pup has received.

Here at the monastery, we follow a variation of the Bio Sensor program during the neonatal period and expand this as the pups mature, scheduling regular periods of handling with each litter, making sure that the pups receive daily attention from different monks and kennel workers. This is possible because all of us are involved in varying degrees with the puppy program. Each monk and kennel worker is known by the mothers, who allow the pups to be touched and handled without becoming agitated. When we observe a pup who is extremely reactive to touch at this early stage, as Yola is, we make sure that she receives a little more stroking and handling than normal, though without overdoing it. Usually we practice this once or twice a day, stroking the pup's body and gently massaging the stomach. We also like to lift a pup up and breathe on her, then hold her next to our face, allowing her to rub against the texture of a beard as well as experience the softness and scent of skin. In general, we find that with such regular exposure even pups who are initially very sensitive to touch show noticeable improvements in reactivity, becoming quieter and more accepting of these mildly stressful experiences over the course of several weeks.

The final type of mild stress we introduce during the later part of the neonatal period involves the reduction of the puppies' body temperature. During the second week of life, we routinely administer a brief thermal stress by placing the pups in a separate, cool room away from the nest. The pups are held in individual cardboard boxes for three minutes. This allows their bodies to sense a temperature fall, causing the pituitary-adrenal system to respond with a brief output of corticosteroid hormones — a process that helps the pups resist disease later on. When we perform this exercise, the puppies begin to squeal and make a ruckus. At the end of the period, each pup is returned to the warm nest and stroked gently. Immediately all signs of agitation stop, and the pups are clearly relaxed and comfortable once again. As an added benefit of this brief separation of the litter, the mother is "reinvigorated" in her vigilant attention to the puppies upon their return.

An additional point needs to be made in connection with early handling and development. Occasionally a whelping occurs that produces only one or two puppies. In such cases, we find that the pups can be prone to greater touch sensitivity because they do not have the ordinary amount of physical contact and stimulation with other pups that is present in larger litters. As we have mentioned, when there are a number of pups, all of them quickly become accustomed to tumbling and squirming over one another, and they adjust naturally to a variety of sensations. When such contact is absent, it is important for the breeder to take the time to handle the pups more often, introducing mildly stressful experiences into an overly sedate environment.

4

Light Shines in Darkness

TRANSITIONAL PERIOD: 13–20 DAYS

On the twelfth day after birth, the first major change becomes visible in one of the puppies. Kairos, Anka's second male, begins to open his eyes. This signals the start of the transitional period of development, a week when many of the pup's sensory capacities begin to function. Contrary to what you might expect, this is no small accomplishment. A puppy's eyes do not open all at once. Instead, this is a gradual process that may take well over twenty-four hours to complete. At first, his eyes seem like dark little slits, begging to be pried open. Then, slowly, as if he is waking from a deep sleep, they become more visible, their grayish-blue, semiopaque color giving them an unworldly appearance. It is only after about five weeks that they will become clear and distinctive, reaching their adult coloration.

By the fifteenth day, all of the puppies in the litter have their eyes wide open, and a parallel increase in activity occurs. They crawl around the nest and continually bump into one another. Despite the fact that their eyes are open, the pups still do not see very well. Shining a penlight into Kairos's left eye causes the pupil to contract; quick gestures in front of him, however, evoke no reaction, and a sudden movement directly toward him does not make him blink. It is not until about twenty-eight days that a pup is able to begin clearly distinguishing forms, though occasionally we have seen puppies become startled by quick, threatening movements as early as the seventeenth day, apparently due to the darting of shadows. Thus, during this time we take care not to make sudden moves that could frighten the pups.

Puppies still need a lot of sleep during the transitional period.

The process of eye opening is symbolic of everything that happens during this stage — a steady, gradual transformation. It is the first clear sign of the passage from the insulated newborn stage to the fully social existence of an adult. This is why we call this period *transitional*. It is a week of dramatic change. By the end of this stage, the pups will have received, albeit at an immature level, all the basic tools of life: sight, hearing, walking, the ability to eliminate by themselves, chewing, and a more refined sense of smell. Because of this, the pups will become much more sensitive to their environment than they were before.

For example, during the neonatal period, puppies have no sense of place. If you remove one and put him in a different room, alone, at the same temperature as the nest and on a comfortable surface, the pup will show no sign of distress, provided he is not hungry. Now, however, since Anka's puppies are becoming aware of one another and of their nest, when we repeat this same experiment with Kipper, we see a marked change. After poking his head around for several moments, he suddenly begins to whimper and show signs of distress. The whimper then turns into a wail. Clearly he has no taste for being alone!

Once their eyes are fully open, the puppies begin investigating the small world of the nest. Looking at them now, we see that they are trying out life for the first time. They start to crawl backward as well as forward, and quickly move on to the first clumsy attempts at walking. This reflects the basic pattern of a puppy's becoming aware of himself and his surroundings.

At the daily weighing session on the sixteenth day, Oka and Sunny are the first to try walking. As they attempt to stand on the scale, they shake the platform precariously and are unable to maintain their balance. This, however, is just the beginning. Their efforts continue when they are returned to the nest. Standing up ever so tentatively, wobbling

Puppies' eyes beginning to open up.

The pups interact with eyes wide open.

from side to side, Sunny finally takes two brave steps forward only to flop over onto a sleeping Kipper, creating a very cranky outburst. Quickly crawling backward, Sunny barks indignantly in a comically high pitch and tries to stand once again. Meanwhile, Oka is a little less adventurous. She simply attempts to remain standing without falling over. Lacking the confidence to actually try walking, she finally crouches back down, crawls over to the other pups, and falls asleep. Throughout all this, Anka looks on from outside the nest with what seems to be mild amusement.

The seed of example has been planted. The following day, all of the pups except Yola are beginning to give walking a try, basically following the same pattern. Together, they are like a group of youngsters learning how to ride bicycles for the first time. They have little coordination and make numerous false starts, but their proficiency improves daily. By the end of a week they will be able to walk around the nest without much trouble at all.

About this time we notice something else: the puppies are beginning to sniff around the nest. The refinement of the sense of smell that has been occurring since birth stimulates their curiosity, and they are soon snuffling one another, the newspapers, and Anka. If we pick them up and hold them close to our faces, they sniff and try to suckle the skin, awkwardly probing our cheeks. To reinforce this contact, we put an old cotton sock or unwashed cotton T-shirt into the nest so that the pups will be continuously exposed to human scent as they grow.

Taking the first tentative steps at two and a half weeks.

Given the fact that the olfactory area of adult dogs is fourteen times larger than a human's and that their overall ability to smell is estimated conservatively at one hundred times more sensitive, we can begin to realize the role scent plays in a dog's understanding of the world. While we depend more on our eyes for information, dogs rely on their noses, learning much about their environment from the currents of air that pass their way.

Connected with this rise in inquisitiveness is the emergence of the upper canine teeth, which can be felt around the eighteenth and nineteenth days. Not only does this development set the stage for a transition to more solid foods, but it is likely that the pressure of the incoming teeth prompts puppies to begin exploring one another. As Sunny's upper teeth start to emerge on the nineteenth day, he begins to chew and suck on the other puppies' ears, paws, and muzzles. This happens in slow motion and is accompanied by the first signs of tail wagging. Like a chain reaction, the other pups begin to reciprocate. Thus the first real sessions of play begin.

From the time the pups are born, we regularly examine their mouths and teeth — important in preparing them for later oral care.

Young pups should be provided with a variety of toys.

Hearing is the last sensory faculty to develop, with the ears opening at about twenty days. Beginning with the seventeenth day, we check for this by periodically clapping our hands over each pup's head. The noise elicits no response until the twentieth day. Then Oka and Kipper both react to it, especially Oka, who yips a little and starts moving backward — an understandable expression of alarm. She recovers quickly, however, taking several steps forward with an inquisitive look on her face as she mutters under her breath.

When testing to see if they can hear, we are careful not to clap too loudly, because what the pups experience for the first time can leave a strong fear imprint. Emerging from a silent world into one of sound should happen as naturally as possible to allow the pups to adjust without excessive trauma.

The type of mild-stress handling that we expose the puppies to during this week follows the same principle. Our purpose is to stimulate the puppy, not traumatize him. We find two exercises especially beneficial. In the first, an elevation exercise, we hold the pup in midair until he begins to squirm and protest. We then draw him close and stroke him gently to allow him to settle down. In the second, a dominance exercise, we place the pup on a soft surface, roll him onto his back, and hold him there for ten to fifteen seconds. Once the pup begins to struggle and squeal (and most do!), we turn him upright again and stroke him gently. After a week of this, the puppies associate gentle petting with the end of stress. It also helps dispose the pups to human presence and handling, which we will increase in the upcoming weeks.

One final observation: during the transitional period we begin a weekly grooming session that teaches the puppies how to be handled and touched—ears are cleaned, nails clipped, and the fur lightly brushed. At first, the novelty of the handling causes some minor protestations from the pups, but after a few sessions they come to enjoy it. We continue this practice at least once a week until the puppies are placed in their new homes. As you can imagine, this type of handling can make all the difference in your early attempts to pick up and groom your puppy.

In this week of transition the newborns become more recognizably puppies both in the way they look and in how they act. They now stand poised for the move into social existence. Yet this phase is transitional

*An elevation exercise during
the transitional period:
at first this is a stimulating
but mild stress.*

Regularly scheduled grooming is an important part of socialization.

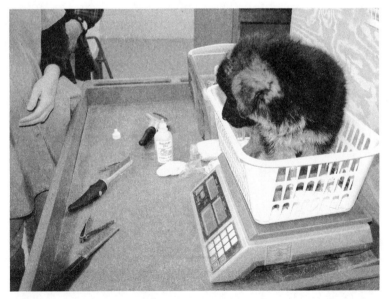

Pups are continually weighed to ensure that they are growing at a steady rate.

*Holding and touching
the puppies helps
prepare them for
grooming and physical
examinations.*

not only for the pups but for Anka, whose behavior reflects a change of role. Before, she was in the nest continuously, jealously guarding and caring for her whelps; now she modifies her vigilance by spending time outside the nest, resting while her pups are asleep. She also wants to play. In the first two weeks, even the sight of her much-loved tennis ball could not coax her away from the pups; at this point, a little bored, she eagerly jumps up at the gate to greet her guardian, trying to get him to play and take her for a walk. She has no worry about leaving her pups briefly. This is the beginning of her natural disengagement from them, which will continue for the next several weeks until they are on their own.

5

Opening Up to the World

SOCIALIZATION PERIOD: 3–12 WEEKS

Twenty-two days have passed. Thus far, the only world the puppies have known has been a small, circular nest that has stood in for the ordinary den found in the wild. For the infant pup, the nest provides the stable, confined environment required for all of his primary needs to be met.

Until now, that is.

For the past several days, the pups have been much more animated in the nest, almost restless, indicating their growing sense of confinement. With Anka spending longer periods away from them, they start pawing at the sides of the nest in an effort to follow her. This morning, Sunny finally resolves to overcome the barrier. Slowly inching his way up the side, enough to place his front paws on top of the edge, he peers over and spots Anka snoozing on her dog bed nearby. He yips impatiently but in vain; Anka ignores his calls. This is just the incentive he needs. With fearless determination and daring, he stubbornly attempts to scale the side. Hoisting himself up, his rear legs pumping wildly against the wall of the nest, he manages to clear the top, only to tumble down onto the hard floor of the whelping room. This unexpected drop elicits a series of high-pitched shrieks that rouse Anka to his aid. Licking him reassuringly, she settles down next to him and lets him nurse. Meanwhile, the commotion rouses the other pups, who now peek over the edge of the nest. They quickly become a chorus of screaming, impatient siblings. It is only a matter of time before each of them will join his or her brother.

Sunny's venture out of the nest occurs near the beginning of the

A mother takes her four-week-old pups out to explore.

all-important socialization period—nine weeks of intensive exposure to life during which the puppies' personalities blossom. Practically overnight their behavior changes. Their growing abilities of perception and movement, which we began to see in the transitional period, suddenly become coordinated. Clearly, they have reached a milestone in their growth. Though still requiring plenty of sleep, the pups are more energetic and awake for longer periods. They now become animated and curious. Their play with one another includes the barking and tail wagging we identify with adult behavior. Though still immature, the brain and central nervous system have developed enough for the pups to interact seriously with their surroundings. Now they begin to learn quickly!

What Is Socialization?

By *socialization* we mean two things: first, the positive adjustment a puppy makes to the many aspects of her life, whether this includes other dogs, people, places, or objects; second, what we do to foster this. A puppy is extremely sensitive to socializing experiences between three and twelve weeks, when the effects are permanent, for better or worse. Previously the puppy was psychologically isolated from her environment, protected by the lack of sensory development. Now that has changed. She is vulnerable in a new way.

Naturally the pups are not aware of this. At the beginning of this stage, their basic orientation is one of openness. Their senses are receiving an abundance of stimuli whereby they gain an immediate perception of their surroundings. Everything is new and interesting, and the pups start to show real curiosity. They are ready to form their first genuinely social relationships with their mother and littermates.

Because of this positive thrust toward life and growth, we keep the pups' environment stable and capitalize on this natural inquisitiveness with a proper blend of new experiences. The mother should still spend the majority of her time with the pups. Since they are in the process of adjusting to their newly found senses, we do not overwhelm them with excessive stimulation and noise during the first week and a half of this period. At this time, though they are naturally disposed to investigate their small world, too much stimulation can cause fearfulness. Normal fear and avoidance of new experiences arise naturally later in the period, once the brain and central nervous system have matured to their adult levels. This is commonly referred to as the *fear/avoidance period* and is discussed later in the book.

Early on, the litter takes great delight in running together through the snow in the exercise yard.

In the wild, this natural rhythm of attachment and avoidance initially bonds a pup to its pack, then later makes it wary of strange animals and new, potentially dangerous circumstances. It is a survival mechanism that instinctively keeps puppies away from predators. During the first twelve weeks of life, the only social contacts a wolf pup has are with its mother, littermates, and immediate pack members. This keeps the pup safe and reinforces attachments to the pack, and thus creates a greater pack solidarity and security. In domestic dogs, the pattern is the same: attachment, then displays of avoidance.

Ideally a pup is raised with a variety of the right kinds of social experiences, first with his mother and littermates and subsequently with the wider world. Since domestic dogs are expected to behave in ways that are socially acceptable to humans, a puppy needs plenty of human contact and exposure to all sorts of common, everyday things. This lays the foundation for a positive attitude toward new people and new experiences and teaches the puppy that human beings and their world are part of his pack. If deprived of these contacts, a pup will develop fearful reactions to people and grow up socially maladjusted and emotionally disturbed. At that point, reconditioning, even if possible, is extremely difficult (and very expensive).

This explains why adult wolves are almost impossible to domesticate. While there have been numerous accounts of wolf pups that were raised and socialized by humans into trusted companions, adult wolves are extremely resistant to being tamed. Lacking any exposure to humans during the critical period of socialization, they have no basis for making the connection. Quite understandably, when an adult wolf is faced with the prospect of an encounter with a human being, its tendency will be either flight or, when cornered, displays of aggression.

In *Understanding Your Dog*, Eberhard Trumler, a noted ethologist in Germany, recounts the story of how he deliberately raised a litter of dingoes (Australian wild dogs) in such a way that they had no contact with human beings between their third and seventh weeks of life. Except for the presence of other pack members, they were raised by their parents just as they would be in the wild. The results were predictable. They developed into shy, wild dogs who avoided any contact with humans and would hide whenever Trumler entered their yard. Since one of Trumler's purposes was to observe the behavior of dingoes in an essentially natural setting, the deprivation was inconsequential. The animals acted as they normally would in the wild. Similar deprivation for domestic dogs, however, has more serious consequences.

When Scott and Fuller raised a number of litters in large, open fields, they found that pups raised without human contact would show fearful reactions to humans at five weeks but could readjust in two weeks' time if handled often. Puppies first exposed to human contact at twelve weeks, however, immediately reacted very fearfully and fled from the researchers. They behaved essentially like wild animals and were socially irretrievable. They had missed the vital contact during the critical period.

A practical application of this discovery was made by Clarence Pfaffenberger at Guide Dogs for the Blind (San Rafael, California) during the 1950s and 1960s. Operating a breeding program specifically designed to produce qualified guide dogs and working closely with John Paul Scott, he confirmed the necessity of regular socialization if pups were to have any hope of becoming successful guide dogs. Pups needed repeated human contact to acquire the emotional stability necessary for such work. Without it, the dogs not only became unsuited for guide work but made poor companions as well. The implications for all breeders were self-evident.

Pfaffenberger also found that the initial benefits of socialization could be lost if puppies were left in the kennel too long after the conclusion of personality testing at twelve weeks. If a properly socialized pup spent three additional weeks in the kennel without deliberate socialization and then was placed in her new home, chances were high (70 percent) that she would be unable to take responsibility for her blind owner as an adult guide dog. Pups placed in homes immediately after the testing, however, had a 90 percent success rate.

These examples underscore the importance of what happens in the life of your puppy before you obtain her, as well as the absolute importance of socialization throughout her life. Socialization accustoms the puppy to a wide variety of new and potentially frightening experiences. The rhythm of first being afraid and then recovering and getting used to the new experience is one of the more valuable lessons that a puppy learns during this period. The pup bounces back and becomes more able to deal with potentially unsettling things later in life.

We believe that we can use this information to distinguish two phases within the period as a whole. The first centers on a pup's interaction with other dogs and takes place between roughly four and six weeks. During this time, though human contact should not be absent, it is not the main focus. Major changes in behavior occur as a result of the puppies' interactions with one another and with their mother. This period flows into the second phase, when the pups begin to focus on socializing with people. This interval extends from five to twelve weeks, thus allowing for a week's overlap when the pups require both forms of social exposure. These two phases highlight the basic social adjustments most puppies need to make if they are to live happy, balanced lives.

An Interesting Exception: A Litter of One

As should now be apparent, we cannot emphasize enough how socialization is a vital process for any pup's adjustment to the world, a stable foundation on which future development greatly depends. What happens, then, in the rare instance when only one puppy is born in the litter? Should we expect such a pup to be at an extreme disadvantage in its growth and development? Not necessarily. While a single puppy presents a challenge, the breeder can ensure that the playing field is leveled by compensating with frequent handling and plentiful exposure to other dogs.

For example, we recall when this happened years ago with a puppy from one of our shepherds. We nicknamed the pup Lit (short for *litter*) and began right away supplementing the attention she received from her mother with plenty of additional handling and stimulation. After the first several weeks, whichever monk was working the kennels during the day would take her with him in a satchel as he did cleaning chores, and as Lit grew we reinforced this by letting her interact with puppies from another litter as well as with older, puppy-wise shepherds of the breeding program who understood how to safely relate with her. We also socialized her with visitors to the monastery, especially women and children, since most of Lit's initial human encounters were with men. By the time Lit left for her new home, she was a thoroughly socialized, self-possessed pup who had also learned some important limits from older dogs.

Had we not done this and instead left her isolated, to be cared for solely by her mother, she would have been seriously undersocialized.

She wouldn't have understood how to react with other dogs and would likely have been a strange combination of pushy and fearful, with a strong tendency to overuse her mouth whenever she was frustrated. The prognosis for such a pup would have been bleak indeed.

Phase One: Socialization with Dogs (4–6 Weeks)

To make these ideas clear, let us return to Anka and her pups. Once the pups start getting out of the nest, we remove it and leave them on the floor, with Anka's comfortable dog bed in the corner to sleep on. As they move around now much more freely, they begin to eliminate on their own, away from the bed, on newspapers that cover the floor. Their instinctive aversion to messing where they sleep is connected with their mother's earlier meticulous care of the nest.

Wildlife biologists observe the same behavior in the wild with wolves: three-week-old pups emerge from their den and start playing with one another in front of the entrance. As they do so, they urinate and defecate on their own, gradually learning to pick spots away from the den. By six to seven weeks, the pups select particular *scent posts*— areas where they will consistently relieve themselves. The movement away from the nest, coinciding with the ability to eliminate by themselves, reveals the natural tendency of both wolves and dogs to keep their sleeping areas clean. Knowing this will help later on when you begin house-training your puppy.

This is why a filthy, disorganized breeding kennel not only reflects badly on the breeder but could spell future health and behavioral problems for your dog as well. When soiled papers are not picked up regularly, the pups wrestle and stomp in their own feces and lose their natural aversion to soiling where they play or sleep. They also quite likely will begin eating their own excrement. This may lead to health problems as well as habitual stool eating (coprophagy) as adults. Thus, kennel cleanliness is essential for proper socialization and should be an important consideration in determining where you adopt your new puppy.

A Gentle Weaning

During the fourth week, the puppies grow so rapidly that their requirements for food increase beyond Anka's ability to produce. Anka

The litter nursing at five weeks. At this stage the mother allows them to nurse for only a few seconds.

becomes more and more impatient with their constant demands. She is reluctant to let the pups nurse and avoids them by escaping into the outside holding pen, where they have not yet learned to follow. If confined with them, she no longer lies down but moves constantly and snaps when they try to nurse from her. When she finally relents, she remains upright, forcing the pups to nurse standing up. But not for long. After several minutes she ends the session and moves away, leaving the pups yipping and barking as they stubbornly follow her for more.

Because their sharp little teeth have begun to emerge, Anka's ability to let them nurse for long periods of time diminishes. It is simply too uncomfortable for her. This is a sign that it is time to wean the pups. During the next several days, we will introduce the pups to semisolid blends of cottage cheese and high-quality canned meat, gradually working up to moistened puppy kibble (dry puppy food). The weaning process should occur gently, giving the pups time to get accustomed to a new diet as well as to prolonged absences by their mother. To grant Anka some relief, we place an elevated platform in the whelping room that allows her to retreat from her pups while still remaining with them. Three- to four-week-old pups still require the stabilizing and secure presence of their mother. Since they are being bombarded with an abundance of new experiences and stimuli, abrupt separations would be harmful.

*Four-week-old pups quickly
gobble up their meal.*

Significantly, in the case of this litter, we do notice something interesting when we bring the pups their first solid meal, a gruel of cottage
cheese and warm water that is easy to digest. As we approach the pen,
we notice that they are already huddled around what we discover to be
Anka's regurgitated food. As they eat, she sits contentedly in the far corner. This strange sight is actually the most natural of procedures, and
the puppies are perfectly satisfied with the fare. Sunny and Oka adapt
to the new diet almost immediately. The others, however, pause and
cough frequently as they chew and swallow.

Soon Kipper tires of the feast. He looks up, pauses, then walks
straight through the middle of the pile toward Anka, disturbing the
others and tracking food all over. Seeing his intentions, Anka curls her
lip and snaps purposefully at him. This show of force has its desired
effect, as Kipper yips and retreats. The others continue eating.

This is precisely how weaning begins with wolves. In the wild, however, the regurgitated meal is provided by other pack members as well
as the mother. Once the pups are about three weeks old, the mother
resumes hunting with the pack while the pups stay in their den. When
the pack returns, all the adult members regurgitate a semiliquid gruel,
which the pups gobble up eagerly—a normal transitory stage until the
young wolves can begin eating solid food. The pups solicit regurgitation from the adults by submissively licking at their mouths. This is the
principal method of feeding for wolf pups, even though the mother
continues to provide milk until seven to ten weeks.

Weaning also initiates a new emphasis in social relationships. By the middle of the fifth week, the periodic absence of the wolf dam* associated with weaning gradually causes the pups to focus their attention more on one another than on their mother, and they learn to be less dependent.

It is the same with Anka's pups. For several days we progressively lengthen the time Anka spends away from the litter, and the pups make the adjustment easily. Now, as we pass by the litter while doing chores, we see that if the puppies are not sleeping together they are playing together, inventing innumerable healthy games, visibly behaving like a pack. As we watch, Oka parades around the pen with a squeak toy. The other pups follow her, eagerly trying to pull it from her mouth. Sunny manages to pry the toy away from her, and the game continues until a noise from outside causes them all to stop and listen. Kairos is the first to go out and investigate, and the others follow.

Puppy play is anything but frivolous. Not only does it develop muscle coordination but it also exposes the pups to spontaneous social situations that they must learn to handle. When Sunny rolls Kairos over on his back and playfully bites him, they are beginning to learn social roles — in this case, dominance and submission. If Sunny bites too hard, Kairos retaliates, letting Sunny know that he has gone too far. This hap-

A mother provoking her pup into a playful confrontation.

---

* *Dam* is the usual way of referring to a canine mother.

A mother gently pinning one of her older pups to the ground as a way of teaching respect for her authority.

pens often with all the pups and teaches them how to use their mouths gently. Play-fighting is usually kept friendly, and, particularly early in this period, pups easily exchange roles as play-fights become highly ritualized periods of learning. For example, during the fifth week, Yola, the most submissive pup in the litter, stands over Sunny with her jaws buried in his neck, growling and shaking her head. Sunny accommodates this, acting out submission by remaining on his back and gently pawing her face.

This constant interaction with one another gradually establishes a loose hierarchy within the litter. The pups learn whom they can dominate and whom they cannot. Were this development allowed to continue uninterruptedly, roles would be completely defined by about four months.

This initial interaction is the basis for the healthy adjustment of pups with other dogs, as well as for their own self-identity as dogs. Puppies need this time of familiarization with one another and with their

The mother and sire are usually indulgent with the pups.

As they grow older, the pups become fearless in their play.

Healthy pups learn to stand up for themselves.

Dominant behavior continues to be displayed as the puppies grow.

Tussling and play-competition are never-ending — here, at six weeks.

Play-fights are highly ritualized periods of learning. Through play, pups discover the basics of appropriate social roles.

mother. If a puppy is separated from her mother and littermates before six weeks, she will not have learned the basic social behavior proper to her species. Serious problems can suddenly develop as the dog matures. One client brought us his seven-month-old American Staffordshire terrier for training after he had attacked another dog in a local park. The horrified owner, totally unprepared for such a spontaneous outburst of aggression, could not understand how this wonderful pet, so gentle and friendly with people, could ever have done such a thing to another dog.

We discovered that the man had obtained the pup from a friend at only four and a half weeks of age. From that time on, the puppy had been raised exclusively with people and had been given no real exposure to other dogs. Since he had formed no social bonds with others, he neither recognized his kinship with them nor learned the basic social interaction proper to his species. The result nearly cost the man his dog.

Between four and six weeks, if the primary social focus is on people, the pup will be oversocialized and tend to identify only with humans. This inclination can even be expressed sexually. One woman contacted us after her young keeshond mounted a guest's leg at a dinner party. The embarrassing incident had not been the first of its kind, although former occurrences had been confined to immediate family members, who were amused. Now, however, the problem had come out of the closet. Again, questioning revealed that the keeshond had been obtained at a very early age. Since the people lived in an apartment in New York City, the dog was always walked on a leash and was prevented from interacting with other dogs. The owner was afraid of his "catching something," even after four months, when all his vaccinations had been completed. Lacking this ordinary experience with other dogs, the keeshond had begun to identify exclusively with human beings, even to the point of displaying overt sexual behavior.

Never adopt a puppy under six weeks of age. The interaction occurring within the litter at that time is too critical to a pup's development. Puppies depend on these natural relationships in order to grow up normally. Then they can enter fully into the next stage of socialization, that of adjusting to the presence of people in their lives and learning to interact with them.

Phase Two: Socialization with People (5–12 Weeks)

The sixth week of life (thirty-five to forty-two days) is pivotal in puppy development. The main emphasis of socialization begins to shift from mother and littermates toward human beings and the world beyond the nest. Building on already developed social behavior, the pups refine their abilities by playing together and manifest new behaviors that help them experience the world. Sexual play now becomes apparent, with mounting common in both male and female puppies. This is an ordinary part of puppy development that teaches them normal sexual responses in maturity. In addition, mounting is used to communicate dominance, even among females. This happens from time to time with Oka and Yola, another sign of Yola's more submissive nature.

By now the pups have developed sharper eyes and ears. They have much clearer depth perception. Their muzzles are beginning to elongate, permitting greater facial expressiveness, and their vocal patterns cover a wider range. Their legs are stronger and more coordinated, allowing them to move where they will. They show an eagerness to explore and investigate everything, approaching new objects and people without hesitation. The monks working at the kennel take short breaks

We introduce the pups to all kinds of surfaces, including steps and obstacles.

The volunteers are extremely gentle when coaxing the pups up and down the stairs.

between chores to play with the pups, and regular times are set aside each day for specific types of handling, with individual pups as well as with the entire litter. During this period, puppies require all the attention they can get, and their reactions help us gauge how they are developing.

Whenever we approach the outside holding pen, our whistling, talking, hand clapping, or jingling of keys brings the puppies charging out to greet us. As we crouch down, they paw at the fence to get our attention and yelp with excitement while we pet them. We intentionally make eye contact with each, since puppies instinctively focus on the faces of those they greet, human and canine alike. As we do so, their gazes are fixed and unconcerned, showing no signs of fear. Our animated, friendly facial expressions and voices, combined with patting and stroking, reinforce the eye contact in much the same way that a human mother playfully coos at her infant. Anyone who has experienced the silent, absorbing gaze of a faithful companion dog during a relaxed moment or her focused attentiveness during obedience work understands its value. Fostering nonthreatening eye contact in puppyhood lays a solid foundation for training and for long-term relationships.

A Special Pup

The greeting ritual with Anka's pups reveals some differences between them. After the initial eye, voice, and hand contact ceases, most of the pups are distracted by other things. Kipper, however, is different. He continues to yip long after we have stopped the greeting. He is very people-oriented and repeatedly tries to weasel in on our attention. He nudges and crowds the other pups out of the way, mouthing and pawing playfully at our hands.

What is remarkable is that Kipper, at six and a half pounds, is the smallest in the litter. With Sunny being the largest, at nine pounds, there is enough of a size difference to disprove the widely held belief that the smallest in the litter, the "runt," is an inferior puppy. While the expression "runt of the litter" is commonly used to designate the tiniest pup, as a technical term it refers to an animal who is stunted, who fails to grow to a size within the normal characteristics of the breed. Though a true runt may have a congenital defect concerning the heart or digestive system, which would explain its small size, this is not necessarily the case. It may be perfectly healthy and normal in every respect other than its unusually small stature.

When the term is incorrectly applied to the tiniest in the litter, it implies deficiency. Variations in the size of newborn pups can be the result of large litters, positioning in the womb, breedings that occur over several days, or the particular genetic makeup and growth pattern of the pup. We know of many "runts" who have matured into marvelous companion dogs — sometimes even the smallest pup in the litter turns out to be the biggest at maturity. One of the more memorable dogs in our program, Caralon's Elko von der Lockenheim, was the smallest pup in his litter, yet he matured into a large shepherd, bigger than all his littermates.

In addition to a marked orientation toward people, Kipper displays a strong survival instinct brought on by his size. At feeding time he refuses to be bullied by his bigger brothers and sisters. As they ravenously attack the food, Sunny suddenly snaps at Kipper in an effort to scare him away from his fair share. Kipper, however, yields nothing, snapping back quickly and convincingly, and Sunny retreats to his side of the dish. Occasionally, when a dominant puppy becomes overly aggressive toward his littermates during feeding, we intervene, pinning the offending puppy briefly at the scruff of his neck, just as his mother would when disciplining him. If necessary, we feed him separately. Kipper, though, knows how to take care of himself.

Puppies need to be considered individually and not prejudged according to simplistic criteria. If you are thinking of adopting a pup of normal temperament who happens to be the smallest in the litter, you should not be concerned, provided you have the option of returning him should a veterinary examination reveal a defect.

A Growth Environment

Full socialization extends well beyond ordinary encounters with people—we contribute actively to the emotional development of each puppy by providing her with as wide a range of safe experiences as possible. There should be plenty of variety, with care taken to offer different sights, sounds, and textures. The pup's world needs to be enlarged by exposure to surroundings different from the familiar whelping room. This important element of puppy growth and development is called *enrichment* and is not limited by a specific time period but continues throughout puppyhood and beyond. Puppies require a variety of different experiences. At this stage, for example, it is of no benefit to the pup to be left cooped up all day in a monotonous kennel room with only a few toys and limited opportunity for play and investigation. Life in the puppy kennel should be balanced by other experiences and environments that will challenge curiosity and intelligence. Because of this, when you are looking for a puppy, you should be sure to discuss with prospective breeders how they accommodate their pups.

We begin by getting the pups accustomed to a variety of surfaces: gravel, grass, woodchips, tile, cement, linoleum, and dirt. Anka helps with this because her charges are inclined to follow her. She leads them over the gravel, dirt, and grass surrounding the puppy building, romping with them, occasionally pinning one playfully to the ground with her mouth or herding an errant pup who has wandered a little too far from the main pack. After several days of these sessions, the pups fearlessly and confidently march around on any of these surfaces.

We can easily lead the puppies on short walks to the edge of the woods to let them explore a new world of sights and scents. The pups do this with obvious enthusiasm, investigating the plants, branches,

Once the pups are out and about, they show an insatiable need to explore a new world of sights, sounds, smells, and things to play with.

In the field during a walk, we condition the pups to come by jangling a set of keys at mealtimes—a practice that will pay off in future training.

insects, and animal odors at their level—things they have no contact with in the puppy kennel. Sunny picks up a leaf and mischievously taunts Yola, who cannot quite get her mouth on the other end. Several yards away, a robin lands on a bare branch close to Kairos. He stares at it quizzically, then backs up and mutters threateningly under his breath. The robin flies off, leaving Kairos bewildered over its sudden disappearance. The other puppies, involved in their own explorations, take no notice.

Since the pups are still young and tire easily, after ten minutes we start jingling keys (a practice we have already begun at mealtimes), and the pups yip excitedly as they eagerly follow us back to the kennel. Before placing them in the pen, we conclude the session with lots of praise and pats on their heads.

This technique of conditioning the pups to sound teaches them to associate a specific noise with a particularly pleasant experience. We like to use keys, since dogs respond well to their high-pitched jangling. At weaning, as soon as the pups begin eating regular meals, we jingle keys immediately before placing the food in front of them. The pups quickly learn to recognize the keys and connect them with food. Soon it is possible to link the keys with any pleasant experience. We simply jingle them and follow up with something pleasurable, like petting and praise. This conditioning also forms a helpful foundation for teaching the recall, which we will describe later.

It is important to vary environments. During the day, we let the pups stay outside to play. In special outdoor fenced-in areas behind the kennel, we create play spaces that are interesting and mentally stimulating. Old tires and large clay conduit pipes make excellent, safe obstacles and tunnels for the pups to explore. They will play for hours with big cardboard boxes; clean, used, large gallon plastic bottles; old tennis balls; and squeak toys.

Even the puppy room itself can be made stimulating. Aside from providing plenty of toys, we also suspend a tennis ball or nylon ring

Puppies love to investigate tunnels in their play yard.

Volunteer Sophia urges a puppy toward the slide in the indoor playground.

Pups get used to new situations pretty quickly.

Puppy rooms and yards should be both physically and mentally stimulating, with plenty of toys and safe objects to help the pups develop.

from a fine chain at the pups' eye level. When the dogs tug at it, a cow-bell attached to the top of the chain rings loudly. Not only does this develop eye coordination but it gets the pups accustomed to unusual noises that might otherwise frighten them.

We tune radios to classical-music stations in the puppy rooms and periodically blow whistles, clap together wooden blocks, jingle bells, or turn on the vacuum cleaner throughout the day. In private sessions with each puppy, we encourage him to sniff, lick, and examine the noisemaker before and after the noise, never praising or comforting a puppy who shows fear. A pup is praised only for reacting positively with alertness and curiosity to a stimulation. Exposure to a variety of sounds is vital to socialization. In our increasingly noisy world, dogs must deal with the constant stress of loud noises — experiencing a wide range of unusual sounds helps them get used to this and prevents fear-ful, nervous reactions later on.

At five and six weeks, puppies will show interest in anything new; here, we wave a leaf to teach a pup to follow.

Clapping your hands and calling the puppy eventually gets him to return to and follow you.

Each litter requires plenty of individual and group attention. Here, smiles and cheerful voices accompany the gentle handling of a group of puppies.

Individual Attention

From the fifth to the seventh week, it is imperative that each pup be handled individually by different people, both men and women, every day. Dealing with the litter as a group often masks significant traits that are more visible when a pup is forced to relate to a human being alone. Puppies derive confidence and security from one another. A pup who appears lively with her littermates and comfortable in her puppy area may act hesitant and fearful when placed by herself in a strange room with an unfamiliar person. By spotting poor reactions early in the socialization period, breeders can ensure that certain puppies receive the personalized attention needed to better adjust to people.

Our practice is to give each pup sufficient individual handling every day at this age. During these sessions we combine simple play with a concluding restraint petting exercise that familiarizes the pups with having their front and back paws touched, mouths opened, and muzzles held. Combined with weekly grooming sessions, this practice helps modify any touch sensitivity.

We also utilize community members who are ordinarily not directly involved with raising the puppies, namely the nuns, the married Companions, the members of our parish, even the retreatants. We bring the pups over to the monastery for a community gathering once a week,

Young pups need endless handling and love. Breeders should ensure that their puppies get accustomed to men, women, and children alike.

allowing them to interact with a wider circle of people in an unfamiliar environment.

This requires time and effort. There is no magical shortcut, no room for compromise when it comes to the emotional growth of puppies. Breeders who are genuinely concerned about their pups set aside quality time for daily encounters, because they understand how much of a pup's future personality is shaped by these seemingly insignificant moments. This play is creative in the deepest sense of the term, allowing the finest elements of a puppy's personality to develop.

Finally, despite the fact that the main thrust of this period is socializing with humans, we don't neglect the ongoing process of canine socialization. Not only do we continue to allow the mother to interact with her pups on a daily basis but we also include older shepherds who are "puppy friendly." This gives the puppies valuable experience with safe, more mature dogs who help refine the pups' bite inhibition and sensitivity to hierarchy. It teaches the puppies to be more aware of canine body language while at the same time reinforcing some of their most crucial drives, most notably those of pack and play.

*Visiting monk Father
Tikhon takes his turn
socializing puppies.*

*Volunteer and pup,
comfortable holding
and being held.*

6

Testing the Puppies

By the time the puppies are six weeks old, much of our attention is devoted to the critical issue of placement: where are they going and why? Puppy placement should never be arbitrary. Rather, it should be the result of careful consideration and planning, something that evolves out of a respect for puppy and person alike. Different pups are suited to different circumstances, and it is important for a breeder to come to an accurate appraisal of each dog's possibilities.

You will want to consult your breeder regarding placement procedures. At New Skete we evaluate puppies in several ways. First, since we take notes on each litter from birth and are fully aware of the genetic background, we have a sizable amount of information on each pup by the time he is six and a half weeks old. His development is looked at in detail, and a general impression is formed about his adaptability to various circumstances.

We also interview many of our clients well in advance of the time they will receive their puppy. This allows us to reach a mutual agreement on the type of dog that will be best for them, as well as to measure how serious they are about certain responsibilities. Unfortunately clients are not always realistic about puppies' true needs. For example, people often say they want a Schutzhund puppy, with no real understanding of what that means. *Schutzhund* is a highly challenging form of training that involves competence in three separate areas: tracking, obedience, and protection. It requires a high level of dedication and knowledge on the part of an owner and should never be undertaken without the support of a reputable club and qualified trainer. Because of its demanding nature, puppies suited for this type of work must be more confident, more competitive, more alert, and much more aggressive than the normal companion puppy. A novice handler could get far more than he bargained for by purchasing a Schutzhund puppy without a serious commitment to the sport. In the wrong hands, a strong, dominating puppy could easily develop into an overly aggressive dog with serious behavioral problems.

We strongly encourage personal interviews before the adoption of a puppy. By understanding what you are really looking for in a dog, the breeder can work more effectively to provide you with an appropriate puppy — one with whom you will be truly satisfied.

Puppy Aptitude Testing

We also administer puppy aptitude tests to each pup at seven weeks. Over the past three decades, there has been a growing appreciation among breeders of the value these tests have in determining what situations best suit each puppy. The test is intended to guide the placement process by identifying general personality traits. As an aptitude test, it allows us to evaluate puppies on the basis of sociability, dominance, and obedience potential.

Such evaluation is nothing new. It goes back hundreds of years to cultures in which dogs were used for specific tasks: herding and guarding sheep, hunting, transporting, protecting, rescuing, even pulling carts and boats. In our mechanized and technological society it is difficult for us to appreciate the vital importance dogs once had for people's survival. Working dogs were critical to the economic well-being of their owners, and farmers and breeders had to learn by experience how to spot puppies best suited for various tasks, as well as how to cull those who lacked promise. People had to acquire a breeder's intuition in order to perpetuate and develop the breeding lines they were using. Puppy evaluation has long been at the heart of selective breeding and the establishment of purebred dogs.

We have used the Volhard Puppy Aptitude Test (see appendix) successfully for many years, finding it an invaluable aid for placing puppies in homes where they will thrive. Though no one test can ever be considered infallible, when combined with all of the previous information accumulated on each litter, the Volhard test gives a clear picture of puppy personality and potential that makes the likelihood of successful placement high.

Testing Anka's Litter

Fifty days after the puppies are born, Debbie Collins, a friend who is unacquainted with Anka's litter, comes to the monastery to test the pups. We always have someone do the testing who is a complete stranger to the litter, in a location the pups are unaccustomed to. This prevents biased results, since the purpose of the test is to obtain an accurate picture of each puppy's raw temperament. Puppies will behave differently in various circumstances, but we can accurately chart a pup's true temperament by observing her reactions during a broad spectrum of new experiences and minor stresses.

The best time to test puppies is as close to the forty-ninth day as possible. Once they are seven weeks old, EEG readings indicate that neurological development has reached adult levels, thus allowing us to obtain a true reading of their behavioral tendencies. If testing is done earlier, results will be inconclusive because neurological development is still too immature; if done later, between eight and ten weeks, pups will be in the fear period, making assessments of temperament subject to serious misinterpretation.

We conduct the test late in the morning, well after the pups have eaten, during a period when they are lively. The exam takes approximately ten minutes, and each pup is tested individually, going through all the phases in one session. To assist the tester, one of the monks watches from a hidden location and records the puppies' responses.*

Yola is the first pup to take the test. The initial phase evaluates social attraction, testing the degree to which a puppy is willing to approach a stranger. Once Yola has been placed in the room, Debbie crouches down several feet away from her and begins clapping her hands gently. Though Yola's tail initially goes down, she approaches readily, and when she reaches Debbie, she circles back and forth between her legs, squirming affectionately as she is petted. This is a submissive reaction, indicating a certain lack of self-confidence that is blended with a gentle disposition toward humans. The other pups are bouncier, coming readily to Debbie with their tails wagging high and licking at her hands. Sunny even jumps and paws at Debbie's leg, displaying a more dominant, self-confident nature. None of the pups bites at her hands.

---

* For clarity's sake, we will discuss individual responses to each phase of the test together rather than presenting each pup's test separately.

We rate the pup's responsiveness to hand-clapping.

Following along with the tester: Is the puppy reluctant or enthusiastic?

After several seconds, Debbie stands up and begins the *"following"* *exercise*, which measures the pup's sociability as well as her willingness to accept leadership. As Debbie walks away, Yola pauses a moment, then continues after Debbie with her tail wagging gently, though she does not get underfoot. She stays behind Debbie and follows her around the room, suggesting a willingness to accept Debbie's leadership. Kairos and Oka score about the same, while both Kipper and

Sunny end up getting underfoot, a sign that could spell dominance with their future owners.

The next two phases, the restraint and social dominance tests, are given in succession and measure puppies' tendencies toward dominance or submission, as well as their willingness to forgive. Debbie crouches down and rolls Yola over on her back, looking at her calmly. Yola remains passive, offering no resistance, and licks Debbie's hand several times. After thirty seconds, Yola is placed upright on all fours and is stroked gently from the top of her head down to her back. During the petting, Yola licks at Debbie's face once and seems to melt. This series of reactions shows a high degree of submissiveness and sensitivity, and suggests that Yola will be a dog who is quick to forgive after being disciplined. Her response differs from that of the other pups, who offer more initial resistance on the restraint test, struggling to escape for at least fifteen seconds before they settle. Except for Sunny. Sunny struggles and squirms to get free for the duration, tossing his head back and forth in protest as he is held to the ground. When time is called, Debbie lets out a sigh of relief, and Sunny immediately rights himself and walks away. He comes back quickly, however, and as Debbie pets him, he jumps up toward her and starts pawing at her arm. Sunny's response to the restraint test shows a high orientation toward dominance, and though he was forgiving after it, he was also somewhat pushy. The other pups did not show this characteristic; they simply allowed themselves to be stroked, cuddling up to Debbie to lick her face.

In the final phase of the temperament section of the test—elevation dominance—the puppy is evaluated in a situation in which she has no control. Cradling Yola with both of her hands under the rib cage, Debbie lifts her up and holds her in midair for thirty seconds. Yola shows no signs of struggle; she is passive, fully accepting of the handling. The other pups score exactly the same, even Sunny. Not one manifests any inclination to struggle, a sign that they will be easy to handle when placed in a situation such as a veterinarian's office or a professional groomer's parlor.

At this point, the tone of the exam shifts to obedience aptitude. The first test is a retrieval exercise and demonstrates a puppy's willingness to work with a human being. Debbie takes a crumpled piece of paper and jiggles it playfully in front of Yola. She then tosses the paper about four feet away. Yola goes to investigate it, sniffs it for several seconds, and then returns to Debbie without having picked up the paper. This indicates a

The elevation-dominance exercise—the puppy is held in midair for thirty seconds.

modest aptitude for obedience, since she did investigate and show some interest but did not bring the paper back. The other pups do, though not in identical ways. Kipper and Kairos trot over to the paper immediately, pick it up, and return with it to Debbie, who praises them enthusiastically. When Oka gets it, she meanders around the room, showing a little independence, but after about thirty seconds she brings it to Debbie, who is still clapping her hands and calling her. Sunny's response is the most precocious. Running after the paper, he picks it up in his mouth and shakes it vigorously back and forth. He paces sideways for several moments, then shakes it some more and brings it back to Debbie, who praises him. All the puppies' reactions show various degrees of obedience potential, with Oka's response being the weakest. Her delay in bringing the paper back suggests a bit of independence that we do not see in the other pups.

After the retrieving exercise, we test the puppy's touch sensitivity. The purpose of this is to determine a pup's threshold of pain, giving us an idea of how difficult she will be to control and train. Puppies who are very touch-sensitive will respond to the slightest pressure from a

Bringing back an object such as a piece of paper or a bone to the tester can be an easy retrieval exercise, even at seven weeks.

collar. Those who are insensitive will probably require more strength and perhaps different types of training equipment. Debbie crouches down next to Yola and lifts up her front leg. Taking her paw, Debbie squeezes the webbing between her toes and begins counting, increasing the pressure as she does so. After a brief two-count, Yola gives a quick yip and tries to pull away. Her pain threshold is low, indicating that it will not be necessary to use a great deal of force with her in training. The puppy with the highest count is Sunny, who yips at six. Nevertheless, this is still a medium sensitivity reading and does not indicate potential problems with obedience training.

The next test centers on sound sensitivity and is intended to measure how a pup responds to sharp noises. This is especially relevant for puppies who will be living in busy cities. Debbie faces Yola away from the source of the noise. She then takes an aluminum pie pan and throws it to the floor. Yola acts a bit startled and very cautiously takes several steps in the direction of the pan. She then stops, looks over at Debbie, and walks away, deciding not to investigate any further. The other puppies are more confident, going over to the pan and sniffing it. The most interesting reaction comes from Kairos. After hearing the sound, he approaches the pan and picks it up in his mouth, carries it to the corner of the room, and lies down. This manifestation of courage and intelligent reaction to sudden noises demonstrates his ability to adapt to any type of living situation.

*Puppies differ in their
sensitivity to sounds and
noises. They can learn to
ignore distractions.*

The next exercise is the sight sensitivity test, which gives us an indication of a puppy's reaction to a strange object. We use an old cloth that
is attached to a string and have Debbie tauntingly jerk it across the floor
so that Yola can see it. She hesitates for a moment, ducking her head
down in a cautious movement and tucking her tail. After Debbie makes
several passes with the cloth, Yola starts to trail slowly after it, though
she does not pounce on it. Her response is very tentative in contrast
with Sunny's. He immediately jumps on the cloth and puts it in his
mouth, shaking it vigorously. Debbie gives a few tugs on the string, and
Sunny pulls back with delight, revealing a feisty, spirited pup who
could become aggressive if put in the wrong circumstances. The other
pups simply walk over to the cloth and try to sniff it, showing self-
confidence but less inclination toward aggression.

The final phase is a stability exercise that determines the level of startle response to a strange object. Holding an umbrella, Debbie stands
about five feet away from Yola. She opens the umbrella and gently
places it on the ground. Yola looks at it, staying in her position for about
twenty seconds, neither retreating from the umbrella nor moving
toward it. She doesn't seem visibly disturbed, just not inclined to investigate the new object. Kairos, on the other hand, walks up to the
umbrella and begins sniffing it. His tail doesn't move as he approaches,
and he seems comfortable trying to figure it out. Sunny, by contrast,
barks when the umbrella opens, and he marches up to it confidently.
He doesn't bite it, just sniffs.

The sight-sensitivity test. We pass a strange object near the pup and observe his reaction.

At the conclusion of each test, Debbie briefly praises the puppy on his way back to the puppy pen. Then she confirms the recorded score with the assisting monk. When all of the tests are completed, several monks and staff workers involved in puppy placement discuss the results and begin planning each pup's departure.

As you might guess, the purpose of puppy testing is not to judge which pups have good or bad temperaments but to indicate where they should be placed to reach their full potential. A pup with a good temperament for an outdoorsman might have a poor temperament for working as a therapy dog in a nursing home. So much depends on an owner's needs and desires.

Analyzing the results of Anka's litter (see appendix for score sheet), we see no real surprises; each pup's scores confirm our own general impressions from the previous weeks. Because the litter comes from two parents of solid working lineage, the pups will require people who are familiar with handling active, intelligent dogs. We can now carefully review the applications of people who are waiting to obtain a puppy from us and try to match them with what is available from the litter.

Sunny, who scored mostly twos on the test, is the dominant pup in the litter. He possesses all the qualities found in a successful working dog: spirit, self-confidence, intelligence, and poise. We place him with an experienced handler who is seriously involved in Schutzhund work.

Kairos, the second male, scored mostly threes, indicating a lively, outgoing dog. Since he shows no difficulties with either people or noise, we choose to place him in a suburban setting, with a family that has three teenagers. They have owned shepherds in the past and are committed to having him well trained.

Oka, scoring mostly threes and fours, is also lively, though with a mild tendency toward independence. We feel she will adjust well in a situation in which the owner is gone part of the day, so we place her with a single woman who spends some hours counseling clients in her home.

Kipper, who also scored primarily threes, is a pup we feel confident can fit into a family situation because of his strong orientation to people. He is placed with a family that has two children and one other dog, an active Labrador retriever.

Yola, who scored mostly fours, is a perfect puppy for an elderly couple. She is gentle and submissive but not fearful, so we place her with a recently retired couple who have plenty of time and love to spend on her.

By the end of the ninth week, all of the pups are gone. Ordinarily, we send puppies to their new homes between eight and ten weeks, depending on particular circumstances. Though some books make a point of identifying the seventh week as the ideal time for placement, we have found that departure dates can be much more flexible, provided regular socialization continues at the breeder's. When puppies stay beyond the seventh week, we still follow a daily socialization schedule, making sure they receive plenty of exposure to people, dogs, and different environments, and we have seen no ill effects from this. By the time the puppies leave, they are ready to make the transition to life with their new owners.

The Fear/Avoidance Period

Earlier, we alluded to a natural part of the socialization process that occurs between eight and ten weeks of age called the fear/avoidance period. During this time, puppies who were confident and precocious a week earlier can suddenly appear tentative and cautious, making you question whether something is wrong. This is especially so for new owners, who fearfully wonder whether such behavior indicates that their breeder pulled a fast one on them or that they are somehow mistreating their new charge. Be reassured that what is most likely occurring is merely the pup's natural adjustment to full adult sensory capacities — this lasts for several weeks. Because most breeders place their pups between seven and ten weeks (the optimal time for puppies to bond with their new owners), you must be conscious of this phase and use it to your advantage. Your patience and understanding strongly encourage the pup to come out of this period having a strong bond with you.

Despite the fact that this phase is normal, it is important not to expose a pup to highly stressful experiences during this time. Specialists have discovered that in this period pups are especially sensitive to traumatic experiences and poor handling, which may result in long-lasting emotional scars. Whereas five- to six-week-old pups bounce back quickly from a sudden fear experience, the impact is much more profound during the fear/avoidance period.

This does not imply that we should keep the pup insulated from new people or new circumstances. Socialization is essential throughout the period. It must, however, be done intelligently, with care. New experiences should be nontraumatic and easy for the pup to deal with. By taking a positive, encouraging attitude toward your pup and safeguarding him from frightening, stressful experiences, you will notice a natural recovery back to his normal self toward the end of the tenth week.

One final remark: the fear/avoidance period is just one more reason why the early environment of a pup must be balanced and healthy to begin with to ensure a positive adjustment and transition through puppyhood. If a puppy was never in a normal, healthy situation early on, if he did not receive the necessary socialization at each stage of his young life, then he will have no solid ground to return to now — the effects of this period will be much more pronounced and long-lasting. Furthermore, if the circumstances and attitudes in the pup's new home are not conducive to guiding him through the fear/avoidance period, the pup usually suffers emotional scars that will affect his behavior for life. Prospective puppy owners must be careful about where they obtain their pup and the manner in which they introduce him to his new home. We will examine these issues in detail in the following chapters.

Inspiration and Perspiration

Perhaps the most enchanting quality of a puppy is possibility. Puppies fill us with hope, giving us a chance to start over again, to shape them and ourselves into long-term companions who will share an intimate part of each other's lives for the next ten to twenty years.

— Dogs & Devotion

Let's pause for a moment to see how we've come to this point. Our purpose in describing the hidden stages of puppyhood so meticulously has not been to burden you with a lot of fascinating but unnecessary information. Rather, our hope is to create in you an informed appreciation of the many factors that have made your puppy the unique creature she is. When new owners understand the complexity and beauty of how puppies develop, they are more inclined to commit to the disciplined process of raising them conscientiously — they won't take their new charges for granted. If an owner can see the pup for the mystery she is and the capacity she has for becoming a great companion, that owner's desire to work hard to realize that goal will increase as well.

This is an important point to remember. Each new or prospective puppy owner enters the process with a vision of the sort of puppy he or she hopes to raise. Think of your own experience here: what are you hoping for? Whatever your specific desires, obviously they won't transpire by magic but will require consistent and conscientious work to make them a reality. If you can keep in mind what your pup is capable of becoming, you can remain hopeful while resisting the temptation to take behavioral and developmental shortcuts with his training.

We're not suggesting this is easy, but the good news is that by being faithful to the first six to eight months of puppyhood, by providing your pup with the structure and experiences he needs to become integrally adjusted to his world, you put yourself in the enviable position of enjoying the fruits of that for the rest of the dog's life. Dealing with puppyhood conscientiously does demand a lot of hard work and sacrifice — but the rewards are well worth the effort. When we raise puppies with an enlightened understanding of the many formative issues that define the first months of their lives — when we provide them with the daily exercise and handling they require to flourish mentally and physically — they are much more likely to reach their potential while also bringing their owners deep and long-lasting joy.

We use the word *joy* here deliberately. Perhaps the biggest surprise in raising a puppy is the transforming effect it can have on you. Performing this service well is not simply about your puppy maturing into a happy adult companion. It is also about you becoming a better human being, more of who you are called to be. Throughout history, the dog-human relationship has shown that dogs can humanize us, and this is part of the magic unleashed in adopting a puppy. One of the biggest temptations we can fall prey to with a dog is hubris, to think of training one-dimensionally as what we do vis-à-vis the dog. That is indeed one element, but not the only one. Raising a puppy, and the training that is a part of it, equally involves our own transformation in the process. Perhaps because New Skete is a contemplative monastery, we've been naturally disposed to consider how living so closely with dogs has changed us for the good. Yet when we have expressed this publicly, many folks from widely divergent faith backgrounds (indeed, even those with none whatsoever) have conveyed similar experiences. This suggests there is a spiritual dimension present in the human-dog relationship that is available to all and that is profoundly enriching. How might we explain this?

First, by virtue of their very otherness, dogs have the capacity to put us in touch with the natural, nonhuman world around us. They are guileless, responding to life spontaneously and without calculation. Because of this, they become windows to the soul, prodding us to pay careful attention to them in a manner that also awakens us to the divine mystery all around us. Something so simple as walking the dog takes us out of ourselves and reminds us that life's beauty beckons to be acknowledged. Or think of a dog greeting her owner after several hours' separation, her body showing effusive yet controlled signals of joy. It is as if she's saying, "This is the high point of my day! You're home." Could we ever merit such affection? It is pure grace, yet its sincerity draws the best out of us, encouraging us to respond by trying to live up to such love.

When we live with our dogs consciously, we become deeply aware of their importance as a reliable source of self-knowledge. Precisely because dogs are so absolutely honest, they mirror us all the time, reflecting how we're coming across, how we are being understood. Bringing home the baggage of a tough day at work? Letting your irritation get the best of you when your dog is soliciting attention? Your companion never fails to mirror that. You'll see her words in her body language and know she doesn't lie. That's crucial information for you to mine and reflect on. It will keep you in touch with reality and prevent self-inflation. It will continually challenge you to be conscious of your feelings while at the same time not fall captive to them. That can lead to a new level of personal freedom that is intimately connected to your own transformation as a human being.

We have often spoken of the fact that the word *obedience* comes from a Latin word that means "to listen wholeheartedly." What we discover in our relationship with a dog is that it is not simply the dog who obeys. The person who truly listens can discern what is needed in the moment, what serves the relationship. When you pay close attention to your dog, the relationship becomes reciprocal even as you assume the role of the benevolent pack leader. By responding obediently to reality with your companion, you'll experience the type of bond that inspired you to get a puppy in the first place. And chances are that if you listen consistently, your actions will carry over into how you deal with reality more broadly, with the whole gamut of your human relationships. Everything interconnects.

So the effort is worth it. Whether you are preparing to embark on a new adventure or are already immersed in the beginning stages of the relationship, you should keep the ultimate goal in mind. Inevitably there will be ups and downs that will test your seriousness and resolve. If you can keep a sense of humor as well as an attitude of patience and faith, chances are very good that both you and your puppy will reap the rewards. This is not a closed process. It grows with each day and has the possibility of being renewed time and again. Trust in the process.

It may seem surprising to associate faith with our bond with a dog, but truly it's an essential component. Faith helps us believe in what is possible, in how deep we can go with the relationship. Each dog is unique, and a good relationship adapts intuitively to the temperament and needs of the particular dog who shares our life. There are likely to be some rough spots where things don't seem to be going as expected and where we can start doubting ourselves. But believing in the process, and having faith in the wisdom of those who have worked with all manner of dogs, can help us relax and listen closely to the needs of the moment, and respond appropriately.

—Dogs & Devotion

7

Deciding to Adopt a Puppy

To form a healthy bond with someone requires that we take into consideration the genuine needs and possibilities of the other. This is true not only of people but of dogs. Certainly dogs should not be thought of as human, but they still have a unique value of their own. Many people fail to recognize that having a dog involves what any true relationship requires. We are most successful at adopting and raising a puppy when we build on a clear-sighted respect for the kind of creature a dog is; then we can understand and accept the responsibilities of caring for one properly. Such an attitude flies in the face of the *me* mentality, a one-dimensional mind-set that fails to respect a dog in its integrity as a dog and instead sees it only in terms of one's own wants and desires.

So before you rush out to adopt a pup, we recommend that you step back for a moment to challenge yourself and your family on the seriousness of this step. Play devil's advocate! Examine your motives. Why do you want a dog? What type of owner will you be? What are you prepared to give your dog in return for the pleasure of her company? Far better to raise the issue of responsibility and care before you get a pup than to learn of your mistake later, when you have a twelve-week-old puppy who is suddenly making demands on you... at 3:00 in the morning!

The One-dimensional Owner

Recently we received a call from a married couple inquiring whether we could find a new home for their five-month-old German shepherd puppy, Wolf, whom they were no longer able to keep. Though we explained that we did not offer that type of service, we asked them why

With twice the attention, this pup knows two friends are better than one. You should introduce your puppy to plenty of children.

they were giving up on their puppy. Embarrassed, the husband said he and his wife lived in a suburb of a large city and had adopted their pup after several local burglaries convinced them that a watchdog would be desirable. They had gone to a reputable breeder and had obtained a bright, affectionate puppy who they assumed would easily meet their needs. "Yet," the man confessed, "we had no idea what we bargained for." This was their first dog.

Being professional people, they had to be away from the apartment at least nine hours a day. In itself, this wasn't a problem, since Wolf had been successfully house-trained in a matter of days, and they had arranged for a dog-walker to take him out for half an hour at midday.

"Then what is the problem?" we asked.

"He won't leave us alone," the man replied.

Having Wolf around, he complained, was like adding four more hours to an already hectic day. When he and his wife got home from work, they wanted to relax and be with each other, yet Wolf's need for attention made that quite impossible. "I mean, he has to be fed, walked, played with.... It's worse than having a kid."

"And all that licking," the wife chimed in on the other line. "It's disgusting! He simply won't settle down and be a good boy. The two of us are even starting to get into arguments because of the dog, and the neighbors are complaining about his barking and whining during the day. It's just a pain having him around. I mean, who needs it?"

What the couple discovered too late was that they did not need a dog but a high-tech alarm system. They never really wanted a dog in the first place; they only thought they did. They were unwilling to accept (because they never dreamed of it!) the real demands a puppy would make on their lives, specifically his need for love and companionship. During our conversation it became obvious that it had never occurred to them to try to see things from Wolf's perspective, to consider his needs in the relationship. Wolf was bought for protection, period. When it became clear that Wolf's needs exceeded what they were willing to give — that Wolf was becoming a pain, an inconvenience — their solution was to get rid of him.

This is a frequent scenario that appears in many different disguises. Though nobody intentionally obtains a dog only to keep it for several months, things can easily turn out this way. Sometimes this is caused by the onset of a specific problem behavior in the dog; at other times it is merely the result of the owner's fading interest. The common thread in so many failed owner-dog relationships is the belated discovery that having a dog is not what the owners thought it would be. Cold reality clashes with their one-dimensional expectations, and so they bypass the responsibility by opting for the easier solution: giving up the dog.

Who Should Have a Dog?

When it comes to dogs, romanticism abounds! Certainly one of the effects television has had on our culture is to create highly idealized images of what a dog should be like. Rin Tin Tin, Lassie, Bullet, Benji, and Big Red are all presented as ideal companions who require no training and are faithfully devoted to attending to their owners' every need. They never have soiling "accidents," they do not need to be taken out for walks, and they are always obedient. They mind their own business when they are not wanted and are always ready to give love and affection when it is asked of them. What could be easier or more wonderful?

The truth is that the Hollywood dog exists only in the movies. What we never hear about is the long and difficult training process these dogs go through to perform the amazing on-screen tricks and stunts, and the patience, love, and perseverance required on the part of their trainers! If you expect your puppy to rise effortlessly to the standards set by Lassie, you will be sorely disappointed.

Many people are simply unprepared for the changes that will take place in their lives once they adopt a puppy. In fact, our experience has taught us that anyone who thinks he or she wants a dog should postpone the decision until after thinking the matter through completely.

Not everyone should have a dog. Because of a variety of circumstances, many people simply do not have the time or ability to care for a puppy or even an adult dog. A pup will take us outside of ourselves and our own little world. Ordinary personal decisions that previously concerned only you or your family will now always have to take into account the presence of the puppy. Free time that was once for yourself alone must now be shared with your pup. How do you feel about that?

Caring for a dog is a lot of hard work. *Canis familiaris*, the pet dog, cannot attend to herself. From the moment of her adoption until the day of her death (which, barring accident or illness, can be fifteen years or more), she is a highly dependent creature who will count on you for all the essentials of canine living: food, water, shelter, exercise, training, and periodic veterinary care. But beyond these, the principal need a puppy has throughout her life is social. She requires an owner who is a companion in the fullest sense of the word. Can you see yourself or your family in such a role?

From this perspective, the old injunction is as relevant as ever: Know thyself! People who are willing to look at themselves honestly and who try to find a dog who blends in with their lifestyle and living environment stand the best chance of developing a healthy, long-term relationship with their puppy. Any normal puppy has a unique personality; he will naturally and actively seek out a relationship. Though there are a number of legitimate practical reasons for getting a pup (working, sport, show, breeding, protection, etc.), none of them should ever exclude or override the chief one: the desire for companionship and therefore the willingness to accept the obligations this entails. Taking the time to consider the choice realistically and listing the demands and responsibilities beforehand will bring rewarding results for both puppy and you.

So You Really Want a Dog?

Frequently visitors to our monastery are interested in obtaining one of our shepherds. On just such an occasion, after meeting many of our dogs and talking at length with one of the monks, a woman asked what she should do next in order to get a puppy. We explained that there would be a waiting period and that she would first have to fill out a puppy application form (see page 94). This is a detailed application that we use to help match prospective customers with individual puppies. As she looked over the form, the woman expressed amazement, saying, "My heavens, you'd think I was adopting a child!"

This is precisely the point. Though a puppy is not a child, the decision to adopt one involves a similar sort of seriousness. It is entirely appropriate for breeders to question potential clients thoroughly, since their answers will help indicate what sort of puppy is best suited for them. Any conscientious breeder feels a personal sense of responsibility for the pups she has bred; her interest is less in selling them than in placing them in the right homes (that is, right for the owner and right for the puppy). Thus, if we prefer to use the term *adopting* a puppy instead of *buying* one, it is only because it puts the emphasis squarely where it belongs: bringing another member into your family.

All canids live naturally in packs, the immediate members of their social circle. With domestic dogs, those human beings with whom they live are considered fellow pack members, even if the "pack" involves only one other individual. There is nothing sentimental in regarding a new puppy as an additional member of your family: this is how *he* will view *you*.

That's why it's important that your choice be more than just a hit-or-miss proposition. It should involve serious thought and planning. Personal circumstances and those of the dog also must be considered. Dealing as we do with a large variety of dogs and people, we have

Puppy Application

*Please note: This is a sample application for this book. Should you wish to contact the Monks of New Skete about a puppy, kindly do so online at www.newskete.org.

NAME: _____ APPLICANT AGE: _____

ADDRESS: _____

CITY: _____ STATE: _____ ZIP: _____

HOME PHONE: _____ WORK PHONE: _____

CELL PHONE: _____ E-MAIL ADDRESS: _____

DO YOU OWN OR RENT? _____

OCCUPATIONS OF ADULTS? _____

PUPPY GENDER PREFERENCE: (Please Circle)   MALE   FEMALE   EITHER

ACTIVITY LEVEL: (Please Circle)   HIGH   MEDIUM   LOW

TEMPERAMENT TENDENCY: (Please Circle)   INDEPENDENT   DOMINANT   AVERAGE   QUIET

COAT PREFERENCE: (Please Circle)   LONG COAT   SHORT COAT   EITHER

COAT COLOR: (Please Circle)   SABLE   BLACK   BLACK/TAN   BLACK/RED   ANY

I AM INTERESTED IN: (Circle One)   SEARCH & RESCUE   HERDING   AGILITY
                                   OBEDIENCE   THERAPY   COMPANION
                                   OTHER (Please Specify) _____

IS THIS YOUR FIRST SHEPHERD FROM NEW SKETE?   Y / N

WHY DO YOU WANT A GERMAN SHEPHERD DOG AS OPPOSED TO ANOTHER BREED? _____
_____
_____

HOW DID YOU HEAR OF US? _____

HAVE YOU READ OUR BOOKS? _____ WHICH ONES? _____
_____

HAVE YOU RAISED A PUPPY BEFORE? _____
_____

WHAT DOGS HAVE YOU PREVIOUSLY OWNED? _____
_____

HAVE YOU OR YOUR SPOUSE EVER TRAINED A DOG BEFORE? _____
_____

DOES ANYONE IN YOUR FAMILY HAVE ALLERGIES? _____

HOW MANY ADULTS LIVE IN YOUR HOME?____ AGES: _____

DO YOU HAVE CHILDREN?   Y / N   AGES: _____

DO YOUR CHILDREN LIVE WITH YOU FULL-TIME? _____

IS ANYONE IN YOUR HOME DISABLED? _____

DO YOU HAVE ANY OTHER ANIMALS? (PLEASE INCLUDE AGES AND M / F) _____

_____

IS YOUR YARD FENCED?   Y / N
WHAT TYPE OF FENCING? _____

ARE YOU COMMITTED TO EXERCISING YOUR DOG THROUGHOUT HIS LIFE?   Y / N

IF BOTH ADULTS WORK DURING THE DAY, WHERE WOULD YOUR PUPPY BE? _____

_____

WHERE WILL YOUR PUPPY SLEEP AT NIGHT? _____

WE DO NOT SHIP PUPPIES BY AIR; HOWEVER, YOU HAVE THE OPTION OF FLYING OR DRIVING INTO
ALBANY AND PICKING UP YOUR PUPPY. WE ENCOURAGE YOU TO PICK UP YOUR OWN DOG. HOW
WILL YOU BE PICKING UP YOUR PUPPY? _____

WE SELL DOGS WITH ONLY LIMITED AKC REGISTRATION. THESE DOGS YOU PURCHASE FROM US WILL
NOT HAVE BREEDING RIGHTS. (Please Initial) _____

ARE YOU WILLING TO SPAY OR NEUTER YOUR DOG?   Y / N

ARE YOU WILLING TO TAKE YOUR PUP TO PUPPY CLASSES?   Y / N

ARE YOU WILLING TO FURTHER YOUR PUPPY'S TRAINING WITH A PROFESSIONAL?   Y / N

ARE YOU WILLING TO SEND THE CONFIRMATION OF THEIR
CERTIFICATES TO THE MONKS OF NEW SKETE?   Y / N

HAVE YOU READ THE NEW YORK STATE SALES POLICY?   Y / N (Please Initial) _____

The cost of a puppy is $3,000–$3,500 (plus NYS sales tax), subject to change according to the value
of the individual breeding. The following payment types are accepted: Visa, MasterCard, American
Express, cashier's check, money order, personal check, and cash. Payment is required at time of
pickup of dog. All payments are nonrefundable. We reserve the right not to sell a dog to anyone. The
buyer is responsible for the appropriate training of this dog.

Please sign and return this entire page, plus an initialed New York State Sales Policy.
I have read the above conditions of sale. I understand and agree to all of the above conditions
of sale, as indicated by my signature.

Buyer's Signature: _____ Date: _____

Buyer's Name (print): _____

Pups need to be socialized in a variety of situations with a variety of people. Here, a family of volunteers finds that time flies when working with the puppies.

files of case histories that repeatedly demonstrate the effects of poor selection on the human-dog relationship. Making a smart decision regarding a puppy is more complicated than most people imagine.

Dogs are the most varied of all the species in the animal kingdom. There are currently 167 breeds officially registered by the American Kennel Club (AKC) plus many in the "Miscellaneous" class that are waiting for official recognition. Natural historians of dogs can identify more than 400 breeds internationally. Of the purebred dogs recognized by the AKC, seven specific breed categories reflect the general orientation of each breed: Sporting Dogs, Hounds, Working Dogs, Terriers, Toy Dogs, Herding Dogs, Non-sporting Dogs. In addition, there are any number of mixed-breed* combinations that draw physical and behavioral characteristics from diverse genetic backgrounds. With all this to consider, what is the best way to determine which is the appropriate puppy for you?

---

* For dogs whose immediate ancestry involves two or more breeds, we prefer the term *mixed breed* or *random bred* to the more demeaning designation *mongrel* or *mutt*.

Mixed-Breed or Purebred Puppy?

There are many opinions within the professional community regarding the desirability of a mixed-breed puppy over one who is purebred. Some veterinarians, for example, maintain that mixed-breed pups make better family pets because they have calmer temperaments and by nature are more adaptable to a wider variety of living circumstances. These veterinarians also point out that mixed breeds are substantially less expensive and are less apt to have congenital defects. If you add to these factors the consideration that adopting a puppy from an animal shelter will most likely save him from being euthanized, taking in a pup of mixed breeding has considerable merit.

Other specialists, however, disagree, noting that random-bred pups are far less predictable with respect to future size and temperament than their purebred cousins. Since the mixed puppies come from breedings that were more than likely unplanned and unwanted, there is often no way of foreseeing what the puppy will be like when he grows up. Thus, an owner may be adopting a puppy for which he is especially unsuited. The advantage of adopting a purebred pup is that you can reasonably predict what the pup will be like as an adult — in size, color, and behavior. This is not necessarily the case with a puppy who is random bred. What may initially appear to be a scrawny terrier mix at eight and a half weeks could well end up being a ninety-five-pound mammoth by the time he is full-grown. Choosing a purebred helps prevent "surprises" that end up badly for owner and dog alike. Also, because random-bred litters are often unwanted, it is likely that the puppies have not been raised with the consistent care administered by dedicated breeders.

So who is right?

The truth is that either a random-bred or purebred pup can become an ideal companion, provided that the right elements are present. We have known too many well-adjusted mixed-breed dogs to doubt the possibility of finding one who can become a wonderful companion. Nevertheless, it is deceptive to state that random-bred dogs are calmer or more intelligent than their purebred counterparts. This is simply not the case. While one random-bred dog may be superior in intelligence and trainability when compared to an individual purebred, there is a basic standard of quality among purebreds (from reputable breeders) that does not exist in the gamut of random-bred dogs. Purebred dogs have a traceable

Two Pomeranian puppies ready for play.

genealogy—conscientious breeders study pedigrees, analyze previous litters, and purposefully breed into lines that demonstrate intelligence, good health, and overall soundness. Unplanned breedings between dogs of differing breeds, however, are much more difficult to predict.

Taking these factors into account, we believe that for the individual who wants to closely match a pup to his or her personality and lifestyle, there are very good reasons to adopt a purebred puppy. It can be helpful to adopt a pup in full knowledge of what she will be as an adult than on the basis of what she appears to be as a puppy. This is most easily done with a purebred.

If you do decide on a mixed breed, however, you should keep several things in mind. First, plan on neutering or spaying your pup between six and eight months of age: no random-bred dog should be allowed to reproduce, since it only perpetuates the sorry cycle of unwanted pups who are annually destroyed. Second, understand that a random-bred dog has the same needs as a purebred dog. He is never, under any circumstances, a second-class citizen. He requires the same commitment, the same amount of love and care from you as would any purebred. Never think that because he is a less expensive investment, the burden of responsibility is also lessened. Regardless of what kind of puppy you adopt, your love and informed attention should be constant.

Pet Shop Puppy?

If you have decided to get a purebred puppy, where is the best place to obtain her? A pet shop? Pet stores are a curious phenomenon in American life. Frequently tucked away in shopping malls, they do a decent job of filling the needs pet owners have for supplies. If you take a walk through a typical shop, a wide variety of colorful specimens will vie for your attention: cats and kittens, reptiles, mice, gerbils, birds, tropical fish, and...puppies. These puppies, all kinds, are in separate cages lined up against the wall for shoppers to view easily; elsewhere, older pups in larger pens lie forlornly on dog beds. While Muzak drifts through the store, the birds in the center of the shop whistle at the browsers, seemingly jealous of the attention the puppies are receiving.

The pups all seem cute enough, like the young of all species. They look up toward their admirers for several moments, seemingly begging for liberation, and then go back to playing with squeak toys provided for their amusement. Maybe a well-dressed couple chat in front of the springer spaniel puppy, putting their fingers through the cage for her to lick as they try to decide if she is the one they really want. Nearby, two children tug at their mother's skirt, pointing to a Labrador retriever pup while they pester, "That one, Mommy, that one!" Shop attendants in practical white smocks move throughout the store, politely answering questions, while another employee routinely makes sure that all the cages are clean. Everything seems so civil. It has all the order of a supermarket and, we might think, all the quality as well!

So what is wrong here?

We could first focus on the source of many of these pet shop puppies: "puppy mills," where dogs are bred in cramped, fetid, factory-like conditions and where basic health standards are nonexistent. These establishments, many of which are located in rural American communities, are often created to supplement ordinary farm income by mass-producing puppies for pet shops throughout the country. The preponderant motivation for any puppy mill is pure profit and not the breeding of sound, healthy animals. Large numbers of male and female purebred dogs, jammed into filthy kennels, are bred as often as possible and with no consideration whatsoever for quality. Dogs who are nervous, hyperactive, shy, or vicious, or who have one of any number of inherited defects, are not prevented from breeding—that would simply be bad business.

The puppies themselves are forced to spend their first critical weeks in abominable conditions: they must walk around and sleep in their own filth; vaccinations are rarely given; human contact is negligible; and when they are shipped out at five to six weeks of age, they must spend up to a week in transit, stuffed into cages or crates with insufficient food, water, and veterinary care. Often they arrive at the pet shop weak and dehydrated, stressed, and suffering from infections picked up in transit. After a superficial cleaning up, they still lack the vigor and spark of really healthy pups. By the time they are offered for sale, customers pay approximately the same price they would to a private breeder, but for a much less reliable dog. Though it is true that some pet shop puppies are purchased from local breeders who raise their puppies in responsible ways, it is more likely that the pups come from outside the immediate area of the store. This makes checking up on where the dog came from next to impossible.

Thus, for the prospective customer looking at a pet shop puppy, there is seldom any reliable information available on her background, her genetic predispositions, or how she was raised. Even if a puppy comes with a pedigree, the names rarely involve top dogs; this is mostly a smoke screen designed to impress clients. More serious is the impossibility of seeing the parents, or at least the mother, firsthand. Without realizing it, the customer may be buying into a host of unseen medical and behavioral problems that will surface months later.

Besides, how humane is it to have a puppy "on display" in the store itself, isolated from its mother and littermates, in a separate cage, lacking adequate exercise and handling, and exposed to any number of germs and infectious diseases? What these pups experience early in life is shameful if not criminal, degrading the humans who abuse them. The only way this can end is for customers to stop purchasing them. Think about it. Who would want to buy a friend at the local supermarket? A pet shop is fine for buying goldfish, gerbils, or supplies, but it is the last place a person should look for a new puppy.

Five-Week Puppy Syndrome

There's more. Connected with the shamefulness of the whole puppy-mill industry is a condition that trainers have been seeing in some young pups, loosely — but fairly — called "five-week puppy syndrome."

The condition involves excessive and troubling behavioral characteristics in young puppies between ten and twelve weeks of age. The most notable behavior is inordinately excessive biting and mouthiness in these pups, whose unrestrained, sharp baby teeth are capable of doing real damage. This isn't just normal puppy mouthiness but something much more serious.

When trainers first noticed the syndrome, they began to exchange information and compare notes, and a very clear profile emerged. What almost all of these puppies have in common is that they have been separated from their mother and/or siblings prior to eight weeks of age. What is more, the closer the separation is to five weeks of age, and the more radical the separation, the more severe the symptoms are because the pups don't learn how to inhibit their bites, much less how to act in relation to other dogs or people. Another interesting discovery: if the pup is separated before six weeks of age, genetic background doesn't matter — the puppy is set up for developmental turmoil.

This is often precisely the time when puppy mills send out pups to pet stores so that the dogs will be on display and ready for sale at seven to eight weeks of age. The puppy mill wants to get their charges out as early as possible to cut costs and enhance profit, while the store wants them sold quickly for the same reasons. No doubt younger pups are cuter and easier to move along. However, they can also mask, or incubate, a disease that will become visible at nine to ten weeks of age. Even more troubling are the behavioral irregularities.

What is increasingly clear is that this condition is related to aggression in older dogs. In taking case histories of adult problem dogs, trainers have often seen the correspondence between dog and people aggression and early separation from dam and litter. These professionals know how challenging it is to reverse such behaviors and how dangerous they can be. Although aggression in older dogs is not always caused by "five-week puppy syndrome," it is safe to say that all dogs removed from their mother and littermates at five to six weeks of age will be highly likely to manifest behavioral problems. Without extreme training and behavioral measures, the problems will not only persist but grow.*

---

* Maryna Ozuna's thorough and insightful discussion of this topic appears in *Safe Hands Journal,* volume 11, issue 1 — the publication of the International Association of Canine Professionals.

Adopting a Puppy: Breeder or Animal Shelter?

We are often asked where the best place is to adopt a puppy. Because we have been breeding German shepherds for close to forty years, we could have an obvious prejudice in steering individuals toward a reputable breeder as the surest way to obtain their dream puppy. For many years, while we never wanted to discourage the possibility of adopting a wonderful puppy from an animal shelter, we suggested that there was a greater likelihood of finding a healthy, happy puppy from a breeder. In recent years, however, our thinking has changed. Many shelters have made a concerted effort in the past twenty years to provide not only humane but safe and conscientious means for obtaining a dog. At the same time we've been deeply aware that simply going to a breeder is no guarantee that you'll find the puppy you're looking for. Sadly, there are plenty of breeders who are in it solely for the money, whose primary motive is financial and not "love for the breed." Rather than recommending one source over another, we now realize that a wonderful pup can come from either a breeder or an animal shelter as long as you follow sound guidelines. What you should pay attention to in either instance is the word *reputable*. Not all animal shelters are equal, just as not all breeders are equal. Plan on spending some time checking out the possibilities, asking pertinent questions, and following up on referrals. Wherever you choose to obtain your puppy—breeder or animal shelter—it will pay to do your homework.

That said, the first question to ask yourself is, how important is it to me to have a purebred puppy? If you are set on a puppy of a particular breed, you may want to work with a reputable breeder whose dogs' bloodlines are clear and who has a lot of experience within the breed. Though this will doubtlessly cost you more, there are plenty of reasons to go this route. Aside from providing you with a guarantee of health and temperament, a pedigree going back at least three generations, and an AKC registration slip, a good breeder will take the time to explain how the puppy was raised and socialized during the important early weeks of growth. She will introduce you to one or both of the parents and accurately describe the results of similar breedings, so that you will be able to judge the immediate temperamental background of your pup. This information will give you a realistic picture of what to expect as your puppy grows. Good breeders are intensely interested in the pups they produce and will want to stay in touch with you to find out how the puppy matures. Because of this, they can be a valuable source of information, advice, and assistance should you run into difficulties down the road.

Now let's look at adopting a puppy from a shelter. While it is likely that different people will tilt in one direction or another on this issue depending on how they view the "nature versus nurture" debate, the fact is that a good animal shelter can be a reasonable source for a new puppy. Adopting a pup from a shelter represents a highly moral choice as well — it saves an unwanted puppy and provides him with the possibility of life. Many of the risks formerly associated with adopting a puppy in this way have been addressed by the better shelters. We find that an increasing number have set in place valuable behavioral and veterinary resources to support new owners. Such shelters are conscious of establishing a relationship with their clients, providing good basic information, planning a spaying or neutering timetable for young pups, and sponsoring training classes to help folks develop a healthy relationship with their new charges. Whereas it used to be de rigueur that no information was made available on either the litter or an individual pup, many shelters now provide this background. Prospective adopters who get a clear idea of a pup's upbringing are poised for success and are unlikely to be forced to give up on the pup when difficulties arise.

In terms of fees, the better animal shelters will usually charge between $50 and $400, with puppies being at the high end of the price range. These adoption fees help offset the costs of evaluating, housing, feeding, and medicating the animals in their care, as well as starting additional programs geared toward the success of the adoption process. Also, given that the majority of dogs at an animal shelter will be older, you may have to wait awhile before a seven- to ten-week-old pup becomes available. That does raise the possibility, however, of adopting an older puppy. The fact that a four- to five-month-old pup lands at the animal shelter is in itself no real indicator of whether he might be a good prospective companion. Often owners discover only too late that the pup is too much for them, that they don't possess the time or skill to raise the puppy properly, or that they didn't know what they were getting into in the first place. Sometimes the reason is simply that the novelty of having a pup has worn off and the owner just couldn't be bothered. Given proper guidance and training, most of these pups can become good pets. An older puppy often has the advantage of some training, and hopefully at the very least some socialization and basic housebreaking. If you have any background or skill in training, you can easily build on that foundation.

Finally, whether you plan on adopting a puppy from a breeder or an animal shelter, you should follow the extended guidelines in chapter eight to determine the quality of your source. Set up a checklist for yourself to ensure that the breeder or shelter meets your basic criteria for health and safety, as well as for honesty and integrity.

Male or Female?

In his well-known book *Man Meets Dog,* the famous ethologist Konrad Lorenz goes out on a limb when he makes this remarkable statement:

> A bitch is more faithful than a [male] dog, the intricacies of her mind are finer, richer, and more complex than his, and her intelligence is generally greater. I have known very many dogs and can say with firm conviction that of all creatures the one nearest to man in the fineness of its perceptions and in its capacity to render true friendship is a bitch.

We respectfully beg to differ! It is futile to discuss gender differences in terms that suggest a companion dog of one sex is superior to another. Not only is this untrue but it fails to account for the many exceptions to gender stereotypes: the highly affectionate and trainable male, the overly protective female, the male who does not fight with other dogs, and the female who does. While some loose generalizations can be made about gender differences, there are no absolutes. Especially when considering puppies, you will find that the general behavior depends more on you and the way you raise your pup than on the particular sex.

Deciding on a male or female is primarily a matter of individual preference, and there are advantages and disadvantages to each. Female dogs are typically smaller than males and tend to mature more quickly. This is why they are easier to train at an earlier age, not because they are more intelligent. They come into season (proestrus and estrus) twice a year for a period of three weeks, during which time they secrete drops of blood-tinged vaginal discharge (spotting) that sexually attract male dogs. During this period, you will have to keep the female locked indoors to prevent "accidental" breedings. This can be a nuisance. Also, when a bitch is in season, she will need to be confined to linoleum or hard surfaces because of her spotting. Bloodstains are difficult to remove from carpets and fabrics. Depending on the individual dog, we recommend that she be spayed within the first year if she is not to be bred or exhibited at shows. This prevents unwanted pregnancies and incidences of uterine and ovarian disease, and it has beneficial behavioral side effects as well. Many owners observe a mellowing in their spayed female dog—a calmer, more focused attitude.

The high spirits and self-assurance of many male dogs lead them to dominate weaker owners, especially with larger breeds, where the males are bigger and stronger. Males generally exhibit more independence than females and, particularly in the earlier phases of obedience training, will require firm yet patient handling. Although males who are not neutered are inclined to roam and fight more than females, owner negligence significantly contributes to this behavior. Still, it is wise to neuter a male you do not plan to breed (see the guidelines in chapter ten), as this will diminish roaming, aggression, and generally boisterous activity.

Which Breed Is Best for You?

Among dog fanciers it is quite common to hear good-natured ribbing over which breed of dog is the best. Understandably, personal prejudices often color these judgments and allow the spread of mistaken notions. There is no "best breed." The principal reason for so many types of dogs today is that they have been bred selectively over the centuries for specific tasks and characteristics. As a result, different breeds emphasize different qualities, and some are better suited than others for specific situations and living environments. For example, a dog who fits in beautifully with a suburban family with several young children may not be the best choice for a single woman living in a high-crime neighborhood of a big city. Or a very active dog may be perfect for a young, athletic couple but would be particularly ill-suited for a quiet and sedentary elderly couple. So much depends on the circumstances of your life.

You should also remember that no dog conforms rigidly to the behavioral standard of his breed. Within the individual breed there can be a wide range of personalities and aptitudes. However, certain bloodlines can be expected to produce dogs with specific behavioral orientations. This is especially important to keep in mind when dealing with breeders. Any conscientious breeder wants the puppies she raises to be placed intelligently and will be more than happy to discuss a particular puppy's family background. She will work to ensure that the puppy she is selling you will fit into your life.

Despite these complexities, there is hope. While no one can provide you with a surefire method for picking the perfect puppy, you can increase the likelihood that the pup you choose will be a good companion by following several guidelines, listed below. The decision to adopt should be made from a sober look at the whole of your life and not simply on the basis of your own personal preference. Face the reality around you and within you. Do not assume that because a particular breed appeals to your aesthetic tastes, it is therefore the right one for you. That decision needs to be weighed in a careful, critical manner.

The following recommendations are intended to help guide you through the complex process of choosing a puppy. They represent an integrated approach to adopting—an approach that we believe will help prevent poor selections and start you in the direction of responsible ownership.

Personality

What is your own personality? What about those of the people you live with? We, like dogs, are individuals with particular characteristics and personality traits, so recognizing our basic personality should always be connected with the decision to adopt a pup. Successful relationships involve mutual compatibility. On a human level, our most lasting connections are with people whose personalities complement or harmonize with our own. It is the same with a dog. Part of our natural preference for a particular breed will often be based on the type of person we are. Matching our own personality with representatives of any particular breed is the intelligent way to decide on a puppy. A quiet, low-key individual, for example, may find a high-strung, always-on-the-go terrier a little too much to handle. Or someone who is lighthearted and affectionate may be more suited to a breed that has a strong need for affection than one that is independent and aloof.

Look at yourself. Ask some basic questions: Are you extroverted or introverted, high-energy or laid-back, strong-willed or easygoing? How affectionate are you, how demonstrative with your emotions? Are you reserved, or do you spontaneously express yourself through touching and physical contact?

As you consider these questions — and others they may provoke — remember that there are no ideal answers, just as there are no superior personality types. What makes us individuals is our variety, our different abilities and talents. Since breeds vary widely, however, in such areas as trainability, playfulness, protectiveness, and the need for exercise and affection, it is important to take our individual characteristics and match them with what we would most like to find in a companion dog. The time spent reflecting seriously on ourselves first will provide a good foundation for considering individual breeds.

Lifestyle

How much time will you have available to spend with a puppy? Whatever your lifestyle, you are subject to a certain routine. The puppy you adopt not only will have to fit into that routine but will alter it dramatically, forcing you to take into account new priorities and needs. Are you flexible enough that this will not be a problem?

It is possible that the way you live may make owning a dog unwise. For example, imagine that you and your spouse are dedicated environmental lawyers who work away from home ten hours a day. You are also socially active, involved in the local chapters of the Sierra Club and Greenpeace, which takes up most of your remaining free time. While this type of lifestyle may be rewarding and desirable, it is entirely inappropriate for a puppy. What will the pup do? Who will take care of him while you are away?

Dogs are social animals who require plenty of human contact and respond poorly to isolation and confinement, unlike some cats and tropical fish. Being left alone in the basement, confined to a utility room for ten hours a day, or stuck outside on a chain is no life for any dog. Even if you have a large fenced-in area for your dog to play in, with a well-insulated kennel, your pup still needs plenty of ordinary social-ization. A play area is never a dispensation, absolving you from spend-ing quality time with your dog.

As an owner, you should anticipate walking your dog at least three times a day (ten to thirty minutes each walk), feeding and playing with her (one hour a day), performing basic training (fifteen to thirty min-utes a day), and attending to grooming needs that will vary according to the breed you select. An Old English sheepdog, for example, may require as much as thirty minutes of daily grooming to keep him free of mats and tangles. How would these needs fit into the way you live? For the daily jogger, the thought of having a dog along might be fine; if, however, you are less athletic and are occupied with other concerns, you may discover that an active breed presents problems.

Most dogs will have to adjust to a certain amount of time alone each day. This should not be a problem if the periods are reasonably short. If, however, your dog will be home alone for ten hours a day, we strongly urge you to consider hiring someone to take him out for a good walk at midday. If you're not willing to do this, you should rethink getting a dog. In most cities, professional dog-walkers can be hired for sixty to one hundred fifty dollars a week, depending on the specific arrange-ment. In suburbs, responsible teenagers can sometimes be hired for the same purpose. Let us say it again: If this sounds unreasonable (or impossible) to you, you should reconsider adopting a pup. "Latchkey" puppies who spend most of the day alone learn to take out their bore-dom on your furniture, linoleum, carpeting, and anything else within reach...and, besides, what kind of a life is that for the dog! Owners should remember that weekends will require extra quality time with their pup for exercise and companionship.

If you have a family, it is usually easier to share the responsibility to ensure that the puppy receives proper attention, but you should not be blind to potential problems. We've found that most children under the age of fourteen are unable to take *full* responsibility for a dog, even when the animal is officially theirs. Mom or Dad usually ends up with the biggest share of the duties of daily care. When parents merely go along with their children's wish for a family dog and are uninterested themselves, they may discover that the burden falls on them anyway once the kids lose interest. Thus, it is important to educate children beforehand to the responsibility they will share once a new pup comes into the family.*

A close look at how you currently live will also suggest characteristics to look for in individual breeds. For example, if you enjoy hosting dinner parties or casual evening get-togethers, you should consider a breed that is confident, good-natured, and not overly protective. Otherwise, you will be forced to isolate your dog every time you have guests. Similarly, if you have children, you should anticipate the presence of playmates romping in and out of the house. Right from the start, you will be looking for a breed that is good with children. One couple we know wanted a companion dog for the wife, since the husband traveled frequently in his work. They also lived in a high-crime suburb, so they were more inclined toward breeds that demonstrated high levels of protectiveness, trainability, and loyalty. An Akita fit this profile, and the well-bred pup they obtained worked out well.

There are endless possible situations. The point to remember, however, is this: an examination of your individual lifestyle can provide you with important information in discerning which breeds are most compatible with you.

Environment

Where do you live? Whether in the city, suburbs, or country, or in different places at different times, be clear about what your living environment offers for walking, exercising, and caring for your dog. While there is no such thing as an ideal setting (every environment presents its own problems and challenges), be realistic about how your living situation will affect the development of your puppy's behavior. All dogs require a certain amount of exercise every day, in every season, regardless of the weather. Depending on the breed, that need may be substantial. Be careful to select a breed whose size and general activity levels do not exceed the opportunities your environment offers. Many canine

* Several excellent resources for young children exist that highlight the basic issues involved in raising a puppy. *Some Swell Pup: Or Are You Sure You Want a Dog?* by Maurice Sendak and Matthew Margolis is currently out of print but available online in used copies. *Just Me and My Puppy* by Mercer Mayer is also a delightful book for young children with a good message. Finally, *The Lessons of Chief Pondy* by dog trainer Scott MacConachie is a fine twelve-minute cartoon that teaches young children how to be safe around dogs. It can be obtained at www.chiefpondy.com.

behavior problems can be traced to pent-up energy, which is then released through destructive chewing, excessive barking, aggression, and hyperactivity — behavior that can abruptly end a dog's welcome.

Many small breeds adapt well to city life because it is easier to satisfy their exercise needs. While it is true that several of these breeds are highly active and demand their share of exercise, they also have a small leg span, making a mile walk for them equivalent to a four-mile walk for a big dog. Their high energy can thus be held in check, preventing many problems from developing.

Still, there are no absolutes here either. Your surrounding environment need not automatically determine the size of your dog. We know many people who live happily in urban settings with large dogs such as German shepherds, Dobermans, rottweilers, and Akitas, because the owners go out of their way to ensure that their dogs are well cared for and properly exercised. We once worked with a young man from New York City who owned a Hungarian vizsla, a highly energetic sporting breed that ordinarily would be poorly suited for city life. This relationship, however, was exemplary. Since the man was a jogger, he went out with his dog twice a day, running five miles in the morning and three in the late afternoon. He also owned a business and was able to keep his dog with him during the day. Since puppyhood, the dog had been worked with faithfully in basic obedience training, and the owner spent weekends at his upstate home, giving the vizsla even more room for exercise. The success of this relationship demonstrates how dogs can adapt to unlikely circumstances, provided you attend to their basic needs.

Another aspect of your environment to consider is your personal living space. Is it an apartment, house, studio, town house, or farm? How big is it? Is there yard space available that could be fenced in to give your dog freedom for play and exercise? Also think about your neighbors. How do they feel about dogs? Are they so close that barking would be a problem? If so, look at breeds that rate low in chronic barking.

Small environments such as city apartments are nevertheless generally incompatible with breeds that are big and bulky, and when forced to adapt to them, some dogs develop neurotic behavior. For example, we met a young woman who lived in a small studio apartment in Boston. When she was a girl, her family always had Great Danes, and when she moved away from home, she decided to adopt a pup whom she named Hulk. When she first got the pup, he was thirty-five pounds and full of fun. In four months, however, he had grown to eighty pounds, with no sign of letting up. Left alone in the studio while his owner was at work, Hulk became extremely destructive, forcing her to crate him for unreasonably long periods during the day. This confinement resulted in general unruliness that made walks unpleasant and contact with people exceedingly rare, and that dramatically increased aggressive, overprotective behavior. The only place Hulk could run was in a small playground several blocks from where his owner lived, and only late at night, when there weren't any people around.

The young woman finally realized that she could no longer keep Hulk. Fortunately, she was able to place him with a middle-aged couple who had a country home and who were experienced in living with Great Danes. With plenty of exercise, consistent handling, and faithful obedience training, Hulk overcame his problems and blossomed into a happy companion dog. Many dogs, however, are not so fortunate.

As we pointed out in *How to Be Your Dog's Best Friend*, dogs can be happy almost anywhere, provided you structure their lives in accord with the demands of your particular environment and with sensitivity to the general characteristics of each breed. Weighing the practical issues of your living situation before getting your puppy will give you a balanced idea of what to look for in a breed.

Do Your Homework

In bringing all these factors to your attention, we don't mean to imply that finding a suitable breed is an impossibly burdensome chore. It is a matter of attitude. The process can be a fascinating and enjoyable one that will involve you and anyone you live with. You may already have a good idea of exactly what breed you are looking for. If you do not, there are several things you can do to help narrow your possibilities.

First, pay a visit to your local library. Most have well-stocked sections on dogs, with books that will give you a general idea of the choices available to you. Start by looking through a dog encyclopedia. Each section will have a short profile and description of a particular breed with a photograph reflecting the standard. Another valuable source is *The Complete Dog Book*, the official publication of the AKC. This outlines the official standards of the breeds recognized by the club and

Older yellow Labrador pups vie for attention and interaction with people.

includes profiles of what their temperament and personalities should be like. Also, be on the lookout for books on individual breeds, which provide detailed accounts of breed history and use, suggestions about proper care, and other valuable tips on each particular type of dog.

Several books offer a comparative look at different breeds as they relate to varying behavior categories and living environments. These are invaluable for helping you determine how appropriate a particular breed may be for you. Though these profiles are not absolute (different books sometimes conflict in their evaluations), they do provide a good idea of how obedience judges, veterinarians, and breed fanciers look at various breeds. We recommend several books that should be easy to locate online, at your library, or at your local bookstore:

Choosing a Dog for Dummies, by Chris Walkowicz. Wiley Publishing, New York, 2001.

The Perfect Match: A Dog Buyer's Guide, by Chris Walkowicz. Howell Book House, New York, 1996.

These books—by Chris Walkowicz, noted breeder, judge, and
writer—provide clear and responsible guidance on more than 250
breeds. Either resource is a good choice; however, our preference is the
first because of its scope, clarity, and wit. It is a fun, informative book
and prepares readers for a realistic adoption of their preferred breed.

Paws to Consider: Choosing the Right Dog for You and Your Family, by
Brian Kilcommons and Sarah Wilson. Grand Central Publishing,
New York, 1999.

The authors, two very talented trainers and writers, bring their
knowledge and expertise to helping the reader make an informed decision about choosing a dog as they review more than ninety breeds. The
strength of this book might also make some people a bit indignant: the
authors include both the pros and cons of each breed so that an individual knows the challenges he or she faces in adopting a dog. This
reflects the writers' long experience of working with a wide variety of
dogs and their owners. We appreciate and identify with their candor.

*The Right Dog for You: Choosing a Breed That Matches Your Personal-
ity, Family, and Lifestyle,* by Daniel F. Tortora. Fireside, New York,
1983.

The scope of this book is broad and complex. It surveys 123 breeds
and ranks them according to numerous behavioral criteria. The text is
packed with valuable information, though it occasionally lapses into
technical jargon that makes it less readable than the other books. The
persevering reader, however, will be rewarded with a multidimensional
look at the breeds reviewed.

The information you uncover in your research will take you a long
way in narrowing down your preferences. However, you shouldn't
make any final decisions based on book information alone. What you
have learned needs to be balanced by seeing the dogs themselves.

Attend some all-breed dog shows. These are usually scheduled on
weekends and make ideal outings for families and friends. Call your

local newspaper or breed club or check online listings for schedules and upcoming events. Going to a show will give you the chance to directly observe adult representatives of the breeds you are interested in and to talk with people who are involved with each breed. Do not be bashful; dog breeders love to discuss the virtues of their particular breeds and can be quite forthright about potential difficulties. Besides learning a lot, you will also have the chance to make personal contacts with breeders from whom you may later wish to adopt your puppy.

Finally, a good veterinarian or an experienced dog trainer can be an invaluable resource for information about the breed you are most interested in. Aside from offering you personal insights, they may be able to direct you to a conscientious and reputable breeder. It is a good idea to call ahead and schedule an appointment to ensure they will have time available to help you with your decision.

8

Finding Your Puppy

Once you decide on a particular breed, you should explore all reasonable sources for obtaining your new pup. Locate the quality breeders in your area, but also be aware of breed-rescue groups and animal shelters as possible sources for a good pup. Both breeders and rescuers can offer good reasons for why you might want to get a puppy from them, so it is wise to keep an open mind, particularly in the planning stages. Also, while the Internet can be a valuable tool to expand your search, it is always preferable to adopt your puppy by personal contact, so that you can see the context from which the puppy is coming to you. You should also understand that puppy mills often sell dogs online with slick, enticing websites that disguise their true "pedigree" by posing as small family breeders. Be wary. Don't be deceived by cute photographs designed to tug at your heartstrings and lead you to make an impulsive purchase. Buying from such disreputable sources only perpetuates the cycle of abuse. And, more personally, a problematic pup can be a huge drain on your time, money, and emotions. To help you avoid these issues and make a responsible choice, we have laid out the following guidelines.

Finding a Good Breeder

Although you may have avoided pet stores and puppy mills, you should also be aware that someone who hangs out a shingle saying BREEDER OF PREMIUM...should not necessarily be believed at face value. It makes sense to deal only with breeders who have established reputations for high-quality dogs and client satisfaction. In addition to checking with local veterinarians and trainers, you can contact the AKC or the national club of the breed you are interested in for a list of registered breeders in your area. As we have mentioned, another good way to make personal connections with breeders (at the same time as seeing the dogs they have bred) is to attend an official dog show. While breeders won't be able to spend a lot of time with you at the actual event, you can get a general impression and find out how to follow up afterward.

Be methodical in this process. While we're not suggesting you have a skeptical, adversarial attitude, we believe it is wise to get as broad a perspective as possible before settling on a particular breeder. Visit several breeders and meet as many of their adult dogs as possible. Compare the various dogs to each other and weigh the different conditions in which they are kept. What strikes you about the dogs' appearance and temperament? Do they seem well-socialized and healthy? In speaking with breeders, you should try to get an idea of how long they've been breeding, how many dogs they care for, and how many litters they average a year. Breeders must have a good understanding of the potential health issues of the breed and be able to explain what they've done to prevent such problems in their lines. For example, a German shepherd breeder should speak honestly about hip and elbow dysplasia, and should breed only dogs who are free of either condition.

If there are puppies on the premises, it is quite normal for you to be shown the litter. However, do not expect to handle the pups, for the conscientious breeder will be aware of the risks of transmitting diseases before the dogs are fully vaccinated. Instead, observe the pups in their pens and ask how they are being raised and what sort of socializing they receive. The breeder should also be able to discuss vaccinations and worming scheduling and explain what sort of food the pups eat and why. You can expect healthy pups to appear curious and lively, with glossy coats and clear eyes. Be wary of breeders whose kennels are a mess. Central to the overall quality of any breeding program is the cleanliness of the kennel. Filthy conditions often mean unhealthy dogs, and puppies who are vulnerable to infectious diseases such as parvovirus and coccidiosis. There also might be behavioral side effects, such as coprophagy and house-training problems. So remember, a dirty, disorganized kennel not only reflects badly on the breeder but could spell future health and behavioral issues as well.

When all is said and done, you should expect that a good breeder

- will be able to show you a clean environment, healthy puppies, and adult breeding dogs with sound temperaments.
- will be knowledgeable and sensitive to health and behavioral issues within the breed and will always use only OFA-certified breeding animals.*
- will place pups in their new homes between eight and ten weeks of age.
- will belong to his or her national breed club (for example, the German Shepherd Dog Club of America) and likely be involved in showing dogs in obedience, conformation, and/or field trials.
- will provide you with a signed contract that explains mutual responsibilities.
- will allow you to return a puppy if a veterinary examination reveals a problem (usually within forty-eight hours of purchase), and will have a sales policy that gives you the right to return a puppy with a serious genetic health problem or genetically unsound temperament within the first year.

Most important, however, the breeder will be interested in you. Good breeders understand the importance of positive relationships with their clients and will not place their puppies with just anyone. They are concerned that the pups go to good homes, and they will spend time planning matchups based on personal interviews and detailed application forms. For this reason, reputable breeders generally prefer to select puppies for their client instead of relying on the client's choice, which can be overly emotional and misguided. Not only has the breeder been living with the puppies for two months and thus gotten to know them well but his or her experience in placement is usually more objective and will serve the client's needs better.

Adopting a puppy from a breeder is much more than a standard business transaction. The pup you take home with you is a living creature who will have a profound effect on your life, so it pays to be careful. If you find a breeder who fits the profile described above, you have an excellent chance of getting a puppy you can live and work with successfully.

---

* The Orthopedic Foundation for Animals evaluates hip and elbow X-rays to determine the presence and degree of a genetically transmitted condition known as *dysplasia*. Dogs who are certified by the OFA are acceptable for breeding.

Obtaining Your Puppy Through Breed Rescue

Another excellent option for obtaining a purebred puppy is by contacting a breed-rescue organization. Most AKC-recognized breeds have such groups that are dedicated to finding good homes for the dogs they care for and are relatively easy to find on the Internet. If you take the time to do your research and are willing to wait as long as it takes for an appropriate pup to become available, you can increase the likelihood of bringing a wonderful dog into your life. Reputable breed-rescue groups provide a vital service in rehoming purebreds who, for whatever reason, are given up for adoption. Perhaps the original owners had an unavoidable change in life circumstances, such as relocation or death. Other cases are more tragic, as when a dog has been abandoned by an owner who simply didn't have the knowledge or patience to deal with a treatable health or behavior issue. No matter the background, once the rescue organization deems the individual dog or puppy "adoptable" and he or she has been neutered or spayed, the animal goes into a temporary foster home. Depending on the skills of the foster parent, this often includes training and rehabilitation work that will increase the chances of permanent rehoming.

Don't be surprised or put off by extensive questioning about your ability to care for the dog. Reputable breed rescues are run by people who love their chosen breed. They are not in this for the money and simply want to ensure that the adoption is mutually beneficial and that the dog doesn't get "recycled." Sometimes rescuers will ask to visit your home to check out your living circumstances. For your part, you have the right to confirm that the rescue organization has 501(c)(3) nonprofit status, all pertinent health records, a basic understanding of the breed, and some sort of temperament evaluation that indicates why they believe the dog is a good match for you. Usually they will also have a clause in the contract stipulating that should the adoption not work out, the dog will be returned.

Something to be aware of: often the dogs at breed rescues are either older pups, at least five or six months of age, or older adult dogs. For some people this is ideal, as often the pup is house-trained. Then again, some prefer to raise the pup themselves and not inherit other people's mistakes. Young pups are placed almost as quickly as they come in, so ask to be put on a waiting list—that way you'll be contacted as soon as a pup becomes available. But you may have to be patient if you want a puppy younger than twelve weeks.

For the client who may not be able to afford the price of a good breeder and who can wait for an appropriate pup, breed rescue is a very worthy means of adopting.

Obtaining Your Puppy Through an Animal Shelter

There is no question that it is not only possible to get a wonderful puppy from an animal shelter but a noble endeavor to do so. Adopting a pup in this way gives a dog who might otherwise be destined for euthanasia an opportunity at a happy life, and this can only be honored. Reputable animal shelters are always striving for better ways to place the dogs who come to them and have expanded their resources to include adoption counseling, behavior counseling, and dog training, as well as medical services. Their facilities are clean, comfortable, and safe, and they do their utmost to save as many dogs as possible. While it is true that the majority of dogs in shelters are older dogs, puppies do become available. If you are looking for a specific breed, get your name on a waiting list. Shelters receive new animals each day, so the wait might not be as long as you'd expect. Also, if you know a trainer or someone experienced with dogs, ask if they will go with you to look at the prospective puppy — a second set of eyes will be invaluable in helping you make an informed decision. To gauge a pup's suitability to your circumstances, you can take her outside to walk on a leash. What is the general disposition of the pup? How social does she seem to be? If you've brought someone with you, what is her response when she meets the person? How oral does she seem to be? These and many other questions can be more easily weighed when you have an experienced friend to dialogue with. By acting deliberately instead of impulsively, you will arrive at a decision that is less emotional, and your chances of success will be greatly improved.

At a time when millions of dogs (both young and old) are given up each year — often due to owner negligence — animal shelters provide a relatively inexpensive and compassionate means of obtaining a pup who will be fully vaccinated, wormed, and spayed or neutered. If you are confident in your ability to deal with a variety of unknowns, and especially if you don't mind adopting a mixed breed, getting a pup at a responsible animal shelter makes a great deal of sense.

9

First Things First

If you choose to go with a breeder, you may have to wait a while before getting your puppy. Often the pups you see during preliminary visits are already spoken for, and your dog will come from a future breeding. This is just as well, for you can use this time for preparation and learning. Your breeder can recommend books on the breed as well as on general dog care and training, such as this one. You should also look for books on your own, choosing those that cover puppy behavior and training. Different approaches provide different insights, and no one book can ever give the last word on training.

During the waiting period, you may find it helpful to observe some local KPT (Kindergarten Puppy Training) and obedience classes to get a feel for what is involved in these types of training. Without the distraction of a puppy of your own, you can learn a lot just by watching different owners and their dogs and listening to the trainers. At local obedience trials you can see the actual results of conscientious obedience training. A well-trained dog at work is certainly a beautiful sight, and it is worthwhile to see for yourself the successful and harmonious interaction of dog and trainer. Check with local obedience clubs for the dates of trials taking place in your area, and make it a point to attend one for some firsthand experience.

Preparation

When you hear that your puppy will soon be ready to come home, you should make some specific preparations. Before you actually pick up your new dog, gather the household members together to discuss future responsibilities for the pup. Make sure that everyone is clear about how the puppy is to be managed, since owner consistency is one of the biggest factors in a smooth adjustment to the home. The separation of your puppy from her littermates will be stressful; everything familiar will be gone. Conflicting signals from different members of the household will only compound this distress. Consistent handling will prevent confusion and give the puppy a clear set of expectations right from the start.

To accomplish this, you should set up some basic ground rules: How many times a day will the pup be fed, walked, and played with? Who will do this? Where will the dog eliminate? Which rooms of the house will the pup be allowed into, and where will she be kept when she cannot be supervised? Where will she sleep? It is best to resolve all of these issues before the arrival of the puppy.

If there are young children in the house, discuss with them their role in welcoming the new pup to her home. Both before and after adopting a pup, owners must educate their children in proper behavior. Kids have a tendency to maul puppies and to contribute to stress by squealing, roughhousing, hugging, kissing, and teasing. Explain to them that it will take several days for the puppy to get used to her home, and that during that time they will have to be calm and quiet around their new friend.

It is best to plan on having the puppy arrive during a vacation, when someone can be with her most of the time for the first week or two. Most puppies are adopted either just prior to or during the fear period (eight to ten weeks), when a close bond with a new owner can most naturally develop. Take advantage of this. It is never wise to leave a new puppy alone for large blocks of time when you first adopt her, since the stress of such abandonment can lead to serious problems.

Naming

It is best to decide on a name for your puppy prior to her arrival in your house. Why not spend some time considering the different possibilities and including everyone in the decision making? Though picking a name is enjoyable, do not take it lightly, since the name is the doorway to communication with your pup. It not only reflects a dog's individuality but reveals the way you look at her.

This is worth serious consideration. Many people do not realize when choosing a name that dogs are not *people*. A dog does not understand a name the way we do. She does not identify herself with it or take her self-identity from it. She recognizes the particular sound we have imposed on her only as a call to attention, having learned to associate it with our desire for attentiveness. A dog, then, makes no judgment regarding her name. Thus its poetic qualities or psychological associations are important only for us, in serving as a sign of our mental and emotional bond with our dog.

Instead of choosing human names for our pups, we should select those that speak to a dog as a dog yet respect her own dignity and uniqueness. Otherwise we can easily fall into the trap of giving her human status. The dog becomes one of us, a "Fred," an "Oscar," or a "Betty," and we end up anthropomorphizing our pets, forgetting how differently they see things.

The chief rule is to pick a name that is easy for the pup to understand and for you to pronounce. In general, we suggest short, two-syllable names that end in a long vowel sound or a soft *A* (for example, Nero, Anka, Ola, Ivy), because they are clear and easy for the pup to distinguish. This allows the puppy to tune in to you quickly and is essential later on when you are teaching obedience, especially the recall.

Naturally, you should avoid names that rhyme with or sound like obedience commands. Also, do not select a name more than three syllables long—complex and exotic monikers can be clumsy or confusing and often must be repeated. Similarly, we find excessively sweet or joke names totally inappropriate for a dog. Dogs are remarkably intuitive; they sense when they are being made fun of or when they are the objects of suffocating sentimentality. When you choose a name that wears well and reflects common sense, you and your pup will be the better for it.

Supplies

Though you should avoid the temptation to go out and spend a fortune on equipment for your new pup, it is still a good idea to have a number of essential items on hand before you bring your puppy home. These include food and water bowls, collars and a leash, grooming tools, a shipping crate (our preference) or metal cage, a deodorizer/cleaner, and toys. Do not wait until you already have the puppy to acquire these items, since you will need them right from the start. Try a pet-supply store or mail-order catalog as opposed to a department or hardware store—the former's products are usually sturdier and of better quality.

Food and Water Bowls We recommend tip-proof bowls, either in heavy ceramic or stainless steel. Make sure the bowls are big enough for the puppy to use when he grows up. Beware of cheap plastic or metal bowls—if the puppy starts chewing on them, they can splinter or develop jagged edges. Remember that certain breeds with long, floppy ears (like hounds and spaniels) do best with a specially tapered bowl that prevents the ears from resting in it as the pup eats or drinks.

Collars and Leash Most puppies grow quickly. By the time they are adults, medium- to large-size dogs have outgrown at least two collars and two leashes, so keep your initial purchases simple. We suggest two collars to start with: a flat nylon or rounded leather collar to hold an identification tag and dog license (in case your puppy gets lost), and an appropriately sized martingale limited slip collar. Martingale collars have two loops: the smaller is the governing loop that tightens the larger one when a puppy tries to slip out of the collar or resist leash-walking. In principle, this works like a prong collar, applying limited, even pressure around the pup's neck. If you need more control later, as

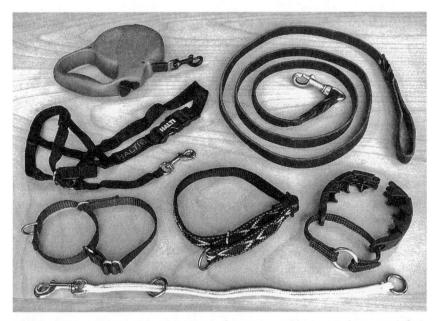

Some important equipment for you and your pup. Clockwise from top left: a Flexi-lead, a six-foot woven leather leash, a Good Dog Collar, a snap-around braided nylon (slip) collar, two martingale collars, and a Halti head collar.

the puppy matures, you can move to a snap-around nylon training collar or a Good Dog modified prong collar (see below).

For puppies, six-foot lightweight nylon show leads are excellent. They introduce the pup to a leash gently, without trauma, and are relatively inexpensive. As pups grow, they require a more durable training leash. For medium- to large-size breeds we suggest a six-foot braided leather leash without sewn parts that can separate. For small and toy breeds a four-foot lead often works well. The width you choose (¼", ½", ¾") depends on what size your pup will be at maturity.

Here are some additional collars to consider:

- a snap-around nylon training collar. These are excellent once you begin working your pup more formally in obedience exercises.
- a Good Dog modified prong collar. These are good for working larger, touch-insensitive pups in basic obedience.
- a head halter. While we ordinarily do not use one, in certain circumstances (particularly when a pup is much stronger than his handler) a head halter is a viable management tool for walking a dog. It fits around the back of the pup's neck and over the top of the muzzle, and when used correctly it allows the handler to direct the dog without having to give strong leash corrections. Head halters can be especially helpful for elderly owners. However, strong leash jerks with this tool can injure a pup. Be sure to follow the manufacturer's guidelines.

Grooming Tools Proper grooming tools depend on the breed you select. Ask your breeder about any items specific to your type of dog. Some basics are a wire slicker brush, an undercoat rake (no German shepherd owner should be without one!), a dematting tool, a comb, nail trimmers, and an ear cleaner (such as Ear-Rite or otic liquid).

Shipping Crate or Metal Cage We feel strongly that shipping crates and metal cages are effective, humane aids in house-training a puppy. They provide the young pup with a secure den and take advantage of his tendency to keep his sleeping area clean. They are also the safest way to transport a dog by car, protecting him against sudden stops. We prefer an airline-approved kennel made of high-density plastic; these provide a safe, denlike atmosphere for the pup while keeping hair inside the crate. Another option is a metal crate. In general, we find these to be less denlike and less sturdy, and if a dog sheds or has an "accident," his hair or mess goes outside the crate. On the other hand, wire crates are lightweight and can be disassembled for cleaning. Several tips regarding both: crates are expensive, so whether you choose one that is plastic or wire, make sure it will be big enough for your pup to use when she is fully grown. If necessary, get a crate divider to fit your pup's size at an early age (see chapter eleven). Also, take off his training collar when he is in the crate, as it can get caught on the metal.

Deodorizers/Cleaners During the house-training of your puppy, there are bound to be some "accidents." Because puppies tend to return to the scene of the crime, where they detect the smell of urine and feces ("scent posts"), it is important to clean these spots properly, using a product that effectively neutralizes the odor. For cleaning puppy "accidents" on nonporous hard surfaces and carpeting, you should use a pet deodorizer/cleaner designed for this purpose, which you can find at a pet shop.

Toys Every pup needs several toys to play with. We like to expose our puppies to a meat-scented nylon bone, a Kong, and a play ring to avoid boredom and control chewing. We recommend nylon bones as opposed to rawhide ones, since nylon is much more durable and less expensive in the long run. We also like Ultra Balls or tennis balls, which can be used with a plastic ball launcher to teach retrieving as the pup grows.

Optional Items These optional items, while not absolutely necessary, can be helpful.

- Pooper-scooper: to make cleanup of the soiling area easier. Even handier if you separate the two parts of the scooper.
- Bitter Apple: a product designed to keep dogs from chewing objects in your house or from licking hot spots on themselves.
- Flexi-lead: a retractable leash that extends up to thirty feet in length. Invaluable for leash-training a puppy in a firm yet gentle manner. Be sure to read the safety guidelines that come with this device or review them online before you purchase. Children should not use Flexi-leads.

- Dog bed: excellent for giving pups a secure sense of place when they sleep. The best dog beds have a combination of cedar chips and fiberfill; cedar chips are a natural repellent to fleas and ticks, and fiberfill helps preserve the bed's shape and softness. Make sure that the cover is removable, washable, and durable.
- Folding gate: to confine a pup to a particular area. The gate should be sturdy, made of a material other than wood (which is chewable), and have slats that are small enough to prevent a puppy from sticking her head through and getting caught.

Finally, before buying a large quantity of dog food, you should speak to both your breeder and your veterinarian. Choosing a high-quality food is an important factor in your dog's health, and it pays to check with professionals before you make your decision. We will have more to say about nutrition in chapter eighteen.

10

A New Beginning

In my beginning is my end.

—T. S. Eliot, *Four Quartets*

The day you go to get your new puppy always has a bit of magic about it. It is a day of anticipation and excitement, dreams and possibilities, hopes and aspirations. Puppies have a way of reducing even the most serious adult to spontaneous displays of childlike delight. This is part of their charm. A puppy touches something very deep in us, and when we first hold one in our arms it is easy to be swept away with blind enthusiasm. Who would suspect the challenge that awaits us?

Nevertheless, a puppy's "magic" is deceiving. Whether this day is *truly* blessed remains to be seen, and so we offer a word of caution: enthusiasm that is not grounded in reality—not supported by knowledge and understanding—has a way of fizzling when ordinary problems develop. Once the puppy passes the novelty stage, once he becomes a familiar part of your household, the true nature of the relationship becomes apparent, and second thoughts may arise. New owners can quickly lose interest. Always keep in mind that a sustained relationship requires a more substantial foundation than mere enthusiasm.

Beyond the joy and emotion of getting a puppy—beyond the good feelings this new bundle of life inspires in us—lies a deeper, more profound reality that should be the anchor of any relationship with a dog: adoption. Adopting a puppy means bringing him into the heart of your home, and developing a healthy relationship demands plenty of hard work and dedication from you—especially now, at the beginning. The day you adopt a puppy begins a new phase in his existence, one rooted in his earliest experiences yet now poised to take fresh expression in your life. How he develops now depends largely on you. The puppy is no longer the breeder's, no longer his mother's. Today he becomes your puppy, a new member of your family, and this means you become parent, companion, pack leader — the puppy's closest friend.

If this sounds sentimental or idealistic to you, think again. Canines are among the most sociable species in the animal kingdom. Whereas a wolf pup is naturally integrated into the wider pack with his brothers and sisters, your pup does not have that possibility. Instead, he adapts himself by establishing his closest social bonds with you and those you live with, treating all of you as his fellow pack members. It is now up to you to teach your pup his proper role in your pack family, a process that begins the moment you adopt him.

As we have seen over and over again, a puppy builds on previous experiences, and this is especially true of his first few days in your home. Good habits start from the beginning. Planning ahead, taking the time and energy necessary to help your pup make a smooth transition to his new home, increases the probability that his good behavior will continue to develop into maturity. The opposite is also true. High amounts of stress, careless house-training procedures, pampering, and improper discipline, to name just a few potential problems, can get the relationship off to a rocky start and lead to serious problems later on. Since it is reasonable to assume that this puppy will be an intimate part of your life for the next ten to fifteen years, you should put serious thought and effort into these first few days in order to establish a sound framework for the future.

With this in mind, let us take a detailed look at your pup's first few days with you. During this time, the guiding principle should be to minimize unnecessarily stressful experiences and to establish a natural rhythm to which your puppy can easily adjust. Since there is so much to remember, having a clear set of guidelines will help bring order and understanding to a potentially chaotic period and reduce stress for you and your puppy. The following suggestions will get you and your dog off to a good start, one that you will appreciate in the months and years to come. "In my beginning is my end."

At the Breeder's

A puppy should be adopted only when someone can stay with him most of the time during the first week to promote house-training and socialization. This may mean sacrificing a week of vacation; however, the long-term benefits make it worthwhile. Speak with the breeder in advance and arrange to pick up your puppy on the morning of the first day of a long weekend or planned vacation. This will allow the puppy to spend most of the first day with you and will hasten his adjustment to both you and your home.

Ask your breeder not to give the puppy food or water on the morning of pickup. Most do this routinely, but it is best to confirm. Fasting will not harm the pup and reduces the likelihood that he will get carsick and vomit on the way home. Also, we advise that you bring at least one other adult with you, since it is difficult to drive and watch the puppy at the same time. If you have a long trip ahead of you, you might consider carrying a crate in the car; however, if you do this, you should have the breeder expose the pup to a crate several days beforehand.

If your puppy has already been selected for you, you will naturally want to spend some time with him when you arrive at the breeder's. When you first meet your pup, sit or crouch down to his level and start playing with him. We like clients to take ten or fifteen minutes to make friends with the pup before we start answering particular questions and going over the necessary paperwork. This gives the new owners' initial excitement and anticipation a chance to subside and helps everyone pay closer attention to instructions during the interview.

New owners ordinarily have lots of questions for the breeder, so it is wise to make a list of them beforehand. In addition to specific questions about the way the puppy was raised and the type of personality he possesses (in the litter as well as by himself), you should ask how he scored on his Puppy Aptitude Test (see appendix). The results will suggest specific guidelines for handling your particular pup and will help you avoid management errors during the first weeks.

Make sure that you get a written record of the immunizations and wormings your puppy has received. If your pup is purebred, you should be given a copy of his pedigree and the AKC registration slip. Though you may have a particular type of dog food in mind for your pup, it is always best to continue feeding the brand that the puppy is currently eating for several more days, gradually changing to the new brand. Sudden shifts in diet add stress and can lead to diarrhea or loss of appetite. If you do not plan to use the brand chosen by the breeder, ask if he can give you several days' supply to help with the weaning process.

The Ride Home

Keep the ride home as relaxed and low-key as possible, allowing who-ever accompanied you to do the driving. Unless you are using a dog crate, cover your lap and the seating area next to you with a towel or old bedsheet in case the puppy gets carsick. Let the pup ride in either loca-tion, and keep one hand in gentle contact with him. It is best to avoid any kind of coddling or doting behavior, especially if the pup starts to whine, since this only reinforces whining as an attention-getting behav-ior. A certain amount of whimpering is to be expected; if things get too noisy, try putting the pup on the floor between your feet: the vibrations of the car often have a calming effect. Do not punish the pup for whin-ing or vomiting. On the way home, stop periodically and let the puppy stretch his legs, but stay away from any area that is frequented by other dogs, since your pup is not yet fully vaccinated and is vulnerable to con-tagious diseases.

Introduction to the House

When you arrive home, first take the puppy outdoors to the spot you have chosen for his soiling area and wait for him to eliminate. Normally after a car ride the puppy will have to relieve himself, and when he does so, be sure to praise him enthusiastically. Then bring the puppy into the house and allow him to walk around and explore, keeping an eye on him from a distance. Do not be surprised if the pup seems a little disori-ented at first. Even the most outgoing puppy will experience strain or confusion in a strange environment, separated from his littermates. Be calm and reassuring, and allow the pup to adjust at his own pace.

If, while exploring, the puppy shows interest in chewing something inappropriate, gently distract him by focusing his attention on a squeak toy or meat-scented nylon bone. *Do not discipline the pup at this time.* Should your dog not seem interested in the toy or bone, entice him with some play-inducing gestures such as quick clapping or rubbing your hands along the floor. If he starts to follow you around the house, encourage him. Tap the side of your leg (or jingle keys if the pup is used to them) and call his name as you walk, praising him as he comes along and investigates the different rooms. During these first days, whenever your pup begins to focus his attention on you — either to follow or simply to look up at you—say his name in a cheerful, pleasant tone that encourages him to hold eye contact. These simple dominance exercises quickly teach your pup his name while presenting you as his leader in a way that builds confidence and trust. Conclude the session by crouching down and playing with him on his level for a while.

Keep the introduction to your household quiet and unforced, allowing the process of bonding to develop in a relaxed and gradual manner. For the first few days, it is important not to overwhelm the puppy with visitors who are curious about the new arrival. Don't introduce your pup to friends and relatives until you are certain he has made a smooth transition, usually after two or three days. Then you may initiate a variety of important socializing experiences, described later.

Usually puppies are not interested in eating as soon as they get home, since everything is unfamiliar. Hold off feeding your puppy for at least a couple of hours until he has begun to settle down. Then offer him some food, and when he has finished eating, take him out to his soiling area and wait for him to eliminate. Puppies typically have to urinate and/or defecate following eating and drinking, waking (short naps included), vigorous play, and chewing a bone. If the pup has not eliminated after ten to fifteen minutes, take him back into the house for several minutes and then try again. Repeat this procedure as necessary. When he does finish, praise the puppy and again bring him into the house. He should now be ready for a nap.

Young puppies require plenty of sleep and should have several naps during the day. Choose an area that is safe for the pup when he cannot be supervised and that is not isolated from family activity. Usually the best location for this is the kitchen, since it is large enough for the dog to move around in and can be easily blocked off with one or two gates. Make sure the area is puppy-proofed for anything that could be dangerous, such as electric cords, small and chewable objects (rubber galoshes, shoes, etc.), and anything made of wood. We also recommend adding a shipping crate to serve as the pup's den during the day. As described in the next chapter, throughout the early stages of house-training you will be keeping your pup alternately in either of these two confined areas. For this first nap, leave the door of the crate open (you can tie it so that it does not shut if the pup knocks into it) and place comfortable bedding or fake fur in the crate itself. Puppies will naturally seek the security of the den atmosphere on their own. Do not be concerned if the pup initially starts to whine in his confined area; wait for him to relax and fall asleep and then periodically check on him to see when he wakes. At that time, take the puppy out to his soiling area and let him eliminate.

During these first few days, you will need to pick the puppy up from time to time to help him get around; young puppies are rarely conditioned to a leash at the breeder's, and it may take at least several days for the dog to be relaxed with the lead. While you should encourage a pup to walk on his own whenever possible, unfamiliar experiences such as going up stairs may initially require some help. There is a right and a wrong way to pick up your puppy. Always use both hands. Place one hand between the forelegs to support the chest and the other behind the thighs to support the rear. This ensures that he is perfectly balanced and unable to wriggle free. *Never* pick up a puppy by his front legs alone (since this could dislocate his shoulder) or by the scruff of the neck (which could be traumatizing). Also, puppies sometimes solicit attention by approaching their owners and whining. A good response to this is occasionally to pick the pup up and pet him briefly, making eye contact at the same time. This reinforces the positive dominance of the owner and is an effective way of having your puppy tune in to you.

The correct way to hold and support a young puppy.

If You Have an Older Family Dog

It is not uncommon for people adopting a puppy to already have an older dog in their household. If this is the case for you, then you need to think through clearly how you will introduce your new pup to your older dog. Simply assuming that the two will get along is inviting disaster.

First, we assume that you have a fairly good idea of how your older dog interacts with both other dogs and puppies, and that he has been social and playful in such interactions. Not all dogs like puppies. Pups can be extremely demanding of attention, jumping up and nipping at an older dog. They often lack boundaries and manners, which can sometimes provoke sudden aggression in an older dog. Since such an outburst can cause serious harm, even death, to a small pup, it is best to go into this with your eyes wide open. If you have seen your older dog show aggression toward puppies, you should not introduce a new pup into your household. Forgo the temptation and be content with one dog. Similarly, if your dog is elderly with arthritis or dysplasia and has to contend with chronic pain, you will need to closely monitor a new pup's interaction with him. While it is true that a pup can sometimes rejuvenate an older dog's spirit, this isn't always the case — he may not enjoy the playful pestering of a young puppy.

On the first day, if your older dog has not traveled with you to the breeder's, plan on introducing him to the puppy on safe, neutral ground. Pick a spot off your property that is not frequented by many dogs and that will not evoke the territorial behavior of the older animal. We like remote and spacious parking lots. Make sure that both your older dog and your puppy are leashed and that two adults are monitoring the introduction. Let them sniff each other, and then — assuming all is well — praise the elder dog and take both for a walk, allowing the older dog to gradually adjust to the presence of the new puppy. Be particularly watchful for any sort of body language that would indicate aggression (e.g., raised hackles, lifting of lip, teeth baring, and low growling). If you see any problems, redirect the older dog's attention off the pup and onto yourself, and have the other adult guide the pup gently away. Think of this encounter as getting into a hot bath. You should be patient and slow, trusting in the fact that dogs can more easily adjust to each other when they are moving in the same direction.

As you walk, you will notice some brief, natural moments of interaction (e.g., the pup brushing into the elder dog) that will help sensitize the older dog to the puppy and encourage a more relaxed attitude.

When the encounter becomes even and relaxed, put each dog in a separate crate and drive them to your home. Walk them into the yard together, again allowing the older dog to get accustomed to the presence of the new puppy. See if the puppy will eliminate as you walk around the yard. If the interaction stays positive and there aren't any aggressive or fearful responses, drop the pup's leash and allow the two to explore the yard together. Make sure that you don't let your older dog get too playful and knock the puppy over. Keep things controlled. When you are ready to go into the house, allow your older dog to be first through the door, with the puppy following. Then place your new pup in a gated area. During the next week, remove all toys from open spaces to discourage any kind of possessiveness, and feed the dogs separately, preferably with the puppy in a crate.

In the coming months you will always need to supervise play. While puppies grow fast, they still can be easily overwhelmed by a larger dog. It is important that you are there to monitor interactions, particularly when play starts to get a bit rough. Gradually, with proper handling, you will find the older dog and the pup becoming not only adjusted to each other but fast friends.

The First Night

The first night a puppy spends away from his littermates is often traumatic for owner and puppy alike. The pup's incessant whining and squealing, restlessness, inability to sleep, and need to eliminate can all contribute to making your initial night together miserable. In the face of such disturbances, you may be tempted simply to isolate the pup in a basement or far corner of the house and deal with the consequences the next morning. We hope that you will not do this. It only compounds the pup's sense of isolation and may make it difficult to teach him to be alone in the future.

It is helpful to understand that when a puppy becomes anxious during this first night, he is reacting naturally, according to a separation reflex. In the wild, when a wolf pup is separated from his pack, he becomes highly emotional and begins to whine, bark, or howl. This is instinctive behavior that helps reunite the pup with his pack, which is essential if he is to survive. This same instinct is at work in your dog.

The best method we have found to prevent night trauma is to let your puppy sleep in your bedroom on an old blanket *or a dog bed,* tethered next to your mattress. This works because the pup will want the security of being with you. We prefer this to using the crate, since most puppies will not be used to it this first evening and will tend to make a lot of noise. Before retiring, you should take your puppy out to eliminate and walk with him around the backyard for a while. Give him the chance to get a little tired. When you are ready to go to sleep, tether the pup with a leash* and place him on his bedding so that he is right next to you. This does two things: First, it helps the pup adjust to you as part of his new pack. In a seven-hour block of time, the pup continuously smells you, listens to your breathing, and accepts the security of your leadership. Second, it prevents the puppy from getting up in the middle of the night to eliminate away from his bed. Remember, puppies ordinarily will not soil in their sleeping area.

As we have said, it is normal to expect some whining this first night. Should the pup start to do so, reach down and quiet him without a fuss. Do this calmly, soothing him at first. If the whining persists, a gentle scruff shake along with a low "No, go to sleep" may be necessary (see chapter seventeen for more details). *Do not put the puppy in bed with you.* The pup will come to expect this, and the practice can lead to a number of behavior problems later in life. If the puppy has been quiet for several hours and then begins to whine, he probably has to go out. Dealing with all of this is part of being a new parent—expect the process to repeat itself for the first few nights.

As soon as you rise in the morning, get dressed quickly and take your pup immediately to his soiling area. Let him empty completely; puppies will sometimes eliminate several times first thing in the morning. When he has finished, praise him cheerfully and return to the house.

Trip to the Veterinarian

For as long as your puppy lives with you, he will require periodic veterinary care for routine shots and checkups, treatment for minor illnesses,

---

* A chain leash is preferable for this purpose so that the pup doesn't chew through the leash while you are sleeping.

and possibly emergency health care. All will mean trips to your veterinarian. Your puppy's first experience at a vet clinic is important, since it often leaves a lasting impression. An initial visit marked by a traumatic, negative experience will most likely establish a pattern, making future visits repeatedly unpleasant. This is one of the most common behavioral complaints we receive from clients. Usually the problem is deeply ingrained, going back to puppyhood.

You can avoid such issues by making your pup's first visit to your veterinarian as pleasant and nontraumatic as possible. Schedule an appointment for the day after you adopt your puppy, so that he can receive a thorough health examination and any required vaccinations. Ask if it is possible to bring your puppy at the beginning of clinic hours, since it is not a good idea for your pup to sit in a waiting room with other people and their possibly sick pets. Having not yet received the full cycle of vaccinations, your puppy is still vulnerable to infections. Be sure to take a fresh stool sample with you (in a paper cup) to be examined for parasites. Worms are a common problem; often puppies require several treatments to show a parasite-free stool sample.

Make the visit itself calm and cheerful. Praise your puppy gently as he is examined, and, especially afterward, keep a happy demeanor and a pleasant tone of voice. Do not be overly sympathetic or indulgent if your pup gets upset, as this will only reinforce whiny, spoiled behavior. Simply try to distract him with playful gestures. You want your pup to form a happy, enjoyable association with the experience.

One important subject to discuss with your veterinarian is microchipping your puppy. Each year millions of dogs go missing, and according to the American Humane Association, only 17 percent are reunited with their owners. The vast majority of lost dogs are either adopted by new owners or euthanized. Microchipping is a means of equipping your pet with permanent identification that can seriously reduce the dog's chances of being lost. This is not a subject to take lightly.

The procedure is very straightforward. A microchip consists of a tiny computer chip housed in a small glass capsule about the size of a grain of rice. It is implanted between the dog's shoulders and is not a painful procedure. Many pups don't seem to feel a thing. Once implanted, the chip must be registered in the microchip company's database (ordinarily for a reasonable one-time fee). It can then be read by a scanner that most veterinarians and animal shelters possess. Should your dog become lost, the possibility of quick recovery increases dramatically.

In the best of all possible worlds, leashes, fences, and doors would be adequate to safely contain our dogs, and microchipping would be more of a high-tech luxury. But statistics don't lie. Accidents do happen — dogs get lost, and microchipping is a big step forward in reuniting them with their owners. If you have a new puppy or plan to adopt one soon, you should consider this option.

Another important topic to be aware of when you see your veterinarian involves the issue of spaying or neutering.* There is a lot of controversy in the dog community about when might be the best time to spay/neuter your dog. Six months of age used to be the routine recommendation based on the supposed health and behavioral benefits. For example, spaying prior to a female's first season does reduce the risk of mammary cancer, and early neutering appears to psychologically dispose the dog to remain in a more permanent juvenile state, something that can be very desirable to pet owners because it helps promote a more positive long-term experience with their dog.

Studies have shown, however, that there are health risks associated with early neutering (e.g., urinary incontinence in females and greater risks for vascular tumors and bone cancer in both males and females as compared with their intact counterparts). Further, hormonal maturation adds to bone density and reduces the likelihood of various orthopedic disorders. And while many pet owners value a more juvenile sort of temperament, those oriented toward serious training prefer the extra boldness and confidence of a dog who is not neutered or spayed too early.

So when is the right time to spay/neuter? This is not a question with a black-and-white, absolute answer. When clients ask us about this, we tend to take our cues from the current state of the dog's temperament. If we're dealing with a high-spirited, challenging dog, we might advise

---

* We are referring here to dogs who are not going to be used for breeding. While we strongly believe in the right of serious breeders to breed responsibly, we are also acutely aware of the pet overpopulation crisis and the owner's accountability in preventing more unwanted puppies and in saving lives. To outlaw breeding is no solution. Instead, we need effective education to help the general public understand the stakes and to prevent accidental or thoughtless breedings. We believe that dogs who are not going to be used for breeding should be spayed or neutered. The question is, when is the best time for this?

the client to trade additional bone density for the benefits of a more juvenile psychological state — the owner will likely be able to live more peacefully with the dog long-term. On the other hand, if the dog lacks confidence or is manifestly juvenile or submissive by temperament, we may recommend waiting until a heat has passed (assuming the owners can be trusted to keep their pup under control at all times and not to breed her) or until the male reaches twelve to eighteen months of age. So, for us, the answer to the question of when to spay/neuter depends on the specific dog rather than on a universal guideline.

11

House-training and Preliminary Obedience Exercises

During the first days, your most pressing task is to see that your puppy acquires proper elimination habits. Nothing is so tiresome as a dog who has not learned to use her designated area for elimination: in fact, statistics show that more puppies are abandoned every year because of house-training problems than for any other reason. You should harbor no illusions about this — starting off house-training correctly is one of the pillars of a healthy relationship with your pup, and it is your responsibility to follow sensible guidelines to establish good habits.

Fortunately, there are natural instincts in dogs that, when combined with understanding and consistency on your part, make house-training a relatively straightforward process. Dogs who are raised properly as young puppies have an innate tendency to keep their den areas clean. As we have seen, pups instinctively move away from the nest to eliminate. In doing this, they naturally create "scent posts," or places where they will consistently eliminate. Whenever dogs urinate or defecate, scent chemicals called *pheromones* are also passed with the waste. When pups smell these on subsequent occasions, it triggers an eliminative reflex that disposes them to repeat the process. Besides being a necessary bodily function, this activity also develops into a form of social communication with other dogs. A pup defines her territory by leaving these scent marks for herself and other canines to sniff out. When your puppy smells her own mark, she repeats the "marking" and makes a habit of using the same area for elimination.

Understanding this allows us to devise a preventive, humane, and effective approach to house-training, outlined below, that avoids the common mistakes new owners make and is in harmony with a pup's natural instincts. Successful house-training depends on several things: sound behavioral principles; a balanced, nutritious diet that produces firm stools; and faithful attention paid by you. The following guidelines will provide you with an integrated program to house-train an eight- to ten-week-old puppy in one to three weeks and help you prepare for the time when your dog can be trusted alone in your house.

Using a Crate

We are decidedly in favor of crate-training puppies. Though many of our clients are initially horrified at the prospect of using such "barbaric, medieval devices" to stuff their puppies into, once they come to understand a crate *from a dog's perspective,* their attitude changes.

All canines are den animals; they naturally seek out spots for rest that are sheltered and secure. This is why family dogs often lie under dining room tables, beneath beds, or in dark closets: they are simply following a deep-seated den instinct.

By using a crate, you provide your pup with her own den and capitalize on her innate tendency to keep this area clean. This is why house-training with a crate is so sensible. A puppy kept in her den for a reasonable length of time (no more than three hours at a stretch during the day) will refrain from soiling and will learn to hold herself until you let her out. Consistently doing this helps your pup quickly acquire a regular schedule for elimination.

Crates come in different sizes. We prefer using airline shipping crates because they are safe and form a denlike atmosphere that is more naturally calming to puppies with a tendency toward separation anxiety. Open wire crates, while convenient because they can fold up, are less denlike, and pups might catch a dewclaw on the wire. In terms of size, use a crate that has enough room for your pup to stand up and turn around. Anything larger than that invites problems. To a puppy, a large crate is like having a master bedroom with a bathroom: she can easily sleep in one end and piddle in the other. However, if you have a pup who is going to grow quickly, you'll soon need the larger version; spending money on several different crates during puppyhood can be costly, so what do you do? The solution is to purchase a "crate divider" at your local pet store so that you can temporarily reduce the size of the crate until you need the extra space.

There are other benefits to crating. A crate prevents a young pup from getting into mischief when you cannot watch her and confines her chewing to objects you have provided. Also, it is ideal for transporting your puppy by car, keeping her safe from sudden stops and swerves, as well as providing safekeeping whenever you stay at motels. Crates are also convenient when your pup has to stay with a pet-sitter, since inevitably there will be occasions when you will not be able to be with her. Having a crate simplifies these situations and provides your puppy with a familiar spot where she will always be comfortable.

Introducing Your Pup to a Crate

As with all things in puppyhood, it is important to work gradually. Go out of your way to make her first experience with the crate a pleasant one. Begin by placing an old blanket over the floor of the crate. *Never force a puppy in, shut the door, and leave during the first session.* Instead, allow your pup to explore around the object. Then place several pieces of kibble inside as your puppy watches. If she goes into the crate after the food, praise her enthusiastically. If not, try luring her in with a scented object or high-value treat such as a bully stick.* If even that fails, gently lift the pup up and place her inside the crate, without shutting the door. You can pet the pup if she needs reassurance. Next, call your dog out and praise her when she comes to you. Repeat this for several minutes. Assuming that your pup shows no signs of disturbance, try closing the door for a minute. Conclude the session by opening the door and praising her.

The next time you feed your pup, do so inside the crate, luring her in with her bowl, then closing the door. When she finishes, your dog may start whining and barking to get out. This should be discouraged by firmly striking the front of the door with your hand and saying *no* in a deep voice. Wait for your pup to be quiet for five minutes before opening the door and escorting her out to her soiling area to eliminate.

As your puppy becomes comfortable with the crate, you can increase the time that she spends there. You should realize, however, that it is important not to overuse it. *Your pup should not live in her crate; she should live with you.* Let her spend periods of time there when she cannot be watched; when she is resting, eating, or traveling; and while she is being

---

* A bully stick is an all-natural chew stick that dogs love.

An airline crate serves as a comfy, clean, and safe den for the litter.

A pup who is gradually introduced to a crate will quickly feel at ease in his own private space.

A roomy den with amenities, located close to the pup's owner-companion.

house-trained, since during this time staying in the crate will teach her to hold herself. Used this way, a crate is an important aid in your pup's adjustment to her new life.

A Consistent Schedule

Dogs are creatures of habit and quickly adapt to scheduled routines. Be a fanatic about your pup's schedule. Starting your puppy off immediately with set times for feeding, watering, and elimination creates a rhythm that lets you predict when she will have to eliminate, thus reducing "accidents."

First thing every morning, take your pup immediately to her soiling area. Do not let her out by herself, even if your yard is fenced. Taking your pup out ensures that she will consistently use the same spot and that your praise is properly timed. Always use the same door and route, and for the first several months leave one or two stools in the soiling area each day for her to smell. Watch her carefully as she sniffs and circles around. As soon as she appears ready to eliminate, softly repeat a simple word or phrase (such as "Do it" or "Hurry up" or "Go potty") to coincide with the act. Repeat it several times; once you begin the command, do not stop until she actually begins to eliminate. When she does, *quietly* change from the command word to soft praise until she finishes. The key is to keep your voice calm and quiet. Some owners make the mistake of being overly enthusiastic when the pup is eliminating, which results in the dog interrupting what she's doing and not completely finishing.

Also, puppies often have to eliminate several times when they first wake up, so make sure your puppy is completely finished before you return to the house. When you are certain she is done, conclude with a "Good girl" and walk her back. Follow this procedure every time you take your pup out to eliminate, using the key word and praise as the conditioning factors. After fifty to seventy-five occasions of well-timed commands and praise, your pup will have a conditioned reflex to eliminate whenever she hears her trigger words. This is a great aid to house-training and avoids long waits late at night or in inclement weather.

Feeding Schedule

Plan on feeding your young puppy three times daily, at the same times each day. An ideal schedule is 7:00 a.m., noon, and 5:00 p.m., because it ensures that your pup will be empty by the time he goes to sleep and can pass the night without having to go out. Keep to this schedule until the pup shifts to two meals daily, between fourteen and eighteen weeks of age.

When you feed, be certain that your pup receives the correct amount of nutritionally balanced, high-quality *puppy* food. Avoid generic or bargain-brand foods from supermarkets, as well as prepackaged, semi-moist foods that contain high amounts of glucose (sugar). These generally lack the proper nutrients necessary for puppies, disrupt their normal growth, and often cause diarrhea. Training manuals frequently underestimate the importance of a good diet in house-training. It is of little value to a pup to go through a detailed house-training program if he is suffering from either loose stools or constipation connected with poor diet or overfeeding. Take the time to find a top-quality kibble designed for puppies; ask your veterinarian and breeder about particular brands and amounts to feed, and consult chapter eighteen for more detailed information.

As we have mentioned previously, we suggest feeding your pup in his crate; this forms another positive association with the crate and allows him to eat without distraction. It also helps prevent the pup from eliminating immediately on finishing his meal. Give a pup fifteen minutes to eat, offer him some water, and then take him to the soiling area.

Sample House-training Schedule for a Young Puppy

6:30 a.m.	Rise. Walk pup briefly.
7:00 a.m.	Feed pup and offer a drink of water. Walk puppy. Return home and play briefly with pup. Pup stays in crate.
Midmorning	Walk pup. After walk, pup stays with owner fifteen minutes. Pup returns to crate.
Noon– 1:00 p.m.	Feed pup second meal and offer water. Walk puppy. Return home and play with pup. Pup returns to crate.
Midafternoon	Offer pup water. Walk puppy. Pup returns to crate.
5:00 p.m.	Feed pup third meal and offer water. Walk puppy. Allow pup to play in kitchen while dinner is being prepared.
7:00 p.m.	Walk pup briefly. Return home and play with puppy. Pup returns to crate.
Before bed	Walk pup. Puppy sleeps in crate or on a tether (preferably with metal chain) in your bedroom.

After elimination sessions, it is a good idea to spend some time playing with your pup in the house. Do this either in the gated kitchen area or in some other part of the house, as you prefer. Since your pup has just finished eliminating, you can be relaxed, without having to worry about "accidents." When playtime is over, lead your pup to his crate and let him rest for an hour or two, leaving one or two toys with him.

During the house-training period, plan on taking your pup to his soiling area once every hour and a half. Before you go out, always offer him some water. Keeping to this schedule, you will discover that your pup will gradually be able to hold himself for longer periods of time, establishing a sense of confidence. This is another reason why adopting your pup during a vacation period makes sense.

"Accidents" Do Happen

Inevitably, some puppy "accidents" are bound to occur. No matter how watchful you are, how careful about looking for warning signals, your pup will probably have several episodes of house-soiling during her first weeks with you. When these happen, it is of the utmost importance to deal with them correctly, in a manner appropriate to your pup's age.

One of the most frequent mistakes new owners make is the tendency to overcorrect for house-soiling errors that have already occurred. Puppies live entirely in the present. They do not "remember" acts of house-soiling, and punishments given after the fact only confuse the pup and harm your relationship. That is why it is important to have your pup either with you or safely confined, and not to allow her to wander around the house unmonitored. Punishments based on poorly thought-out "folk remedies" such as rubbing a pup's nose in her mess, beating her belatedly at the site of the elimination and then isolating her, or letting her lie in her own mess when she has soiled her crate are absolutely inappropriate ways of dealing with the problem. These punishments give the pup the wrong message and ultimately produce a pup who is terrified of you.

You are responsible for monitoring your puppy in a way that tilts her chances toward success. Make sure that you always allow her to eliminate regularly. That said, some pups will still eliminate unpredictably. For a correction to be meaningful, you must catch your pup *in the act*. If you see her starting to eliminate in the house, quickly raise your voice enough to startle her (use *no* or *ahh*), sweep her up in your arms, and take her immediately outside to the soiling area. Wait for her to eliminate, following the method we have already described under "A Consistent Schedule" in this chapter. Most pups will stop what they are doing as soon as they are startled. If your pup requires more than just your voice, throw a set of keys near her or rattle a shaker can (an old soda can with some pennies in it).

When they are not confined, young pups have to be watched constantly. Learn to look for telltale signs that your puppy needs to go out. These include restless pacing, intense sniffing of the floor, whining, and scratching at the door that leads to the soiling area. If you should come upon an "accident" that has already occurred, count it as your mistake. Take your pup to her den so that she does not see you cleaning up the mess. You do not want her to think of you as her maid.

From our discussion of scent posts in chapter five, you should understand why cleaning up "accidents" thoroughly is so vital to the success of house-training. With scent capacities estimated conservatively at a hundred times greater than those of human beings, dogs can easily detect lingering odors of feces and urine in areas that have been already cleaned with conventional products such as detergent or ammonia. The result can be a distressing pattern of repeated "accidents" in the same spot.

To prevent your pup from making scent posts of locations in your house, neutralize odors with a dog deodorizer/cleaner that breaks them down chemically. Whether the mess is on carpet, vinyl tile, linoleum, or wood, after you thoroughly clean up, spray the spot with a dog deodorizer and cover the area with an overturned chair until it is completely dry.

The City Puppy

For a new puppy owner living in a city, house-training presents specific difficulties that require different techniques from those used in suburban or rural environments. While it is always preferable to house-train a pup in a safe outdoor location (usually a spot in your yard), in urban environments this is often neither possible nor advisable. Aside from the difficulties of getting a pup outside quickly from the fourteenth floor of an apartment building, city puppies are particularly vulnerable to diseases such as parvovirus and canine distemper, which are communicated through urine, feces, and vomit. City veterinarians are rightly insistent that clients not walk their pups on the street until they have received their full series of immunization vaccinations, at sixteen weeks of age.

In these circumstances, paper-training is the only real alternative. Begin by placing several layers of newspaper over the entire confined area (if possible, over a large plastic sheet) to prevent urine from seeping through onto the floor. Make sure the confined area has easy-to-clean surfaces such as linoleum or ceramic tile — never use an absorbent surface such as carpeting. We advise keeping a crate available for the pup's use in this area, since it gives her a secure spot of her own.

Instead of taking the pup outside to her soiling area after feeding and watering, you should simply wait for the pup to eliminate, praise her, and change the papers. When you first put out a fresh batch, leave a soiled paper underneath in the area where you wish the pup to relieve herself. The scent will draw her to the spot, helping her to eliminate exclusively in that location. Leave a little bit more of the floor by the papers unprotected after each change, until you have an area with only four sheets of newspaper. In a few days the pup should be conditioned to seek out that spot to relieve herself. Keep in mind, however, that once your pup is fully immunized, at sixteen weeks, you will want to shift her soiling habits to an outside location. This is usually done by strictly confining a pup to her crate as described in the original schedule. When the time for elimination arrives, whisk her out and wait for her to soil outdoors. Praise her effusively if she succeeds. If she does not relieve herself in a reasonable period of time, take her back to her crate, wait five minutes, and then take her back out. Patience is important here. For a pup who has difficulty making the transition, try bringing one of her soiled papers outside until she gets the point.

Leash-training and Preliminary Obedience Work

Puppies are rarely accustomed to a collar and leash when they first arrive home, and though it is important to begin using them right away, if you do this too abruptly and without adequate preparation, the puppy's first reactions will probably be fearful and belligerent; she will balk and fight all your efforts to get her to walk with you. A more sensible approach is to make the introduction gradually, over the course of several days, building up the pup's self-confidence as she learns to accept the leash. This way, the leash becomes a means of bonding, of communicating with your pup, and not an instrument of compulsion.

Begin by having your puppy wear her flat-buckle collar around the house for a day or two. Do not be concerned if she initially scratches at the collar or shakes her head. Though a collar might be uncomfortable at first, your puppy will quickly forget she is wearing one.

Introducing the leash follows naturally. Let your pup begin dragging the lead around the house, getting her used to the feel of minor pressure on her neck. As she walks around, follow her, then gently pick up the lead and walk with her, keeping the leash held high and speaking in a friendly, encouraging manner.

You can follow a similar routine in your backyard. Start by following your pup around the yard without a leash, praising her as she investigates. After a short while, reverse the roles, getting your pup's attention by clapping your hands and enticing her in cheerful, encouraging tones. Praise her enthusiastically when she follows. Next, try the same sequence with the lead attached. If the pup should balk and start to play tug-of-war, crouch down with your arms wide and call your pup in a pleasant voice (that is, say her name and the word *come*). Do not force the puppy toward you as if you are reeling in a fish, since this will only cause more fight and resistance. Simply clap your hands and encourage your pup to come. Most dogs will return immediately. This is excellent foundation work for the *come* command discussed later.

This exercise can be easily adapted for several family members through circle work. Begin by having the participants sit in a large circle or triangle, about five feet apart from one another. Attach a light nylon line to your puppy and then toss the end of the line to one of the handlers. Have that person call the puppy, praising the dog enthusiastically as she comes and gently easing her into a sit. The end of the line is then tossed to the next handler, and the exercise continues around the circle for five to ten minutes.

Retractable leashes (Flexi-leads) are now widely available and can be a very effective tool for preliminary leash-training and teaching the *come* command; they allow a pup to get used to the leash and an occasional tug without feeling the constant pressure of a lead on the neck. This eliminates virtually all rebellion, since you can immediately release the tension on the leash after a mild tug. The result is a puppy who quickly learns to walk with the leash in a relaxed, unthreatened manner, and to come willingly from a distance of up to twenty-five feet.

However, we also need to point out a number of caveats about Flexi-leads to ensure they are utilized safely. While Flexi-leads are a very effective tool when used with understanding, they can be dangerous when used incorrectly. Here are some important considerations:

1. The Flexi-lead needs to be held tightly. If a pup starts moving away from you quickly, tap the brake button several times to interrupt the dog's bolting and redirect her attention toward you. Otherwise, the pup might build up so much speed that when she hits the end of the cord, the handle will be yanked from your hand. In this scenario, the plastic handle flies across the ground toward the pup as the lead is recoiling, potentially frightening or even injuring her. For this reason, children should never be allowed to use these devices.
2. Never grasp the Flexi-lead by the cord. This can result in a very serious skin burn.
3. When your pup is walking well with the Flexi-lead, you can then transition to a regular leather or nylon leash.

After about a week, your puppy should be walking nicely with you on the lead. You can now try this effective exercise for bonding while you are in the house: Simply keep your pup with you on-leash as you move through your day (preferably after he has eliminated). Hold the leash in your left hand and have him follow you around. When you need to be in a fixed position for a time, either sit on the leash or put your foot over it on the floor to hold the pup in place. You can even clip the lead to your belt loop; however, you must not let that be an excuse for not keeping your attention on him at all times. Simply because the pup is tethered to you does not mean that you don't have to watch him. That holds true regardless of whether you are carrying the leash or attaching it to you.

If you ensure that your pup has eliminated before beginning this exercise, you will be able to go about your business for an hour or so without having to worry about taking him out. As the puppy accompanies you all around the house, he learns to stay with you and to focus his attention primarily on you. This exercise is great for doing house-

When your pup is nine weeks or older, you can practice this effective bonding technique: tie your leash to your belt and have your puppy accompany you throughout the day.

work and will naturally develop a pup who will choose to be with you in a calm, collected manner, while also laying the groundwork for polite leash-walking, described later.

An observation: At this early stage, do not look for the disciplined precision of a formal heel. Your goal is simply to get your pup comfortable with the leash, walking with you without protestation. For this informal walking, instead of the command *heel*, use the phrase *let's go* — your pup should walk with you without pulling, though not necessarily at heel. Be animated and encouraging. If he starts to pull out in front, gently reverse your direction and say your puppy's name and "Let's go" in a happy tone, clapping the side of your leg. Everything should be geared toward conditioning your pup to remain close to you.

Right from the start, in addition to introducing your puppy to coming when called and to preliminary leash work, you can also begin teaching the *sit* and *down* commands. We will outline simple, noncoercive techniques that will familiarize her with these positions without the use of force. At this early stage, it is always wiser to refrain from compulsive techniques; we are concerned with only a gentle, positive introduction to the exercises.

The easiest way to teach the concept of *sit* is to link the command with one of her most pleasurable activities: eating. Since you will be feeding your pup three times a day, you can simply begin associating the two activities. As your pup waits for her food, lift the dish above her head. When she looks up, say, "Sit." If she jumps, stand up straight with the dish held away from you. It may take a second, but her rear will naturally go down into a *sit* position. As soon as this happens, put the food down and praise her gently. With regular practice, your pup will learn that the quicker she sits, the quicker she gets her meal. Not only is she learning how to sit but she is also discovering that you are the one who is in control and she must pay attention to you. You are reinforcing your role as leader.

A variation on this exercise can apply to non-mealtimes. Get your pup's attention by snapping your fingers above her head or by using a ball as an object of attraction. When she looks up toward your hand, wave it slightly over her head. By following the movement of your hand, your pup will shift naturally into a *sit* position. As she does this, say, "Sit," following immediately with lots of praise. If after several attempts

Teaching the sit *command and reinforcing it as the pup grows. Get the puppy's attention with a tennis ball or toy and move it back and forth slightly above the pup's head. As she follows the movement of the ball, say, "Sit," at the same time as she begins to move into the* sit *position. Be sure to reinforce this with praise.*

your pup is still standing and simply looking up at your hand, repeat the exercise, tapping her rear end lightly with your free hand. Follow up with praise. With these techniques, most pups will quickly become conditioned to sitting.

For teaching the concept of *down*, you can use another noncoercive method. With your pup in a sitting position, get her attention by

Lower your hand to the ground to teach the puppy the down *command.*

The pup will follow your hand down; as she does so, say, "Down," and praise her.

showing her a ball or toy. As she focuses on it, dramatically bring it down to the ground about six inches in front of her feet, saying, "Down," at the same time. As your pup follows the object to the floor, praise her gently. You may have to pat the ground several times to get her all the way down — do not be concerned with making her stay down at this time. This is simply a preliminary exercise. If your pup does not follow the object to the floor, simply put a small amount of pressure on her shoulder as you give the command. Once she is down, immediately release her with plenty of praise. This will gradually teach her to be comfortable with the position.

Remember, a house is only as good as its foundation. Taking the time to start off right with your pup is in everyone's best interest. It sets the stage for teaching your puppy the basic elements of obedience and companionship in the weeks and months ahead.

12

The Foundations of Training

The first months of puppy rearing pass so quickly that before you know it your puppy is practically full-grown. From adoption to six months of age, your pup will grow to three-quarters of his adult size and pass through a series of developmental stages that will have a strong effect on his future behavior. Do not let this growth catch you off guard. Understanding how this period of development unfolds will allow you to anticipate your pup's behavior and plan effective training methods. You must learn to harmonize your handling of your pup with the particular stage of growth he has reached, thus giving him the best chance of maturing into a happy, well-adjusted companion.

The Socialization Period Concludes

As we have seen, most people adopt their pups between seven and ten weeks, in the middle of the socialization period. Because of this timing, new owners often notice their pups manifesting fear and avoidance shortly after being brought home, usually in connection with new experiences. This fear/avoidance period (eight to ten weeks) is a normal part of socialization and is indirectly responsible for puppies' bonding quickly with new owners. A puppy who experiences this touch of insecurity tends to seek the presence and security of his owner; he gladly follows you around and stays by your side.

Through this close contact the puppy's self-confidence grows steadily, so that when he enters the final two weeks of the socialization period (ten to twelve weeks) he acts like a little adult. This is a particularly enjoyable time to spend with your pup. He learns quickly yet still looks upon you as the central figure in his life. Occasions of fearfulness are infrequent. Even though the pup appears to be well-adjusted, it is important not to adopt a careless, laissez-faire attitude with him. Within the parameters of safety, you should continue intensive socializing: invite friends and neighbors to your house to meet your puppy. Be sure to plan these encounters ahead of time so that your friends will know what to do. A good practice is to set up a greeting routine that your pup will quickly become accustomed to. When the doorbell rings, bring your puppy to the door on a leash, so that he is under control. After you open the door and greet your friend, have the person crouch down to meet your puppy, praising him in a pleasant voice. It is much easier for pups to approach a crouching figure than a person who is towering over them. Make sure your guest makes no sudden movements toward the pup that could be frightening.

Also, take the puppy on short car trips around the neighborhood to get him accustomed to the car. Use a portable crate (or have a friend stay in the backseat with him), and keep the trips short enough so that he does not get sick. If you follow up each excursion with praise and a session of play, he will learn to associate the car with a pleasant experience. Pups who are conditioned to riding in the car early in life become quite comfortable as adults and rarely have difficulties with motion sickness.

If you can walk him safely (remember, until your pup is fully immunized you must be careful about exposing him to other dogs and areas where animals defecate), let him explore the area around your house while on-leash, and take him to meet people in the neighborhood, especially children. We cannot overemphasize the importance of socialization: providing your pup with as many new experiences as possible should be a major priority for you at this time in his life. This also includes conditioning to a wide variety of common household appliances: electric blender, dishwasher, garage-door opener, waste-disposal system, and vacuum cleaner. Keep the initial exposures gentle, switching on the appliance when your pup is well away from it and letting him make a gradual approach. Do not force or drag him. Instead, let your pup get accustomed to the noise and movement in his own time.

These daily episodes of socializing build his self-confidence and foster a healthy attitude toward life. Also, if you have not already started to teach your pup basic obedience exercises (see chapter fifteen), now is the time. Although a puppy at this age has a short attention span and

A training class is helpful for puppy and dog socialization, teaching good behavior, meeting new people and other dogs, and learning good training habits.

requires plenty of patience, he is quite capable of learning and will benefit from short training sessions that are kept positive and nonpunitive.

The above holds true for city pups as well, though it is easy to imagine how socializing a puppy under these circumstances can be a real challenge. Since urban apartment dwellers most likely will not be walking their puppies in public until at least sixteen weeks of age, they must provide safe alternative social experiences. Why sixteen weeks? Because many city veterinarians worry about the risks of allowing puppies to interact before they have completed their full cycle of vaccinations. The primary concern is canine parvovirus, a potentially lethal disease that is contracted when an unprotected puppy comes in contact with infected feces or with other contaminated organic material such as soil, where the virus can survive for more than a year. With the high population of dogs in our cities, the parvovirus threat on the street is very real. An even greater risk, however, is that of an undersocialized pup being euthanized or surrendered because he exhibits serious behavior problems related to lack of socializing. Since the critical socialization period ends at fourteen weeks, it is vital that newly adopted puppies be thoroughly socialized from the day they come into your life. Quite literally their lives may depend on it.

Fortunately, city owners are not without viable options to safely accomplish this. For clients living in apartments without private yards, we recommend several procedures to ensure proper socializing without jeopardizing a puppy's health. As part of your daily routine, take your pup on walks around the neighborhood, using a large tote bag in which the pup can be comfortably carried. Small and medium-size breeds have no difficulty fitting in these kinds of carryalls throughout puppy-hood, and large breeds can be easily carried until they are between ten and twelve weeks of age. Toting your pup around prevents him from coming into contact with urine and feces while also exposing him to the sights and sounds of city life. Urban puppies have to get used to honking horns, jackhammers, sirens, and busy traffic, as well as to large crowds of people walking along sidewalks. Often if an owner is sitting with a puppy on a park bench, people will ask to meet or pet the pup. These experiences will provide your dog with controlled exposure to the world and will nurture his normal development.

Another safe socializing exercise for pups in cities involves using the lobby area of your apartment building for random encounters with all sorts of people. With your pup on a leash, you can walk him around the lobby, letting him investigate and mingle naturally with the whole environment. Simply offering your pup the opportunity to see people coming in and out of the building has a very beneficial effect. If people come over to greet or admire your dog, introduce your puppy to them, taking care not to allow him to jump up. After the adjustment of the first several days, you can invite friends and relatives over to meet your puppy. This step is extremely important if a large number of your pup's social experiences prior to sixteen weeks of age will occur in your apartment.

Finally, puppy classes are widely available for socialization pur-poses, although the safety of these has been called into question. Some veterinarians caution their clients not to participate until their pup's vaccinations are complete. In a roundtable discussion sponsored by the American Veterinary Society of Animal Behavior (AVSAB) and printed in the December 2009 issue of *Veterinary Medicine*, four veterinarians with expertise in animal behavior weighed in on the risks versus the benefits of puppy classes. Without exception, each of these experts underscored the importance of early socializing in puppy develop-ment, the minimal safety risks associated with attending puppy classes before the full cycle of vaccinations has been completed, and the absolute benefits to puppies in participating. The veterinarians believed that getting puppies properly socialized was paramount, even with the potential health risks of puppy classes. They discussed the safety protocols that most puppy classes have in place — such as requiring vaccinations (i.e., those appropriate for the age of each puppy), health certificates, and good hygiene, and not allowing ill puppies to attend class — and they reported the few, if any, instances of serious sickness they had witnessed as a result of puppy classes. They also encouraged socialization dates in safe areas with adult dogs who are known to be healthy and who are friendly with puppies, as well as car rides that can expose pups to a broad number of sights and sounds. The experts discouraged visiting dog parks and walking on sidewalks until a pup's vaccinations are completed at sixteen weeks of age.

The Juvenile Period (12 Weeks to Sexual Maturity)

The juvenile period of development corresponds to that time in the wild when wolf puppies make their first excursions away from the nest area, showing a new curiosity about their surrounding environment. They become increasingly independent, and existing behavior patterns are refined as the pups grow in strength and skill. Prior to this, the pups have stayed within twenty yards of the nest, and their primary focus has been their mother. Now that changes: the nest is abandoned and the pups are taken to "rendezvous" sites, where they stay while the pack is hunting elsewhere. At these sites, which can be as large as a half acre, they become adventuresome and begin learning how to hunt, practicing on field mice and other small animals. Their running skills improve steadily, and their gait progresses from awkward bunny-hopping to a smoother, more coordinated trot. This results in greater stamina and higher activity levels. Social behavior also matures: by fourteen weeks the dominance order of the litter is fixed and the pups have developed a keen sense of their rank and status within the pack. Over the following months their permanent teeth will come in, and they will be introduced gradually to adult life — hunting with the pack around ten months of age, when their bodies have grown strong enough.

These same behavioral changes occur in the life of your puppy, though they can make for trying times in a domestic context. Many owners are quite unprepared for the challenge of these months, when puppy behavior fluctuates dramatically. Beginning at thirteen weeks, a pup will show more pronounced expressions of independence: the dog who only last week was your shadow, who seemed well on his way to being trained, now begins to ignore you when you call, and during training and play sessions you have to work extra hard to keep his attention. His rapid growth produces a corresponding increase in activity that makes him highly excitable and difficult to manage. While he does need plenty of exercise, for most owners this translates into walks with lots of pulling and lunging. Bad habits develop quickly. When guests come to the house, the juvenile pup turns into a juvenile delinquent, jumping up and making himself a pest, continually demanding attention. It is also common for pups of this age to become very mouthy, so that by the teething period (four to six months), they are chewing on everything, people included. To top things off, your puppy will probably go through a *second* fear period, when his behavior will swing from being independent and bratty (twelve to fourteen weeks) to periodically cautious and fearful (sixteen to twenty-four weeks), even of things with which he had formerly been comfortable.

Patience alone is not sufficient to get through these months. Now, more than ever, your pup needs the guiding, stabilizing presence of a competent and understanding pack leader (see chapter fourteen). Take an active role in this process. Preliminary training, appropriate discipline, and a reassuring attitude are all key elements in helping your pup through this challenging period of his life. Perhaps the biggest mistake you can make with your pup is to put off this early training under the mistaken assumption that training should occur *after* six months. This common misunderstanding is responsible for all sorts of unnecessary behavior problems. When owners fail to begin puppy training as soon as they adopt their pup, the dog begins to train himself. After several months of the pup doing as he pleases, "untraining" will most likely involve sterner techniques that, while effective, could have been avoided had puppy training begun immediately. To illustrate this, we bring you the case of Rory.

Rory

A six-month-old German shepherd puppy lunged through our gift-shop door with his owner in tow, a young graduate student desperately begging the rambunctious pup to "heel." As she pulled the leash back and forth in an attempt to restrain him, the puppy forged around the room, excitedly sniffing the carpet and furniture. When the student finally managed to get the pup under control and collect herself, she nervously looked up at the attending monk and said, "Hello...uh...I have an appointment to bring my pup, Rory, for training."

When she had first contacted us by phone, the woman had described the bind she was in: she had unexpectedly received an important grant to study in Europe for two months, which left her no choice but to board Rory during that time. Since Rory had not yet received any training, the woman was looking for a kenneling program that could do two things: board Rory, and train him in a "kindly, gentle way." She confessed that the idea of training made her very wary, but she also admitted that she was having real problems controlling Rory—among other things, he was becoming highly destructive.

In response, we outlined the services we could offer, and we were frank about what would be involved in training him. It appeared from her description that despite his basically friendly nature, Rory was spoiled and used to getting his own way. He was the boss in their relationship, and if a real change was to take place in his behavior, he would have to learn to become a follower. In all likelihood, this would mean firm yet fair discipline, particularly early on.

This response made her nervous. She did not like the idea of training Rory by force. We explained that it was she who had inadvertently made that choice by delaying the process until now. By allowing Rory to grow up without proper direction and leadership, she had made training a more difficult proposition. She said that this had never occurred to her and that she was under the impression training should not begin before six months of age. We then explained why this was not true. Finally, almost reluctantly, she agreed to bring Rory to us.

As the monk greeted owner and pup, Rory playfully tried to jump up several times, and the student had to use all of her strength to restrain him. Soft-spoken and polite, she kept pleading, "Stop it, stop it," but Rory seemed completely oblivious to her corrections, merrily tugging away at the leash and making hoarse, straining sounds as a result of being pulled. Unable to reach the monk, he wrapped himself around his owner's legs several times, and when she finally managed to free herself, he began to mouth and nip at her hands. Her pleading only encouraged him further, until at last he began to bark continuously for attention.

The monk finally suggested that it might be best to get Rory settled in his kennel area before proceeding with the interview. The woman agreed, but before handing over the leash, she said, "Wait just a few seconds." Crouching down to gather Rory to herself, she anxiously began hugging and kissing him good-bye. The emotional farewell proved too much for the young puppy. Overwhelmed by the intensity of her affections, Rory squatted helplessly and let go with a minor flood, making the student groan in frustration, "Oh, Rory!" The scene could not have been more predictable.

When the monk returned from placing the pup in the kennel, the student was in tears. She looked up and remarked awkwardly, "I know that all of this must seem rather silly, but I feel absolutely distressed about leaving him. We're very attached and the thought of leaving him for training...well...please tell me, is the training going to break his spirit?"

In response, the monk walked her over to the window and pointed to the front yard, where one of his confreres happened to be working with a seven-month-old Labrador retriever who was just completing a three-week training course. The two walked harmoniously around the yard, their pace and rhythm so measured that their movements seemed choreographed, like a ballet. The unhesitating attentiveness, wagging tail, fixed eye contact, and perfect pace of the dog were utterly captivating. His responses to the obedience commands were precise yet not mechanical, and the monk's soft, encouraging praise brought out energy and enthusiasm in the dog's work.

The student watched silently for ten minutes. When the session ended, the monk beside her said, "Three weeks ago she was just like Rory. Now look at her. *That* is spirit!"

What Is Training?

Rory arrived at New Skete unruly and dominant, unresponsive to the leash, and unable to focus on anything for more than several seconds. His owner had raised him with the mistaken notion that obedience training should not begin until six months of age, if at all. The result was a puppy out of control and impossible to live with. As we suspected, during Rory's first training session with us he initially tried to domi-nate his trainer, fighting the leash and bolting in different directions. Had the graduate student witnessed this first session, she might have frantically "rescued" Rory from the kennel and sped off, convinced that the monks were too unsympathetic. No doubt she would have been upset by the absence of any coddling, and the firm, uncompromising leash corrections Rory received in his first lesson. She likely would have been disturbed by the physical correction his trainer used to discourage his initial attempts at dominance. What she would not have imagined, however, would be the rapid transformation that would occur over the following weeks, as Rory changed from a willful, spoiled, stubborn puppy into a calmer, obedient dog. When she returned to pick up Rory, she stared in disbelief as he moved flawlessly through his paces, happy and attentive. After the demonstration, she turned to the monk next to her and exclaimed in an astonished voice, "That's not *my* dog!"

Happily, Rory responded to the training commendably, and the stu-dent was able to get a new insight into the value of a properly trained dog. Nevertheless, the whole process could have been so much simpler. By no means does obedience training have to be harsh or disagreeable. Much of the challenge of Rory's first sessions could have been avoided had his owner understood that "training" is much more than a formal set of exercises a dog learns once he reaches a certain age. Six months is a reasonable time to commence *formal* obedience training, with regular daily sessions; however, this will have its greatest value only when it flows naturally from a basic foundation of socialization, puppy condi-tioning, preliminary obedience exercises, and play that begins early in puppyhood. All of these factors naturally dispose a puppy to accept the human leadership so necessary for more advanced training.

Make no mistake about it: *training is never just optional.* If you have a new puppy, she will be trained one way or another—either into an unruly, dominant, spoiled dog with real possibilities for serious prob-lem behavior or into a companion who is friendly, well managed, and obedient. It all depends on you. Had Rory been raised with this type of understanding, his formal training would have begun with much less compulsion and discipline, since it would have flowed naturally from a healthy leader-follower relationship. As we explain in *How to Be Your Dog's Best Friend*, we understand training as a dynamic process that begins at the puppy's birth and continues throughout her life. It enables a puppy to reach her full potential as a dog and companion, in a manner completely in harmony with her canine nature.

Training is educating. Significantly, the word *education* comes from the Latin *educare*, which means "to draw out, to call forth what is already present as a possibility." Applied to your dog, this concept is not limited to the mastering of five basic commands; it is an ongoing process. We have seen this holistic understanding of puppy development borne out in watching litter after litter grow and learn, conscious of our own role in that process. From the perspective of theory and experience, we view training as a way of relating to a dog that involves a person's whole life with it, not simply ten-minute sessions in the morning or evening. Many new owners fail to perceive that their puppy begins her training the day she arrives home and not three to four months later, when she reaches that magical age of six months. She is not in a state of suspended animation until then. Rather, your puppy is reacting, responding, learning, and forming habits, if only by default.

A pup learns how to meet other dogs in a natural but mannerly way, with oversight by the people.

Me? A Trainer?

Since your dog is always learning, for better or for worse, it is to your advantage as an owner to give direction to the training process in a manner that enhances your life together. Only by taking a deliberate, active role in training your pup will you have the opportunity to develop a smooth and enjoyable relationship.

However, let us emphasize that you must do this with sensitivity, intelligence, and thoughtfulness. All the good intentions in the world are of little value if the way you treat your pup is unsuited to his immature stage of development. A young puppy's emotional system and physical structure have not matured enough to handle the stress brought on by less-than-thoughtful compulsory obedience training. For example, some dog owners, knowing they must be the boss in their puppy's eyes, go to the opposite extreme of Rory's owner. They make the mistake of being overbearing, misusing dominance in a heavy-handed, stressful way. When a puppy errs, these owners deal with it severely, convinced that punishment is the best way for him to learn. This approach can result in a pup who is passively submissive and fearful, lacking any self-confidence. A more patient, guiding, and correcting approach to training, one stressing encouragement and praise, is much more effective in preparing a puppy for a future of companionship and learning. Remember, a pup *must* develop confidence in adolescence.

Puppy training, therefore, is different in tone from traditional formal obedience training. Very young puppies (seven to ten weeks) have no innate impressions of training; their slates are basically clean. Possessing brain waves already at adult levels, pups lack only experience. This is the ideal time for them to acquire positive attitudes about life and about training, since there are no bad habits to undo. In puppy training we are less concerned with demanding precise responses to obedience commands than with nurturing basic character traits: respect for leadership, attentiveness, curiosity, playfulness, and an enthusiastic attitude toward your relationship. The emphasis here is on fun. Puppies learn best in the context of play, just as young wolves and young humans do. By keeping the focus of early sessions positive and pleasant, with lots of play, you can lay a solid behavioral foundation that will prepare your puppy for advanced training later on and will serve him throughout his life. You will be amazed at how easily formal obedience and advanced training follow from a program of interesting and fun puppy training, in which you exercise your leadership in a manner that stimulates your pup's growth.

Being a Leader

All dogs need discerning leadership. Remember, in the wild they will function as pack animals who are very sensitive to social hierarchy: they discover their place in the pack naturally and learn to respect leadership. This is a primary reason dogs have been so successful from an evolutionary point of view. On the domestic front, the dynamic remains the same, only now your household is the pack, and you must assume the role of leader. Be sure of one thing: if your pup does not learn to perceive you in this way, she will assume the role herself and try to lead you. Don't take it personally — it's simply part of her nature: she'll rise as high as she can in the pack. If you don't assert your leadership clearly and consistently, before you know it your pup will have you fetching the slippers, so to speak. She'll be in control, and you'll be frustrated.

Part of being a benevolent leader is learning the characteristics of good training: patience, fairness, consistency, attentiveness, and intelligence. Good trainers might occasionally *feel* impatient with a dog, but they always do their best to avoid showing it. They take a long view of the training process and don't try to do too much too quickly, building methodically one step at a time. They keep their anger in check when things aren't going as planned and realize that a calm and quiet approach vis-à-vis their pup is more helpful. With that sort of self-possession a trainer can be flexible, responding to what the dog needs instead of reacting to mistakes.

Let us be clear here: this doesn't mean being lax. In training, letting the dog ignore known commands or get away with unacceptable behavior is always a formula for future problems. Take the time necessary to be fair and consistent. If you give a command, make sure to enforce it, and use only commands that you know the dog understands and that you can impose. For example, don't try recalling a puppy without some sort of light leash or tether to guide the pup's response. A pup who learns that she doesn't have to come every time you call will return only when she feels like it, which will lead to much frustration and consternation.

You can do this, but first you must be aware of how dogs do and do not learn, how they communicate, and which of your own attitudes draw out the best qualities in your dog.

We remember one client who came to us for advice regarding his four-month-old rottweiler puppy, who was starting to growl at strangers. When we went to meet the client and his dog, they were sitting on a bench in our front yard. As we approached, the pup started to growl in a low, threatening tone, and the owner quickly tried to reassure him with a soothing voice, saying, "It's okay, boy, it's oookay. Gooood boy, gooood boy, eeeeasy," gently rubbing him on his side as he did so. Naturally, the growling only grew worse, and the man looked up helplessly, wondering what to do. Fortunately, we were able to settle the puppy down by taking a short walk with him, and after several minutes he became very accepting and friendly. The owner then complained, "I don't understand it. He's such a good pup, and yet he has this thing about growling." We explained to the baffled owner that the pup was merely doing what he was told. Reviewing with him his reactions during the incident, we showed him that he was unintentionally rewarding the puppy's growling by his soft praise and petting. The only message the puppy was receiving was "This is the way to act."

We cannot say that this pup was "disobedient." Instead, we can see that the owner misunderstood what he was communicating and was ignorant of how to show his true intent in a clear, authoritative way.

To Obey Is to Hear

In dog training, most people understand obedience as something the dog does in response to his handler: the dog is the one who is obedient or not. This is only half true. *Obedience* comes from the Latin word *oboedire*, which in turn is cognate to *obaudire*, meaning "to listen, to hear" — by extension, this implies acting on what is heard. Contrary to popular thought, obedience is as much your responsibility as it is your dog's — even more so, since you are accountable for shaping your pup's behavior to fit your living circumstances. The problem with many owners is that they fail to listen and to respond to the real needs of their dogs; unknowingly, the owners are disobedient.

To be a good companion to your dog, *you* must be obedient — that is, fully alert and focused on your pup, flexible enough to adapt your approach instantly to his needs. As odd as it may sound, your dog does not know what is best for him; you do, but only by being truly obedient to him.

Brother Thomas, who was the driving force behind the training program here at New Skete until he died in a tragic automobile accident in 1973, had this insight into obedience:

> Learning the value of silence is learning to listen to, instead of screaming at, reality: opening your mind enough to find what the end of someone else's sentence sounds like, or listening to a dog until you discover what is needed instead of imposing yourself in the name of training.

This kind of obedience comes only with time, practice, and study, by learning different techniques and methods of training and using them in different circumstances and, if possible, with different types of dogs. Because dogs are individuals, not all respond in the same way to particular training methods. Remember Anka's litter: were we to train Yola in the same way as Sunny, we would probably only compound her submissive, shy personality. In education, teachers discover from working with different children that they must be flexible, adapting a variety of teaching methods to individual students. A rigorous, highly structured program that is effective with one child may be disastrous with another. The same is true in dog training. Part of training means that you become a student of your dog and employ an approach that brings out the best in him.

In discussing training, we will not present you with one absolute method of teaching your pup. We will try instead to point out some general principles that are important cornerstones for all good training and then show you how these can be applied to different dogs. This will help you understand and deal with the particular requirements of your own puppy. Working with dogs of all sizes, breeds, temperaments, and personalities, we have learned that limiting yourself to a singular method of training is a serious mistake. Trainers who insist that only one kind of training works (their own) betray their own ignorance and pride, and close themselves off from a real understanding of dogs.

One last observation, especially for those who have never owned a dog before: Novices often experience feelings of awkwardness and uncertainty at the prospect of training their pup. This can discourage them from even beginning the process. Intimidated by a lack of understanding of techniques and canine behavior, they often fear that their effort will only manifest their own incompetence and lack of coordination while also ruining their puppy. You will be surprised, however, what hidden talents come to the surface if you approach training honestly. Your attitude is what is crucial. Take advantage of the opportunity to learn as much as you can about training, and then practice regularly with your pup, beginning with quick sessions in keeping with his short attention span, then gradually working up to more structured lessons. Get involved with a local obedience club or Kindergarten Puppy Training (KPT) class in your area for some hands-on experience, and listen to the insights of more accomplished handlers. Do not be afraid to ask serious questions. Good trainers are usually very generous with their knowledge. Their advice and encouragement can give practical support to the different ideas you come across in your study.

This last point bears some expansion. While part of the purpose of this book is to provide a reliable road map to establish a solid basic training foundation with your pup, there is no reason why you cannot benefit from professional help as well. Aside from possessing a wealth of experience, a good trainer can coach and encourage you in ways that are hard to realize when you are working alone. This is true whether you are attending a class or working privately. Over the years we have had the privilege of meeting many talented trainers, and when you find a good one, it can dramatically impact your relationship with your puppy.

However, simply having the title "dog trainer" next to one's name does not a dog trainer make. Often there is a vast difference between an experienced professional — who may have certification from a reputable training school or organization, who has attended advanced seminars and conferences, who is a member of a trainers' organization such as the International Association of Canine Professionals (IACP), the Association of Pet Dog Trainers (APDT), or the National Association of Dog Obedience Instructors (NADOI), and who has apprenticed with a more experienced trainer — and an amateur, who may have done none of the above. The collective strengths of the experienced trainer are worth any extra money you may need to pay for his or her services. Take the time to find a trainer whom you feel comfortable with and who has a track record for success in the field. Here are some suggestions:

- Your veterinarian is a good resource for training referrals. Veterinarians appreciate well-behaved dogs and are usually happy to refer their clients to trainers who have worked successfully with a wide range of dogs.
- Ask owners of well-mannered dogs where the pups received their training. Nothing impresses like good behavior, and owners are typically more than pleased to refer people to the trainer who served them so well.
- Training methods differ among professionals. Call or schedule a visit with potential trainers in your area and ask about their particular approach and the tools they use. Where did they get their experience? Inquire if they have worked with your breed and whether their programs can be tailored to your specific needs as a new puppy owner.
- If possible, observe the trainer working with a class or with a dog. Does the trainer communicate clearly and respectfully? Is he or she patient in explaining concepts? How does the trainer work with the dogs in the class? Do the dogs seem happy and responsive? Does the trainer seem too rough? What is the expert's own dog like? Does he or she embody an approach to dogs that you can emulate and learn from?

Working with a skilled trainer can be an enriching experience for both you and your dog. While it won't lessen your responsibility as an active participant in the training, it can make the whole experience more successful and enjoyable. But keep in mind that whether you choose to work with a professional or not, ultimately you will have to stay committed to the training process if you hope to get the dog of your dreams.

Most important, never be satisfied with mediocrity; work hard to bring out the best in your pup by striving each day to make your training something more alive than the day before, something more than a mere mastery of techniques. Our culture is obsessed with technique, and technique is essential in training; however, if the training process is to deepen your relationship with your dog, it must be wedded to intuition. The point of practicing regularly and faithfully is not to create a robot. It is to strive toward a level of freedom and understanding with your dog that speaks of true companionship. When that occurs, training reaches the frontiers of art.

From a Monk's Journal

Looks Like a Puppy Is in the Cards

I have always loved the name Zoe. It comes from a Greek word meaning *life* and has a thoroughly biblical pedigree in both the Hebrew scriptures and the New Testament. Life is the gift that has been given by the Creator, who has freely chosen to share this with his creatures and with creation. Whatever lives, whatever has life, points by its very existence to the mystery that ultimately brought it into being, and that mystery is fundamentally good.

All of this is relevant to me today because Brother John told me this morning that I will be raising a female puppy from the "Z" litter, a breeding between one of our top studs, Dux, and a beautiful brood bitch named Xenia. Throughout the years that we have been breeding, we have assigned letters to each litter in order to keep track of it in an orderly fashion. Every time we go through the alphabet, we add a number after the letter to indicate the next cycle. For example, "B19" would indicate the nineteenth "B" litter in the history of our breeding program, the four hundred seventieth litter, to be precise. To further keep track of puppies, we usually suggest that our clients pick a registered name starting with the letter of the alphabet of the litter their pup belongs to. Granted, this makes for some interesting registered names (e.g., "New Skete's Xcellent Cherry Pie"), but it helps keep records straight while allowing our clients freedom in naming their pups. In the above example, the dog's call name is Cherry, but her registered name lets us know that she is from an "X" litter.

The puppy I am to raise is from the "Z19" litter, so we have decided to call her Zoe. The name definitely seems to fit her. When I've taken her out to play over the past couple of days, she has been spunky and full of fun, and without an inordinate amount of mouthiness. I've been able to redirect her attention to appropriate objects for her mouth and haven't noticed any sort of reticence or fear of people. She seems eager to investigate new objects and environments, and her curiosity amuses me when she gently *ruffs* at something unusual, like the oil truck making a delivery, as it did today. I am excited about the prospect of raising this pup, and the fact that her name is one of my favorites makes me all the more eager to get started with her. But, more than anything, I am aware of the possibility of the gift she can become and how her success or failure depends largely on me.

Zoe and the Crate (9 Weeks Old)

I've been pleased to see how "by the book" Zoe has taken to the crate, as this has made house-training a breeze. Given that there are crates in each of the rooms in the puppy kennel, Zoe was obviously used to the idea from the day I brought her over to the monastery. The only difference now is that I have to shut the door for periods. But even with this, there's been very little whining, and she seems relaxed in the crate.

This is definitely a grace, since I realize from experience that it's not always the case. Some pups I've raised have been very vocal initially and have thrown temper tantrums trying to get out of the crate. During those times, I've had to be really disciplined in making sure never to give in when a pup is vocalizing like that, letting the puppy out only when she is quiet. Given the noise an irate pup can generate, sometimes this can be most trying. But even in these cases, I have found that simply closing the door to the room and letting the puppy wait for a time works wonders. She quickly figures out that quiet means the possibility of being let out of the crate.

One thing I have been very vigilant about is keeping Zoe on a strict schedule. She stays in the crate no more than two hours at a time and then is given the chance to relieve herself. After she's successfully eliminated, I keep her with me for a while before putting her back in the crate. I've been doing this now for ten days, and she has been perfect: nary a mess in the crate. But when I let her out to take her to the run to relieve herself, I have to be very quick about it. She is absolutely a pup with a mission. The second she gets out in the run, she squats and goes potty.

Zoe at the Dinner Table (10 Weeks Old)

This pup does have a pair of lungs on her! Zoe is turning out to be a name that fits her in spades. While she is mostly quiet and content in the crate, restraining her at the dinner table these past several days has become something of a challenge. Fortunately the other monks have been relaxed and understanding about it, not paying attention to the extra vocalizing. Typically we like to have our dogs present with us when we eat. In fact, one of the pictures from *How to Be Your Dog's Best Friend* that gets the most comment shows all of our dogs on *down-stays* around our dinner table. It's really not rocket science. We simply train the dogs to be included in that part of our lives. Once we have taught a dog a down-stay, we can easily practice it in any number of situations that mimic real life. In this fashion we can easily correct a pup when she gets up and simply enforce the command in a very calm way.

With a puppy who doesn't really understand *down*, however, the situation changes. Rather than wait until she does grasp the down-stay, we bring the pup to meals pretty much right away. In this case, I'm keeping Zoe right next to me at the table by using a metal leash (it's the only time I'll use this material because it prevents her from chewing on the lead). I gently move her into a down and put my foot on the chain. After a couple of minutes, she settles. But for those first few moments she tends to raise a bit of a stink. So far I've simply ignored it, but if the behavior continues I'll probably do some specific work with her.

Zoe and Her Dinner (12 Weeks Old)

The speed at which a young, voracious puppy can devour her dinner never ceases to amaze me. The second I put Zoe's dish before her in the crate, the food seems to vanish. You'd think I was a gourmet chef! No doubt this stems from her competing with her littermates for food over the course of several weeks, but it has remained a particular feature of

Zoe's temperament. This does, however, offer an opportunity. Instead of simply feeding her in the crate, lately I've been using mealtime as a preliminary training lesson. I prepare the food as she watches and then simply lift the dish slightly over her head as I say, "Sit." Immediately she goes into a *sit* position (because she has to look up at the dish in a manner that makes her rear touch the floor), and then I place her food in front of her. Zoe has caught on to this very quickly, and soon I'll expand the training, making her hold the *sit-stay* position until I give her permission to dig in. Initially I'll use a light tether to help with this, but the important thing to remember is that we can often use everyday occurrences to reinforce training. There is nothing artificial about good obedience work, and it can start as soon as you get your puppy.

Zoe and Loneliness (13 Weeks Old)

I've been concerned that Zoe is spending a little too much time by herself during the day. My work schedule simply prevents me from having her with me all the time, so she has to be alone for about three hours a day. Ideally she could be in a big pen with one of the other shepherds, but because she is significantly younger and so much smaller than our other pup, Xerxes (and because Xerxes plays way too rough with her even in a monitored situation), we've had to keep Zoe by herself until she gets a bit bigger. Even putting her with one of the placid older dogs without monitoring would be premature, since puppies can be overly demanding of attention and elicit a sharp rebuke from an older dog. I could easily picture that happening with Zoe: a couple of hours alone often results in her eagerness for some playtime with another dog, to the point that she could become a pest. Even when I come to get her at the end of the afternoon, she tends to be incredibly animated, jumping up and down excitedly. While I'm flattered by her unrestrained display of affection, I've had to keep these reunions low-key lest she turn into a jumper. I stay very still and quiet until she calms down and rests for a couple of moments in a *sit* position. Only then do I open the gate.

I believe this situation will require a little bit of imagination and effort. I'm going to have to set up additional play sessions with some of our other dogs so that Zoe can interact with them in a supervised context. I'll also plan on taking some extra walks down our road with various monks and their dogs. Fortunately this won't be difficult, as the others are pretty cooperative. They understand how vital it is for the pups to be thoroughly socialized.

Zoe and the Culvert (14 Weeks Old)

Puppies tend to get into everything, and today Zoe proved the rule. We were coming up the road on the homestretch of our walk when suddenly Zoe became intrigued by the culvert. Perhaps she heard the water gently coming out of the drain, but in no time she had stopped in front of the drain, smelled it thoroughly, and proceeded to enter the tunnel. Naturally I clapped and called for her to stop, but it was to no avail. Zoe was in exploration mode. She went in about five feet, stomping through the water, ignoring my pleas for her to come out and save me the inconvenience of giving her a bath. In fact, as I gently tapped the edge of the culvert for her to come, it only made her more playful, and she jumped up and down until her whole body dripped with water. What a game it was for her! Fortunately, after a few more minutes she bounded out, shook herself, and proudly walked alongside me as we headed toward the kennel for a bath.

Regression (18 Weeks Old)

This morning I was taking Zoe through some basic obedience exercises, and it suddenly seemed as though she had forgotten everything she had learned over the past two months. She appeared distracted and bored, and a number of times she looked at me as if to say, "I haven't a clue what you're asking me to do." If I hadn't experienced this before with a number of the puppies I've raised, I would have thought she had suddenly gone brain-dead. While pups have their good days and bad days, this was something different, and it challenged me to work patiently to regain her focus. Whether Zoe was tired of the routine or simply becoming engrossed in other things, I don't know. I decided to pick up my pace and move my body in a more animated way, and I broke down the sessions into smaller, more positive segments, using items she associates with fun. I kept my voice quiet, resisting the temptation to speak louder, in a way that conveys low-grade panic. Rather than using heavy corrections, I find that at this stage a lighter strategy works better because it doesn't turn the training session into a battle of wills. After a brief working segment with Zoe, I did a couple of retrieves with her, then let her relax a bit in the crate.

I may well go through a week or so of this sort of regression and apparent confusion, but my experience tells me that it will soon pass if I hang in there and trust in the process. There's no need to push perfection down her throat, as long as I don't use this as an excuse to get lazy with her training. She'll come around.

Zoe and the Deer (19 Weeks Old)

Given that we sit on five hundred acres of wooded land, it is hardly surprising when we encounter a variety of animals on our walks. But it's fascinating to see Zoe respond to the novelty. Her "dogness" comes out spontaneously, as happened this morning when a deer bounded out in front of her. She barked reflexively and immediately started to chase after it. Interestingly, however, when the deer went into the high brush, Zoe simply paced back and forth around the point of entry, somehow knowing that it wasn't wise to proceed. Another dog, Sasha, trotted up in the aftermath and also didn't continue, simply raising her head to sniff the wind.

I found all of this striking: many a young pup would have bounded right into the thicket, but somehow Zoe refrained. Of course, it helps that I'm raising a pup with an older dog: there is no question that Sasha has been a real advantage in showing Zoe the ropes of being a New Skete shepherd. Sasha's sensitivity has been striking—how tolerant she was initially of Zoe's age and the reserve she exercised in interacting with her, and how the activity has gradually increased as Zoe has gotten bigger. It is almost as though, with each new day, Sasha has become more animated with Zoe, more of a friend. That said, the unique personality of the puppy is also an important piece of the mix, and I'm beginning to think that I've really got a gem in this pup.

Zoe and the Photo Shoot (20 Weeks Old)

Today I worked with Brother Marc and our friend Kate Hartson on preparing some photographs for the new edition of the book. We decided to use Zoe for the pictures, and I was interested to see how she would do with the photo session. Over the years, I've learned that puppies are sometimes hard to work with on camera. Since the pups are so young and have a short attention span, the photographer's need to get "just the right shot" and to set things up with the proper angle and light can cause a puppy to get distracted and cranky pretty fast. But at nearly five months, Zoe was the perfect model for what we were trying to show, and I had a hunch that she would do well. As it turned out, she was rather remarkable. Zoe took immediately to the agility equipment in the training arena, going up and down the ramp with obvious pleasure and coordination. She was able to handle the tunnel without a problem, as well as the mini-ramp, all because of the early socializing exercises we did with her when she was younger. She displayed no tentativeness whatsoever, just a joyous exuberance to learn. To top it off, after a little break, Zoe did very well on some elementary obedience exercises, which Brother Marc caught on camera quite easily. We didn't have to fuss with her; she was totally cooperative and actually seemed to enjoy herself immensely. You could almost observe her little brain working, figuring out what was next on the "to do" list. The fact that she took to everything without any problems was a delight, since I know how often this isn't the case.

Brother Christopher with Zoe at five and a half months.

I felt really good. Taking a relaxed approach to raising Zoe has certainly paid off. She is just a lovely, lovely puppy: so bright, so friendly, so normal. Given that it had been a while since I had raised a puppy, I wondered at the beginning of the process how things would go. Well, they've gone better than I could have imagined. My only concern now is her preliminary X-rays. Please, God, let them be good. After investing so much emotional energy in this pup, I know how hard it would be if her hips were not suitable for a breeding animal. I take comfort in the fact that her movement, to my untrained eye, seems beautiful, and she hasn't limped at all throughout puppyhood.

Zoe and Basic Training (21 Weeks Old)

Training with Zoe this morning in an obedience session, I was struck by how easily she worked with me. I was very gently using a small Good Dog Collar with her, but the effect was pretty evident: no stress, and a very clear understanding of what I was asking. Given the fact that she's five months old, I'm a bit surprised at how quickly she's getting this. We've been keeping the sessions short, and I always conclude them with some play and retrieving, which she seems to love. I do see a mild tendency in her to try to hold on to an object and not bring it directly back to me, but I suspect this will be an easy problem to solve. I'll simply work with her, using a light line to guide her in.

I'm starting to realize that I can begin increasing the length of individual sessions. Now that's she's maturing a bit, I also need to move naturally into a more consistent training schedule that reinforces her learning. I've seen in Zoe a real willingness to take in information, but an equal level of stubbornness if she is bored. When that's the case, she takes it upon herself to find entertainment, and inevitably that means getting into mischief.

This raises the important issue of knowing your dog. Ultimately, the proof of the training will be in how the dog develops. Can she be included in your life without a high degree of stress? Does she seem happy and well-adjusted? How well-socialized is she, and does she show good manners in meeting new people and dogs? I believe that if a dog is able to pass such tests with balance and calm, then the training has worked well and I'm not going to second-guess the results.

Zoe and the Snake (22 Weeks Old)

This morning on our walk I learned a lesson on the need to pay close attention to my puppy at all times. Before Zoe came into the picture, I could simply trust that my other dogs, Astro and Sasha, would casually accompany me on a walk and stay out of trouble. Indeed, whenever deer, squirrels, chipmunks — even the occasional bear — would cross the road unexpectedly, a simple word would bring their attention back to me and keep them from chasing the wildlife. That isn't necessarily the case with a puppy. However, Zoe had been doing very well on walks, and her recall was such that I was increasingly letting her off-leash on our private road. Nevertheless, this morning was a perfect example of how quickly that "perfect recall" can change. Zoe made the surprising discovery of a small garter snake that had been run over by a car on the road. As it happened, I was thinking about other things and only noticed too late when she triumphantly picked the snake up in her mouth and stared directly at me, inviting me to behold her prize. Without thinking I instinctively responded, "No, Zoe! Drop that!" as I started to move toward her, a reaction I immediately realized would trigger her flight. Sure enough, she started to prance away from me haughtily, swallowing the snake in several stages as she went. There was no way she was going to allow me to deny her that prize. Seeing the grotesque scenario unfold in front of me, I knew I was helpless to prevent it. All I could do was seethe in frustration as I finally caught up with her. If I were to describe her expression as I approached, it would be a confused *What?* Thankfully my anger went no further than that, and I simply leashed her and continued the walk.

Thinking on the event afterward, I realized how important it is to pay close attention to reality when you have a dog. Far from being an unwelcome chore, this is actually an invitation to greater aliveness, to being more in touch with reality as it occurs. We are the ones who are responsible for our dogs at all times, and if we accept this, our dogs will lead us to a greater degree of consciousness.

Zoe and the CGC (23 Weeks Old)

Today we tested about six dogs for the Canine Good Citizen title, and Zoe was among them. Canine Good Citizen (CGC) is a program devised by the American Kennel Club to evaluate and test the behavior and good manners of companion dogs. The certification is something that we've begun hosting periodically as a service for our dogs and those of our clients. Janine was the tester who evaluated Zoe, and though I expected her to do well, I was still interested to see how she would handle some of the novel distractions the test would present, such as walking on a loose leash by a noisy baby carriage, or locating a sudden loud sound without serious discomfort. Fortunately she came through both situations with flying colors, and indeed passed the test quite easily. This confirms for me the basic tenets of our approach to puppy rearing: simply working with pups in a calm and consistent manner and including them in our daily lives.

One of the reasons I like the CGC test is that it is totally oriented to companionship training. It's open to both purebreds and mixed breeds and is not conducted in a competitive environment. The dog is simply being evaluated against a reasonable baseline that applies to every dog. Each of the ten required exercises is geared to the skills any pup will need in everyday life. For example, the dog is not required to do a perfect heel; as long as she is walking in a controlled manner with a loose leash, she passes the particular exercise. This makes sense to me, given the fact that most owners aren't interested in the precision of competitive obedience and tend to freeze and become self-conscious in such an environment. CGC, while not as rigorous as formal AKC obedience, nevertheless gives any owner a legitimate opportunity to certify their dog as a canine good citizen and to do their part toward increasing the level of sanity and balance with our dogs. What CGC allows for and encourages is a high degree of inclusion, something that most owners dream about but that too few realize.

A Walk in the Woods (28 Weeks Old)

Today was a brilliant, mild summer day that unfortunately was busier than I would have liked it to be. Aside from attending a morning community meeting as well as taking the training dogs through their exercises, I had to spend a longer-than-expected session helping a client who was having trouble managing her yellow Labrador. It was satisfying to see her finally "get it" in working with her dog, but when I said good-bye I suddenly felt tired and drained, quietly wondering where such a promising day had gone. Fortunately there was still enough time for a walk in the woods, so I got Zoe, who was all for my idea.

One of the blessings of living here is that our monastery is in the middle of a large acreage of wooded hills. Simply taking any of the several trails that abut the grounds puts you in deep layers of trees and undergrowth, giving you a sensation of being enfolded by the woods. No matter my stress or exhaustion, renewal is as close as a quiet walk through these corridors. It also appeals to Zoe. On such a hike, smell becomes her most dominant sense as she relishes the endlessly fascinating task of exploration. It is something she never seems to tire of, and her heightened sensitivity makes me more aware of the simple beauty surrounding me. I've come to such a level of trust with her that I don't have to worry too much about her running off — what a gift! Even the occasional flushed-out turkey or pheasant precipitates only a brief chase, more of a game than something conducted with deadly seriousness, and she reliably returns to my call. This is something I'll be able to count on in the months and years to come — it will enhance the ways we can spend time together, because I won't have to worry that she'll get lost.

13

Reading Your Dog

Though dogs have no capacity to communicate with words, they do have a rich language of their own that uses sight, sound, and smell to eloquently express their intentions and emotional states. Your ability to understand this language and its particular social setting is the cornerstone of a good relationship with your dog. The apt expression "reading your dog" means really understanding what she is saying to you and not just what you think it might be. By taking into account the dynamic interaction of various forms of body language, you can avoid problems that occur in the human-dog relationship when owners misinterpret their dogs' intentions and moods.

For example, one of the complaints we receive from puppy owners involves submissive urination, demonstrated by a puppy who runs up to her guardian and excitedly greets her by urinating on the floor. This behavior is common in puppies, a natural outgrowth from when their mothers cleaned them by rolling them over to lick their genitals and anus. As puppies mature, submissive urination becomes a reflexive sign of their acceptance of dominance and authority. If you observe a young pup greeting an older, more dominant dog in a similar manner (crouching low, wagging tail tucked underneath, excitedly licking at the elder's muzzle as she leaves several drops of urine on the ground), you will *never* see the older dog punish the pup. The expression of submission is received gracefully, with an attitude of dominant composure by the older dog as she stands erect, holding her tail high. She understands the sign completely.

Unfortunately, many owners misunderstand its significance and treat it as either a behavioral disorder or a housebreaking problem. We recall a frustrated owner who asked us, "Is she just a masochistic puppy? Doesn't she understand? Every time I come home she piddles at my feet. I spank her, tell her how naughty she is, that she's to do this outside, but it only gets worse. Now all I have to do is enter the house and she pees. Why doesn't she understand?"

The man did not realize what his pup's behavior expressed. By misinterpreting submissive urination as neurotic, cowardly behavior, and by punishing her with scolding and spanking, he had set the stage for a serious, long-lasting behavior problem. Punishment was the *worst* possible response to her behavior; it deepened the issue by making her even more submissive, since her body language had already acknowledged his authority. The proper response to this problem is outlined in chapter seventeen.

Expecting your dog to rise to the level of human thought and communication will lead only to frustration. Instead, learn to read her by taking what you know about dogs and stepping into her world, trying to view life from her perspective. This may require a different way of thinking than you are accustomed to.

Try a simple exercise: Imagine looking out of the eyes of your ten-week-old puppy. Do not attempt to verbalize; simply imagine being the dog. Now look up at the big human being next to you (yourself). With the increasing abilities you have as a dog to interpret human body language, what do you "read"? How do you react? Look closely at the eyes, the face, the body. Is the stance imposing and towering, or inviting? Consider the voice—you do not understand the words, but what is the tone? Is it cheerful and pleasant, or harsh and abrupt? Does it sound whiny or anemic? Now look around the room from a dog's perspective. Observe the pair of leather shoes by the door, the large potted plant, the various pieces of furniture, and the inviting electric cords plugged into the sockets at puppy eye level. With your olfactory powers of incredible sensitivity, what is of greatest interest?

The point of this "pup's-eye view" exercise is to till the soil of your imagination responsibly, to help you sense, in some small way, what things are like from a pup's perspective. A good companion and trainer can enter imaginatively into the dog's reality, interpret it correctly, and then adjust various handling procedures to fit that knowledge. Captain Max von Stephanitz, the founding father of the German shepherd dog breed, was very perceptive in this regard:

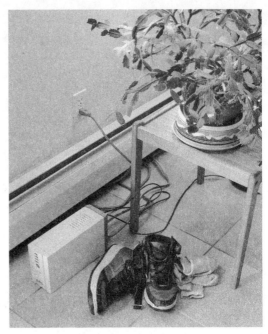

Tranquil domestic scene? Not with a puppy around. Pick up shoes and socks, electric cords, books and magazines, plants (which can be toxic), candy and snacks, and . . . anything else your pup could get into.

The trainer must himself be a psychologist; he must learn to read the soul of the dog, *and his own, too.* He must observe himself closely so that he shall not only be prevented from underestimating the dog in human arrogance, but also that he may be able to give the dog suggestions and help in an intelligent way. Whoever can find the answer to the question "How shall I say this to my dog?" has won the game and can develop from his animal whatever he likes.

When you approach your dog in this way, the experience is surprisingly multidimensional. Not only does your dog become trained but you become skilled as well, and the ongoing knowledge you acquire from your dog's behavior has the potential to teach you as much about yourself as it does about your dog. An often neglected aspect of the training process is how your dog becomes a mirror, reflecting you back to yourself, helping you achieve greater self-awareness by drawing out greater degrees of patience, sensitivity, and emotional self-control. This is the heart of training.

In *How to Be Your Dog's Best Friend*, we spoke of *inseeing* and its importance in your relationship with your dog. *Inseeing* is getting inside your

Inseeing *is being conscious of how your pup sees the world and you. To a puppy, shoes and hands can appear much larger than you imagine, and can even seem frightening.*

dog's psyche, putting yourself at her center, where she is a unique, individual creature, and understanding her from that perspective. This is possible only when you genuinely want to know what your dog is saying. To get inside a dog's head, to understand her from her point of view, you must continually watch, look, and listen, since a dog communicates through her body movements and vocalizations. Inseeing is not a romantic projection of human thoughts and feelings; it takes into account the whole dog by reading what the major centers of communication—ears, eyes, mouth, tail, and body carriage—are saying.

In this chapter, we will examine the significance of these centers of communication and the different meanings associated with various gestures. Your friendship with your dog will mature into real and compassionate understanding when you learn to blend intuition with science in a serious grasp of canine communication and behavior.

Canine Communication

Besides becoming a keen observer of domestic dogs, you can also acquire an authentic sensitivity to a dog's language by paying careful attention to the lessons available from a natural tutor: the wolf and its pack. Scientific evidence strongly suggests that domestic dogs are closely related to wolves, either as direct descendants of several species or as cousins, possessing a common ancestry in some earlier, unknown canid that is now extinct. Either way, studies performed on communication and social behavior in wolves are enormously illuminating for what they teach us about dogs, since the meaning of various postures and vocalizations are generally consistent throughout the canine family. Despite the fact that artificial selection and domestication have emphasized certain characteristics while suppressing others (for example, by promoting pendulous ears or by the unfortunate practice of tail docking and ear cropping in some breeds), all of the behavior patterns we observe in dogs are also present in wolves. Thus, in the following discussion, we gratefully acknowledge the research in canine communication and behavior carried out by wildlife biologists, ethologists, and animal behaviorists, and we include references to wolves where relevant.

Communication, simply stated, is the passing of information from one individual to another. In canines, this involves hearing, vision, and smell. As we have seen, puppies are born with inherited reflexes that are the basis of instincts — natural behavior patterns that are the means of communication. In the initial phases of life, a young puppy is limited both physically and behaviorally in how she expresses herself. As the brain develops and the pup has the opportunity of interacting with her mother and littermates, however, she becomes more and more capable of expressing a variety of different moods and emotions. These abilities continue to develop long into adulthood.

Vocal Communication

A dog, like a wolf, generally vocalizes in one of several ways, each apparently tied to various body postures that communicate different meanings and moods: whimpering and whining, growling, barking, yelping, and howling, all in a wide variety of tones.

The first vocalizations that puppies make are mewing sounds that indicate need (e.g., for food or warmth). Pups also make high-pitched grunts and squeaks when they nurse. As they grow older, the mewing sound changes into a whine, which carries over into adulthood as an expression of greeting, submission, or desire. Whining is more character-

istic of dogs than of wolves (which whine only when expressing submission), and this is probably due to unintentional reinforcement by owners.
Young puppies learn quickly what whining will do when their owners
continually reinforce this behavior to get them to stop. A classic illustration of this is the puppy who whines the first night she is separated from
her littermates. The owner, feeling sorry for her, takes her into bed and
lets her sleep there. The puppy learns a fateful lesson in communication,
and her whining quickly becomes generalized to any situation of want.

A growl communicates threat and antagonism. It is a warning and
may be accompanied with a snarl (i.e., baring of teeth). Young canine
puppies growl when they play, thereby learning proper canine etiquette;
as they mature, the growl is usually serious. With wolves, it is used by a
more dominant wolf over a subordinate and is usually enough to elicit
submission. Dogs can utilize the growl in the same way, and if it is
directed toward an owner, it signifies the dog's attempt to assume dominance. An example of this might be an owner getting too close to her pup
when she is eating. The puppy may utter a low growl as if to say, "Stay
away!" If the owner backs off, the pup easily begins applying this behavior to other situations that challenge the person's position of authority.

Most domestic dogs bark much more frequently than wolves, probably as a result of selective breeding. Since an early goal of domestication
was to have dogs guard and warn, it is clear why they were bred for their
barking ability. Wolves, being hunters that do not wish to alert potential prey, bark only in specific situations, such as a warning to other
pack members or to the pups that a stranger is approaching. The bark is
a short, quiet *woof* and is generally not repeated.

Domestic dogs bark anytime they are excited. Barks are short and
sharp, and the tonal quality reflects meaning. High barks are associated
with greetings, such as your puppy's excited welcome when you come
home; when prolonged and frantic, these vocalizations will accompany
pain and/or stress and are described as yelps. Warning barks are deeper
and alert you that something is up, such as the preliminary bark of the
watchdog. The aggressive bark is deeper still and communicates threat.
It alternates with growling to send an unmistakable message.

Howling is more common in wolves than in dogs and is their major
form of vocalization. It is a prolonged tone, lasting from two to eleven
seconds, and may fluctuate over a wide range of notes. Each wolf's howl is
distinct, which seems to suggest that individual wolves can be identified

by their vocalizations. Specialists feel that wolves howl for a number of reasons: to reassemble the pack after they have been scattered during a hunt, to advertise territory, or simply to perform a collective celebratory rite. Wolves howl both alone and in chorus, and when they howl together they avoid unison, apparently preferring chord tones.

Dogs howl much less frequently than wolves, though the sound is normal in northern breeds such as huskies and malamutes, as well as in hounds. In our kennel work, we notice that many huskies and malamutes howl shortly after their owners leave them, presumably as an expression of loneliness, and we have periodically experienced the howling of our shepherds, most frequently while we ourselves are singing. Evidently the harmonies they hear encourage them to join in with their own notes.

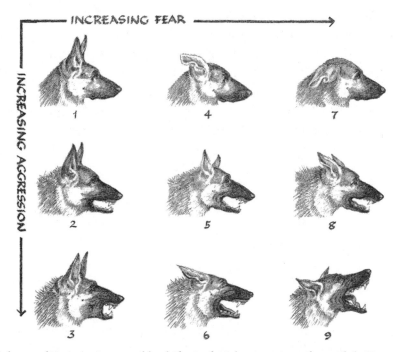

Schema showing nine possible shifts in facial expression of an adult German shepherd. In 1, 4, and 7, note the increasing fear or submission, reflected by the ears flattening out against the head and by the lips forming a submissive grin. In 1, 2, and 3, note the increase of aggression, with the ears erect, hackles up, and teeth bared, forming a snarl. In 3, 6, and 9, aggression is mixed with fear, sending mixed signals. The ears are flattened submissively, yet the teeth are bared in threat, and the hackles are up. Number 9 is a classic illustration of a fear-biter.

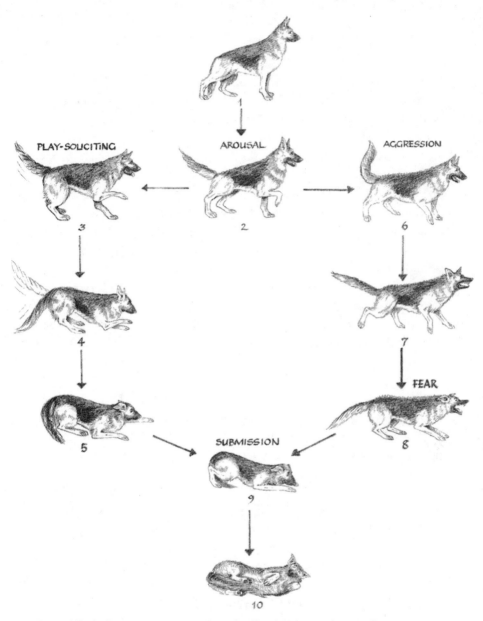

Types of body language. In 1 and 2, the dog becomes alert and attentive. A play-soliciting gesture in 3 is followed in 4 and 5 by active and passive submissive greetings; 9 shows passive submission, with the dog eventually rolling over and showing the genital region to the dominant dog/person. The gradual shift from pure aggression to a mixed fear-aggression posture is shown in 6–8. (Art adapted from Michael Fox's Understanding Your Dog.*)*

Visual Communication

Accompanying all vocal communication yet also independent of it is a large variety of postural communications that clarify for us a canine's internal state. Through her gestures, a dog can communicate a great deal without making a sound. Canine body language involves the interaction of facial expression, ear and tail position, and the carriage of the body. Thus, to read a dog you must be aware of all of these elements at the same time.

In a peaceful and relaxed state, a dog holds her ears slightly back and carries her curved tail out at a downward slope, hanging loosely. The body position is the same front and back, and the musculature around the forehead and muzzle is smooth. The mouth may be slightly open with the tongue panting, and the eyes are clear.

As a dog becomes more attentive, her ears prick up in a forward position and her tail rises, wagging just a little. Some dogs lift a front leg slightly, as if in readiness for what is to come. It is common for a dog to express curiosity from this position by cocking her head, holding her ears forward, and showing concentration and alertness by the minor skin creases around the eyes.

When a dog tries to solicit play, the front half of the body lowers, with the front paws, elbows, and chest touching the ground, causing the back end to rise high in the air; the tail wags furiously. The ears are raised and the mouth is held open in a relaxed way; the dog may bark spiritedly. A lively bearing in a dog communicates joy and enthusiasm.

With the onset of threat, the body language of the dog changes on the basis of her personality and perception of the situation. When a confident, dominant dog perceives a threat, her posture becomes aggressive; her ears stand erect, pointing forward, and her mouth is open slightly, with the upper lip curled to expose the canine teeth. The facial musculature around the nose and forehead wrinkles and the eyes are dark and piercing, with the eyelids raised. Her tail is lifted straight up or slightly over the rear, a sign of dominance, and the tip may be wagging in very quick circles. Her neck and body are erect, with the hackles up to give her an inflated look, akin to a man pulling in his stomach, puffing out his chest, and flexing his muscles. The dog's legs are stiff, and she may even walk on tiptoe. The whole posture, in addition to communicating size and strength, surges and strains toward the

*In the context of play, dramatic and noisy canine body language takes place
from very early on.*

threat. The ears, eyes, tail, and body carriage all signal courage and
confidence.

As a dog becomes more suspicious and fearful, the signals begin to
change markedly. The head drops somewhat, the ears flatten out hori-
zontally or are pulled back against the side of the head, and the tail
tucks down between the legs. The mouth may be open in a grimace
combined with the curling of the lip, and the eyes become glazed, looking slightly away from the source of the fear. The hackles are still raised,
but the body lowers and moves away from the threat. This is the posture of the fear-biter, who signals a potentially confusing mixture of
aggressive and submissive body signals.

Purely submissive body language in canines occurs in one of two
ways, active or passive, depending on the circumstances. In nonfearful,
more *actively* submissive postures, the ears point backward against the
side of the head, the mouth is held in a long grin, and the body crouches
low to the ground, with the tail tucked under and possibly wagging

A puppy engages in energetic and active game-playing with an adult male—neither wants it to end until each is exhausted.

nervously. Active submission is frequently demonstrated at greetings and, in the case of wolves, may involve the entire group, as when an alpha wolf (the pack leader) returns to the pack after an absence. In such group ceremonials, the pack gathers around the alpha, posturing submissively while affectionately licking at its muzzle. This communicates friendliness, loyalty, and allegiance.

Passive submission is a more extreme form that communicates helplessness and vulnerability and does not carry as much of the friendly enthusiasm present in active submission. It is manifested by a subordinate in the face of a threat, such as self-assertion by a more dominant dog. When posturing, the passively submissive dog lies down on the ground and rolls over on her side, exposing her genitals and abdomen, and the front legs are bent at the elbows. The tail is tucked under tightly and wags only slightly, if at all. The ears are plastered backward against the side of the head, and eye contact with the source of dominance is avoided. This posture of total trust and homage is an attempt to make the dog look much smaller than she really is. The gesture of humility placates the dominant, self-assertive dog or wolf.

Even younger pups show active submission and respect to older dogs by licking at their mouths.

A puppy colorfully displays passivity and submission to a dominant adult.

Olfactory Communication

Because a human's sense of smell is so limited in comparison with that of a dog, it is especially difficult for us to know exactly how dogs communicate using their olfactory sense. Though scientists are convinced that smell gives canines more information about the world than any of their other senses, it is the least understood component of canine communication. We can only observe various behaviors associated with scent and then speculate on their meaning.

In the wild, scent seems to define territory, with the alpha wolf generally urinating on objects aboveground that will preserve the smell. This seems important for several reasons. First, it clearly defines territory for the resident pack, especially for the younger, inexperienced wolves, who are able to form mental maps of the territory from the scent markings. Second, it communicates to neighboring packs boundary lines that keep them from trespassing in the resident pack's territory. Scent marks are also important when members of a wolf pack have been separated during a hunt, since the markings tell an individual wolf whether an area has been recently traveled through by the rest of the pack.

Within the pack itself, smell seems to be intimately connected with canine social life. Dominant male wolves frequently present anal areas to subordinates for inspection (as if to broadcast themselves), and the subordinates respond by withdrawing theirs, apparently an acknowledgment of the other's dominance and a way of saying, "I'm not really here."

The smell of urine also communicates sexual readiness in the female, who marks frequently when she is in season, as if to publish this fact for a potential suitor (generally the alpha male).

We have already alluded to the importance of scent marking in defining territory for dogs (see chapter eleven). Dogs will also try to cover the scent marks of others intruding on their territory. Scent says, "This is me; this is familiar," which explains why, when people move, they often have problems with their dog marking in their new house (particularly leg lifting in males). Apparently this is the canine way of making oneself at home.

Anyone who owns a dog quickly discovers that dogs are most interested in urine and feces. Animal behaviorists tell us that from a drop of urine or a small amount of feces, a dog can determine the sex of an individual dog, whether or not it has been castrated or spayed, how

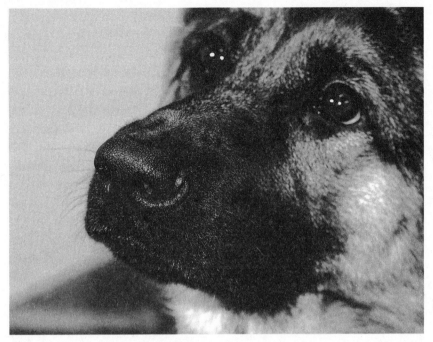

Dogs possess approximately two hundred million olfactory cells, compared with five million in humans. Their sense of smell is estimated to be at least a hundred times more powerful than humans'.

recent the mark is, the direction the dog was going, and, if it is a female, whether she is in season.

Another interesting behavior visible in domestic dogs is scratching the earth after urination or defecation. Traditional folk wisdom says that this is the dog's attempt at covering the odor. In fact, it appears to be just the opposite: the dog is spreading the individual scent around a wider area.

When dogs meet in public, their smelling rituals seem to resemble those of wolves, and because the rituals do not take place within the context of a single pack, displays frequently go beyond simple dominance/ submission. For example, two male dogs meeting for the first time may both assume postures of dominance and become progressively more threatening, trying to get the other to back down. Each one allows the other to smell the anal area, a sign of confidence and courage, and if the dogs are left on their own, the encounter could result in a fight.

Dogs well acquainted with each other, who acknowledge a certain dominance order, greet each other in a more relaxed way, with the dominant dog thoroughly sniffing the subordinate and then presenting himself to be sniffed, at the same time raising himself "higher" than the other dog.

As with other canines, a female dog in season broadcasts this fact by urinating much more frequently than usual. Local male dogs, extremely sensitive to this, become highly agitated when they catch the scent. We see this when they congregate outside the house of a female in season. This is one reason spaying your pup before her first season may not be a bad idea. Male dogs can be unbelievably persistent in trying to breed a receptive female.

Pack Dynamics

"Dog talk" is easiest to interpret in its natural context: the pack. Like wolves, dogs are pack animals, and they respond naturally to the laws of pack existence. Living with a large group of German shepherds here at the monastery gives us a firsthand look at behavior that closely resembles that of wolf packs. It is quite routine—a five-month-old puppy meeting an older female dog, submission and dominance. Or a mother disciplining her pups out on the lawn, teaching them a proper respect for authority. These and many other behaviors point to a common ancestral past with wolves and help us understand why dogs behave the way they do. Just because your puppy does not live in a wild pack does not mean that he will not instinctively adapt these behaviors to his new domestic environment. We assure you that he will. Living with your puppy will be much more enjoyable and meaningful if you understand the basic principles of pack life and apply them to your relationship.

Packs do not hold together automatically. Since wolves are carnivores and have to hunt to survive, a great deal of cooperation must exist for the pack to achieve its food requirements. Most of the wolves' natural prey (moose, elk, caribou, and reindeer) are too large to be brought down by a single wolf and require a strategic, coordinated plan of attack. Refined communication, as well as a tight social structure wherein each member knows its proper role, is essential.

This explains why leadership is so important for wolves. Every pack has a pair of leaders, one male and one female. These alphas are dominant over the other members of their particular sex. Generally, though not always, the alpha male is the overall head of the pack and is responsible for governing and directing activities such as traveling, hunting, feeding, and sleeping. His firm dominance preserves order by eliciting submission and respect from subordinate pack members, who use appropriate deferential body language.

Beneath the alpha wolves, there is a loose dominance hierarchy into which each pack member fits with a particular spot and role. This social structure is dynamic, changing when younger wolves mature, when older wolves get sick or injured, at the onset of mating season, and so on. Wolves appear instinctively to strive for the highest possible position within the pack, continually "testing" more dominant wolves until the question of rank is settled. Thus, to preserve or increase its status in the pack, an individual must constantly assert itself, fending off upstarts or attempting to move up in the hierarchy. You might suspect that this kind of social tension would set the stage for many fights, but surprisingly actual fights among wolves are infrequent. Challenges are usually settled ritually, without a fight, since submissive postures are enough to end the dispute. Should a lesser-ranking wolf challenge the alpha, the latter may threaten the upstart by posturing in an aggressive, dominant manner, growling and staring directly at the other wolf. By staring down the ambitious subordinate, the alpha is often able to get it to back off without an all-out fight.

Interestingly, it appears that wolf packs are stronger, are more secure, and run more smoothly when the alpha is secure and confident in its leadership, for such dominance inspires fewer challenges. When there is no clear authority within the pack, however, as in times of leadership change, the group becomes unstable and may break up. This dynamic is just as true in your relationship with your puppy.

Dominance and submission are absolutely central to pack life and are taught to wolf puppies from the very first. As we saw with Anka and her pups, discipline begins naturally at weaning, when the mother growls and snaps at the pups who are trying to nurse. The pups learn to respond with submissive postures and to direct their oral attention toward an adult's mouth, which provokes the regurgitation of food. This behavior then evolves into expressions of active submission given at greetings. With wolves, the older pack members help rear the pups both through feeding and through discipline. Correction is kept basically good-natured; the pups do not fear their elders but always try to stay with them.

This attitude of balance, a blending of leniency and instructive discipline, is a key factor in the way wolves raise their pups. Puppies are presumptuous, taking liberties with adults that would never be tolerated in older pack members. They playfully wrestle and grab their elders around the muzzle, mouthing and biting them. Occasionally this provokes a well-timed response of dominance, with the elder grabbing the pup's muzzle and pinning him to the ground. The purpose is only to educate, to guide the pups in the ways of canine etiquette, teaching them the vital art of submission.

Training in the Pack

During the juvenile phase (twelve weeks to sexual maturity), besides learning the basics of communication and social structure, wolf pups are gradually trained in the serious business of survival. Though it is not entirely clear how hunting is taught, experts believe that games are an important part of the process. Because wolf pups are physically immature, fatigue quickly, and keep their milk teeth until at least five months, they do not hunt until they are nine to eleven months old. Instead, as we have mentioned, they stay behind at rendezvous sites, or base camps, often with an adult babysitter who is the lowest-ranking member of the pack, the omega. While the rest of the group hunts, the pups play with one another and practice hunting field mice. These activities slowly develop and hone their innate abilities to stalk, pounce, and run. When the pack is not hunting, adult wolves may initiate games of pursuit, teasing the pups into chasing them around. This simulation teaches the younger wolves many hunting skills within the context of a game and provides another clue to how dogs learn naturally: fun is paramount.

In our exercise yard here at the monastery, it is quite common for comparable games to take place. An example: Uli, a mature female, approaches a precocious five-month-old pup named Kali. Uli stares at her for several moments, tail wagging and ears up, then moves her eyes off to the side mischievously. Kali crouches down, gazing back at Uli. Suddenly Uli tears off in the opposite direction, and Kali chases after her wildly, following her through quick turns and all-out sprints, and when Kali finally runs even with her, Uli playfully nips at the side of the puppy's neck. This type of game can go on for an hour, keeping the full attention of both, and it is an important element in Kali's development.

All puppies, wild or domestic, love to play. You can capitalize on this by making play sessions with your pup part of her training. This conditions your dog to be enthusiastic about learning and to enjoy being with you. By mixing training with games, you can bring out a healthy attitude in your pup that will carry over to conventional obedience work when she is older.

The treatment of canine communication in this chapter is by no means exhaustive. Much about a dog's language and behavior remains mysterious, and what we do know seems to suggest the presence of deeper levels of communication that are still beyond our abilities to recognize and understand. This is why studying your dog can be so fascinating: the process is open-ended. Learning to read your dog is something that should continue throughout your life together. By developing more sensitivity to your pup's manner of communicating and a fuller understanding of canine behavior, you will see your appreciation and enjoyment of each other continue to grow.

14

Lessons from the Pack: Becoming Pack Leader

Now we can apply some basic principles of wolf-pack life to the way you handle your puppy. By using certain exercises, we can mimic the natural integration of pups into a pack. Remember that puppies learn their proper place through constant contact with their mothers and the other pack members. Body language, proper physical dominance, and eye contact teach puppies the meaning of leadership and their role as followers. They are happiest when this is clear and consistent. Since every puppy needs a leader, the success of your relationship rests on your being a benevolent alpha figure to your pup. Start right away; leadership is much easier to establish with a twelve-week-old, twenty-five-pound puppy than with a sixty-pound adolescent.

We will concentrate first on physical contact. New owners often try to get pups to behave by explaining what is expected, by reasoning with them. They forget that puppies have no verbal skills, and when the pups fail to respond to spoken instructions, the owners become impatient and exasperated. Only later, through training, does a pup learn the meaning of specific words and commands. You will be a much more effective leader if you concentrate less on what you say and more on what you do.

Our first series of handling exercises focuses on teaching a puppy to be calm and relaxed when handled. Before advancing to obedience training, your pup must first be calm enough to pay attention to you. This may seem self-evident, but the majority of dogs brought to us for obedience training completely lack attentiveness. Their owners cannot get their focus. The dogs arrive unruly—dominant—and in human-dog relationships, that always spells trouble. To avoid this, you must

A basic exercise for restraint: Put your right hand across the pup's chest and your left hand under her muzzle and begin massaging gently.

train your pup to focus on you right from the start. Genuine leadership presumes attention, and when you get it, you will be close to becoming the alpha in your pup's life.

The following exercises are designed to establish you as leader in your puppy's eyes and can begin a week or so after you obtain him. By teaching him to be calm and to hold still while you are handling him, you will show your puppy that you are the dominant figure in the relationship, and that you are a benevolent leader, worthy of his trust.*

Exercise One: Restraint

First, sit down on the ground with your pup comfortably placed between your knees or legs, facing away from you. Put your right hand over his chest and your left hand under his muzzle. This is a basic exercise in restraint. If he accepts this handling calmly, praise him in a soft, reassuring

---

* In the following discussion, we are highly indebted to the insights of Jeanne Carlson, a trainer/behaviorist from Washington State and author of the commonsense video *"Good Puppy!"*, available from www.goodpuppydog.com.

voice and gently massage him. If he squirms and fights to get free, hold him firmly and put him right back in position, saying in a firm voice, "No, stay!" As soon as he settles, resume massaging him, gently petting him from the top of his head down the back of his neck. Any additional struggling can be handled in the same way, with a quick shake that, though startling, does not hurt him. Make sure your hold is firm, since the message you want to give your pup is one of control, with no indecision. Do this for several minutes per session. We find that most puppies come to accept this handling during the first or second session and to see it as very pleasant. This also forms the basis for the *stay* command later on.

Exercise Two: Examining Mouth and Ears

When you are able to restrain your pup in a calm, relaxed manner, move on to the second exercise, which includes examining his mouth and ears. Throughout his life, it will be necessary at times to give your pup medicine, take inappropriate objects from his mouth, clean his

Once your pup is comfortable, massage the top of her head and neck, and slowly move her head from side to side.

ears, and check his teeth. Puppies who are not sensitized to this when they are young can grow very defensive about being examined when they are older, and may even bite. To prevent this from happening, you need to familiarize your puppy with examinations now, while he is still easy to handle.

Begin by practicing the calming exercise we have described. Allow your pup to relax his head in your hand as you massage him and then gently begin wrapping your dominant hand around his muzzle from underneath, gradually getting him used to the sensation. This may take a little time — there is no need to rush things. Be gentle, and when he accepts the hold, praise him encouragingly as you manipulate his head from side to side. If he becomes restless, go right back to the calming exercise to settle him.

Once he allows you to hold his muzzle and move his head around *in a calm and relaxed way,* you are ready to open his mouth and take a quick look inside. To do this, put your dominant hand under his muzzle and your other hand over it, and lift his lip briefly. Praise and pet him. Then, to open his mouth fully, place the fingers of each hand between his jaws and carefully pull them apart. Take a quick peek and then release, giving him plenty of praise. Be brief at first, since your pup will not be used to this maneuver and may initially dislike it. After several episodes, however, he will accept it without protest. If you find your pup tries to mouth or nip at your hand, clasp his muzzle lightly and give him a swift shake, accompanying this with a firm *no.* Open your palm for him to lick, and if he does so, praise him cheerfully. This exercise is particularly useful for gaining control over your pup's mouth and inhibiting the oral, nippy behavior common in puppies.

With your pup still relaxed, begin to examine the ears, first by massaging around their base with your fingers, then working over the surface of the ears themselves. This conditions your pup to having his ears touched and is invaluable for grooming sessions. Puppies should have their ears thoroughly cleaned once a week to prevent infections.

Exercise Three: Full-Body Massage and Repositioning

The third handling exercise, a logical extension of the previous two, involves examining your puppy's whole body and moving him safely when he is in a reclining position. This is a valuable skill to have if your dog is injured or if you need to move him while he is resting. We know of a number of biting incidents that occurred when an owner tried to get his dog to move while the dog was sleeping. Conditioning your puppy ahead of time is a sensible way of preventing such accidents.

Start in the relaxed position of exercise one. To make your pup lie down, grasp both front legs and move them out from under him, gently taking him into a *down* position as you praise him. Move your hands around his neck and back, massaging him in a soothing manner, making sure that he is totally relaxed before proceeding any further.

When you sense he is completely at ease, kneel beside him, roll him over so he is lying on his side, and continue with your massage. Talk to him in a calm, reassuring way. If he starts to struggle, push firmly against his shoulder and say, "No, stay!" Then follow immediately with praise when he settles. At most, your correction should be a quick, gentle pin by the scruff, enough to let him know that you are in control. Continue lightly massaging his entire body with your fingers, paying particular attention to the feet and tail areas, which will help accustom your pup to having his nails clipped and temperature taken. Use eye contact to reinforce the connection with your pup, giving a firm glance when he is restless, and a kind, affectionate look when he is relaxed and accepting.

While he is comfortable, grab both sets of paws and calmly roll him

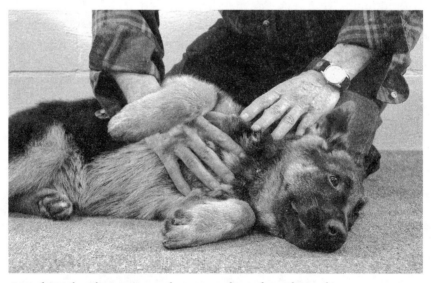

A soothing, bonding massage that moves down from the neck.

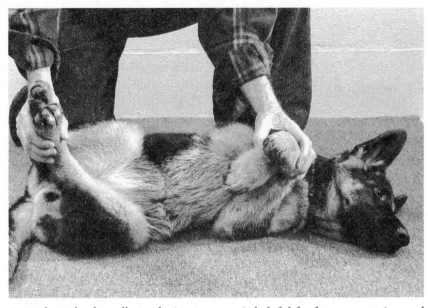

A gentle and calm rollover during massage is helpful for future grooming and examination. When your pup is comfortable, take hold of both sets of paws and slowly roll her over.

over, continuing to stroke and pet him, then roll him back, praising him as you make eye contact. Finally, slide him around as if you were moving him out of the way. Conclude the session with an "Okay" and his name, plus plenty of praise.

We have long known the benefits of canine body massage and described our approach to it at length in *How to Be Your Dog's Best Friend*. Massage is a valuable bonding technique that helps both owner and dog relax in each other's presence. Aside from using it as a relationship-enhancing exercise with older dogs, we also introduce it here as a preliminary training exercise with young puppies to develop their sense of trust and confidence in a human leader. A puppy who allows you to handle, examine, manipulate, and groom him is one who trusts you and accepts you as leader. He acknowledges your dominance as he experiences your kindness, and becomes comfortable with giving you attentive, responsive eye contact.

These preliminary exercises are invaluable foundations to the training process. They can be started shortly after you obtain your puppy and can continue on indefinitely, since they will become mutually relaxing exercises that both of you will look forward to. They communicate dominance and leadership to your pup in a relaxed, nontraumatic way and establish a level of trust that will make formal obedience a smoother process than you ever dreamed.

One last observation: These exercises are suitable for most puppies; occasionally a puppy will be unusually touch-sensitive and may react poorly to the handling. If this should happen and you experience extreme reactions of trauma, biting, and/or agitation, *stop* and seek the advice of a trained professional. Such a pup may require special types of handling that go beyond the scope of this book.

15

Basic Training for Puppies

Often when we adopt a new puppy, we have a vision of the type of relation-
ship we hope for. Based in part on past experiences, or on what we have
read about or witnessed with friends, we can easily put more pressure on
ourselves and on the pup than is wise. Patience is a key virtue in nurturing
a relationship, to keep us relaxed and moving forward step-by-step. With
patience we can stay in touch with the bigger picture, realizing that the
foundations of a healthy relationship are laid over a broad period of time.
No relationship of any real depth matures overnight — human or canine;
trusting in the process will give us a calmness and flexibility in the face of
challenges that arise naturally from time to time.

— Dogs & Devotion

Retreatants at New Skete often comment on how impressed they are
with the behavior of our dogs and the gentle and friendly way in which
the dogs receive them. Since we include our shepherds in as many daily
activities as possible, they are a highly visible part of our life, and guests
encounter them frequently throughout the day. Such contact makes it
imperative for the dogs to be easygoing and obedient, totally lacking in
aggressive outbursts or skittish, freaky behavior. The best way to
develop this behavioral soundness is to start early on by constantly
exposing the dogs to everyday situations in a controlled manner, using
basic training.

A typical example: At dinner there are often a half dozen dogs calmly
on *down-stays* around the dining room table, not begging for food but
simply happy to be there. During the meal, they either watch quietly or
fall asleep, and often people forget they are there. If occasionally one

A three-month-old pup can learn the stay by example and constant oversight—even in the dining room or kitchen.

As puppies mature, they can learn to live safely and comfortably in social situations.

dog should break her down-stay when her guardian gets up to collect dishes or serve food, the monk quietly corrects her and puts her back in her original *stay* position. Rarely is anything more required.

In this type of atmosphere, even a young pup can learn to stay for an entire meal. Initially, to prevent her from wandering around, a pup's guardian simply keeps her on a leash next to him, with one foot on the lead. If the puppy tries to get up during the meal, the monk corrects her gently by pushing her back down with a quick *no*. Experiencing this consistently over a period of several days and seeing the example of the older dogs, most pups quickly learn to relax and not fight the tether. Then, in the following months, the puppies can gradually learn the down-stay away from the table.

At the conclusion of the meal, the dogs wait for grace to be sung and an "Okay" that releases them from their down-stays before they walk over to their guardians. Each monk typically responds with an affectionate pat on the head and some soft, reassuring praise.

Apparently guests see something remarkable in all of this. On one recent occasion, a retreatant remarked, "Brothers, how do you get them to do it? What's your secret? I have only one dog, and Max would never be able to lie still for an entire meal. I'm amazed."

An Overview of Puppy Training at New Skete

There is no secret about how our dogs are able to stay so relaxed during meals and other community functions: quite simply, we train them, steadily and progressively. Since monasteries are by nature quiet, reflective spots, the chaos brought on by an unruly pack of dogs would be completely out of place. For a group of dogs to fit into this environment, they must be properly *trained*. This process is most successful when it begins early, as soon as a puppy starts living in the monastery. An eight-week-old pup has had little chance to develop bad habits.

Initially, besides house-training and the preliminary handling procedures, we begin a gentle introduction to some basic obedience exercises: *sit, stay, come, let's go* (precursor to *heel*), and *down* (see chapters eleven and fourteen). The training gradually becomes more structured and challenging as the months go on. When we start working with a pup, we keep the two to three daily sessions very brief, under five minutes each. The tone of the lesson is intentionally relaxed and pleasant.

There is no fixed timetable for the puppy to "succeed," no pressure on the pup (or handler) to get everything right all at once. We also take advantage of repeated natural training opportunities that come up in daily life, such as sitting before the door or holding a *stay* before feeding, which can be done in as little as thirty seconds.

Our goal is to introduce each exercise in as simple and as natural a way as possible. To avoid unnecessary stress, we begin with noncompulsive methods that condition the pups to respond correctly to commands. For example, in addition to using the aforementioned food-dish exercise to accomplish a *sit,* we also randomly raise our fingers from the pup's eye level to above her head to create the same effect, or we pass the pup's favorite toy from eye level to the ground to get her to follow willingly into a *down* (see chapter eleven). Repeating these exercises often while rewarding the correct behavior with reassuring praise quickly puts the pup at ease with moving into these positions, making it relatively simple for her to learn the more structured commands later on. During each session we keep our gestures animated and lively to maintain the pup's interest, and we break up the various exercises with short moments of eye contact. We always conclude training with a short play session that is fun for the puppy.

Over the course of a month, these daily sessions prepare the puppy for more disciplined training as she enters the juvenile stage, the phase when she starts "testing her wings." By now, the pup will be comfortable with the lead and will respond positively to quick, attention-getting leash checks that can gradually allow the training sessions to become more structured and challenging. Though we are careful to keep the training enjoyable and the pup highly motivated, we leave no room for doubt as to who the alpha figure is; if a correction must be made, it is done swiftly, with *just enough force as is necessary* to change the behavior. Then we immediately reinforce the correct behavior with sincere praise. Eventually, through brief ten-minute training sessions, we work on each of the obedience exercises. By quickly shifting from one exercise to another, we maintain the pup's attention and avoid boredom — the chief malady of all obedience training.

Again, we cannot overemphasize the fact that as the puppy displays a growing understanding of each exercise we use it repeatedly in practical situations throughout the day: down-stays in the living and dining rooms, sit-stays to greet guests, long down-stays at night in the bedroom, and so on. Training needs this practical focus. In turn, it enables the pup to spend greater blocks of time with the monk who is caring for her.

When puppy training is combined with proper management — daily exercise, frequent socializing, balanced diet, and regular grooming — it allows the pup to fit smoothly into the life of our community. The easiest way to lose enthusiasm for a puppy would be to fail to provide her with the practical skills necessary to mature into a friend and companion. If a puppy is not taught how to behave in a calm, relaxed manner, she inevitably becomes an energy drain and a burden, and it is likely that her *guardian* would end up spending less and less time with her. The real point of obedience training is to allow the young dog an optimal amount of inclusion in her guardian's life, with the pup being calm and under control. Pups are always happiest when they are with those who have the responsibility of caring for them.

That is the "secret" of how we raise and train our puppies. Following this program, our six-month-old puppies are well-socialized, have a solid foundation in the basic obedience exercises, and perform these tasks happily and reliably in everyday life. What's more, there is nothing extraordinary or exceptional about this.

Training Your Puppy in Basic Obedience

There is no reason this same sort of program cannot be applied successfully to your relationship with your puppy. Though training is not "easy," it is within the capabilities of owners who set their minds to it. You must combine behaviorally sound principles with actual training of your pup in regular practice, preferably both at home and at a weekly KPT class, which will foster important socialization skills. While it is true that the quality of puppy classes varies widely (from those that are simple socializing sessions with no real training to those run by dedicated professionals who not only socialize the dogs but help with preliminary obedience), in general the positives far outweigh the negatives. If a more structured class is available in your area, we strongly recommend it (usually courses begin at twelve to sixteen weeks of age), in addition to following the guidelines described in this book. Our methods coincide with many puppy programs, and the overall benefits are well worth it. Besides basic puppy obedience and valuable socializing experiences with other pups and people, a structured class will give you important feedback on how you are handling your pup. A professional can spot mistakes in the way you are training that you might not be aware of. Also, seeing other owners work with their pups and exchanging ideas and experiences are great ways to gain a proper perspective on your pup's behavior. It is very good for morale.

If a KPT class is not available in your area, you can carefully implement the program described in the following sections on your own. Begin working with your pup several times daily, no more than ten minutes each session. Before you start, read through the exercises *several* times and mentally visualize them in sequence. You *cannot* train your pup with a leash in one hand and a book in the other. Imagine the session beforehand: think about the brisk pace, the animated tone of your voice, the attention-getting checks on the leash, the sincere praise you will offer when your pup responds to you correctly. If you are not confident in how to proceed *prior* to the actual training session, you will project indecision and awkwardness — cues for the puppy to start acting unruly and unfocused, heightening your sense of frustration. When you clearly understand what you are going to do beforehand, and anticipate mistakes the pup might make as well as your responses to them, you will communicate a greater sense of presence and leadership that will help to focus your pup.

In the following sections, we assume that you have worked with your puppy for several weeks on the preliminary exercises described in chapters eleven and fourteen, and that your pup is now comfortable walking informally on a leash. The exercises that follow are intended for puppies between three and five months. They serve as a preliminary introduction to the training that we have already described at length in *How to Be Your Dog's Best Friend*.

Training as an Art

Good training involves more than simple obedience. The central issue in all puppy training should be how to teach the particular obedience skills in a way that brings out the best elements of the pup's personality. This is why training is an art — it is the process of drawing out your puppy, evoking behavior that will allow her to live peacefully with you. A puppy's knowledge of the five most basic commands — *sit, stay, come, heel,* and *down*—is no guarantee that the training process has been successful. A six-month-old puppy may indeed be able to execute the commands in a training session; however, if she won't do them naturally in everyday life, how successful has the training been? Or, let's say she does them but in the process shakes fearfully and cowers, has her tail tucked under and ears flattened, and shows no animation or enthusiasm. At what price has the training come?

Therefore, we can conclude that good training involves not only the precision of a dog's performance but the attitude she displays in working. When a dog is animated and happy in her exercises, she also projects nobility, self-confidence, and a sincere desire to please. This does not happen automatically. *It is learned by experience.* Despite what most people assume, dogs do not have an innate desire to please their owners. This popularized bit of wisdom is simply not true. Your dog has a natural desire to please herself, to receive pleasant sensations, and she is quite capable of learning how to bring those about. In the training process, she must be taught to associate pleasing you with something pleasant, with receiving praise and affection. This inspires her to work diligently for that reward.

The reverse is also true. While a certain amount of proactive redirecting of attention away from undesirable behaviors to desirable ones is entirely appropriate at the beginning of training, ultimately there will be occasions when your pup will challenge you, and a mild leash check will be very helpful in teaching focus, consistency, and respect. When your dog associates an action with something unpleasant or uncomfortable, she will try to avoid it. In puppy training, a minor leash correction with a simultaneous clipped, firm *aah* or *no* is just unpleasant enough to get her attention without harm.

These are the rhythms in all dog training, both for puppies and for older dogs; with puppies the unpleasant sensations are kept deliberately at mild, nonstressful levels. When your pup does the right thing, praise her *immediately,* in an encouraging, animated tone that is sincere. Properly timed praise is essential; your pup needs to know that she has done what you want as soon as the behavior occurs so that she can make the proper association between the two.

Similarly, when a correction is necessary it must be well-timed, at the very moment of the infraction. An immediate check on the leash with a clipped *no* will get her attention, giving you the chance to repeat the command and then reinforce her compliance with praise. Remember, correction is not punishment; it is communication between you and your pup. It carries with it no anger, and it is just unpleasant enough to help her change her behavior. Once that occurs, it is over, forgotten. In this work, you are the initiator, the leader, and as each day passes you'll express your leadership by clearly and consistently applying the rhythm of praise and correction, letting your pup know what is and is not desired. This must become second nature to you.

Having the right attitude may take an emotional adjustment on your part. To train effectively, you must learn to be flexible enough to redirect your pup's attention in the preliminary stages of teaching, as well as to be at ease with giving quick leash corrections later on, seeing them as helpful guidance and information for your pup. It is perfectly normal for your dog to make mistakes. Puppies learn by trial and error; hence, mistakes are simply opportunities for them to learn. When your pup errs, you have the chance to show her what you are asking her to do. As long as your response is well-timed, she will make the proper connection between the two. Then, as her behavior changes, your praise pleasantly reinforces her obedience. By repeatedly strengthening the pup's good behavior with praise and affection while discouraging unwanted behavior with appropriate corrections, you can humanely teach the obedience exercises and gradually shape your pup's behavior to fit smoothly with your domestic requirements.

Learning How to Use the Leash

For the sake of your relationship with your pup, you must learn how to use the leash fluidly. People who do not know how to do this invariably have major problems with training, since the pups never learn to pay attention to them. A leash used correctly gets your pup's undivided attention and enables her to respond to your request. But be careful! It is not sufficient to simply pull on the leash and expect your pup to respond to you. That usually results in a tug-of-war that confuses the issue of leadership and has the potential of harming your puppy. A *combination* of related elements must all work together:

- a properly fitted training collar that is put on correctly
- a leash that is held so that there is always some slack between you and your pup

■ a three-step correction consisting of a *no* or *aah* with leash check, repetition of command, and immediate praise upon compliance

Let us look at each of these elements.

The Training Collar Once your puppy has been on a flat-buckle collar or a martingale collar for one to two months, it is time to shift to a more formal training collar. Every training approach has its collar preferences, and we have described the range of possibilities in chapter nine. For our purposes here, we will focus on two collars that we have used to great benefit with our pups: the snap-around nylon collar popularized by Jack and Wendy Volhard, and the Good Dog Collar developed at Triple Crown Dog Academy.* Depending on the individual dog, there are also occasions when we will use a traditional steel training collar, as with a puppy who has a long coat (e.g., a bearded collie, an Old English sheepdog, or a long-coated German shepherd). The flat-pounded metal links glide easily through the hair, unlike with the snap-around collar, which can tangle.**

Rule number one is that the training collar must fit properly. Often a new owner purchases a collar many times too large for her puppy, and it hangs like a woman's necklace at the base of the pup's neck. Two problems result from this mistake. First, any kind of leash check will not be immediate, thus affecting the proper timing of the check and the pup's understanding. Second, a low-hanging collar is positioned at the least sensitive part of the pup's neck, where the muscles attach to the rest of her body. Thus, for a leash check to be felt, the owner will have to *overcorrect*, using much more force than would normally be necessary. Remember, a properly fitting collar lessens the force necessary to keep the pup's attention and interest.

That is why the snap-around collar works so well. It fits precisely to the size of the pup's neck and stays up high, facilitating a gentle but effective communication with the leash. Similarly, the Good Dog Collar is a good choice for strong and energetic pups (as opposed to highly touch-sensitive pups, for whom it might be too much). Mimicking the

---

* The snap-around collar and the Good Dog (StarMark) Collar are available from various online retailers and from some pet-supply shops.
** The specific brand we favor is the Herm Sprenger toggle choke, because you can fit it precisely, much like a snap-around collar.

grasp of the mother on the pup's neck, the plastic prongs provide an evenly distributed correction that pups respond to. Good Dog Collars lack the harsh appearance of prong collars, which, while legitimate training collars for some older puppies (eight months and up), often make owners uncomfortable because of their somewhat medieval look.

The correct position of a Good Dog Collar.

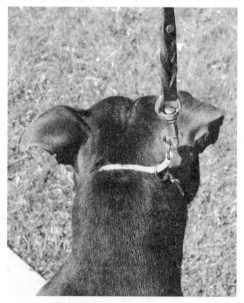

A snap-around nylon collar fitted correctly.

Putting on a Snap-Around Collar Correctly There is only one way to put on a snap-around collar so that it releases when you give a leash check. The most common mistake owners make is to put the training collar on upside down. In this case, the collar does not release when it is pulled, the pup resists and chokes, and the snap-around loses its value and causes your pup unnecessary discomfort.

First, make sure the collar fits properly. To measure your dog, put her in a standing position. Use a tailor's measuring tape and measure under the chin, around the neck, and then up behind the ears. You will want a snug fit but not so tight that it chokes. Add an additional half inch for flat-coated dogs and an inch for fuller-coated dogs. These collars come in whole and half sizes (e.g., twelve and a half inches) to promote an exact fit. The extra half inch to an inch will allow for the necessary check with minimal effort and help the collar stay in place.

Here is how to put on the snap-around collar correctly every time, keeping in mind that the collar has a stationary ring, a moving loose ring, and a snap:

1. Have your dog on a *sit* facing you.
2. Hold the stationary ring and the moving ring in your right hand so that the collar hangs straight down next to the dog's head.
3. Take the snap in your left hand and bring it up around the left side of the dog's neck. Attach it to the moving ring at the top of the neck.
4. Attach the leash to the stationary ring.

We have found this collar to be very humane because of where it rests on the dog's neck, above the trachea. Very little effort is needed to use the collar; a slight flick of the wrist gets the pup's attention right back on you. Check the photograph on page 216 to make sure your pup's collar is fitted properly. If you notice that your correction is not releasing after a leash pop, immediately recheck the collar. Chances are you have it on backward.

Putting on a Good Dog Collar Correctly Before you put this collar on your dog, practice taking it apart and then reconnecting it. Connecting the plastic links takes some getting used to, so be patient. To unfasten the collar, use your thumb and forefinger to angle the links so that the points are nearly touching one another (tepee style). Then firmly rock them in a left-to-right motion until they come apart. To fasten the collar, simply reverse the process. Angle the links so that the points are nearly touching one another and then snap them together by rocking them back and forth in a left-to-right motion.

This collar should fit snugly and rest high around your dog's neck. For pups we usually use the smaller size (fifteen inches), which typically has enough links to fit the collar precisely. Additional links can be purchased separately if your puppy outgrows the provided length.

How to Hold the Leash   When you are working with your pup on a leash, hold the lead in a comfortable, relaxed manner that gives your pup enough slack to make a mistake. This will probably feel awkward at first, going against your instincts, since most people are inclined to hold the leash taut to maintain some sort of control over their pup. In reality, however, this accomplishes the opposite. When the leash is taut, the constant pressure on the pup's neck causes him to resist, resulting in more straining and pulling. There is something Zenlike in this—in training, more control proceeds from less control.

We suggest holding the leash in the following manner:

1. Put your right thumb through the loop, letting the leash lie across the open palm of your right hand.
2. Close your right hand into a fist.
3. Lift the first two fingers and use them to grab the leash a quarter of the way down, resting your right hand against your right thigh.
4. Grasp farther down the leash with your left hand, knuckles facing forward, letting it rest on your left thigh.
5. This is your starting position. Whenever you walk with your pup, keep your hands below your waist and leave your pup some slack with the leash.

A Word About Corrections   In a politically correct universe, the word *correction* has nothing but pejorative connotations as it relates to dog and puppy training. Many folks would like to think that we can teach a puppy using entirely positive reinforcement, without ever having to make a correction. Some believe that the very idea of a leash correction is abusive. We take a very different view. While we are entirely in favor of positive methods in puppy and adult training, we also have found an appropriate place for skilled leash corrections. Effective train-

*Holding the leash in the
starting position.*

ing always serves the relationship, and a balanced use of both positive
reinforcement and helpful leash correction does just that. We say this
to be honest. Each dog is a unique creature with his own personality,
and owners will need to be sensitive to that in helping their puppy
learn. To excise the notion of corrections from the training vocabulary
does a disservice to the dog and puts the owner at a serious and unnecessary handicap. Think about it: what would your own life look like
without appropriate corrections at various points along the way?
Granted, *how* such corrections were given makes all the difference in
the world, suggesting the importance of an owner learning to make
them appropriately and helpfully, always encouraging the puppy forward. Such "corrections" are more like interruptions that redirect a
puppy toward the desired behavior. And while we do see a role for gentle corrections in dog and puppy training, we do not advocate any type
of training that uses harsh pulling or jerking of the puppy at any time.
Through the years we have found that effective signals can be given
with a minimum of effort and, done wisely and skillfully, can promote
the very relationship that conscientious owners seek. Thus, in the following section the terms *check, snap,* and *pop* are used interchangeably

in connection with leash work, with the understanding that they are never heavy-handed and that they serve the overall goal of a healthy relationship with your dog.

The Three-Step Correction Effective corrections communicate clear information to your pup, guiding her into desirable behavior. The quicker you become familiar with the sequence of a proper leash check, the more success you will have in training your pup and the quicker she will fit into your life. To clarify, *leash work* has nothing to do with crass, "yank 'n' spank" techniques that force a puppy to obey. When a pup is jerked repeatedly this way and that—even if it is out of incorrect positions and into correct ones—the whole training process becomes forced and unpleasant, and the puppy's attitude suffers.

With a constructive correction, the focus is different. You are clarifying what you want as well as motivating and conditioning your pup to respond correctly to you. The emphasis here is positive—getting your pup to look willingly to you for leadership. When your dog consistently does this, you can draw the best out of her.

To begin the correction, get her attention by giving a quick "pop" with the leash, then immediately release the tension on the collar. A clipped *no* or *nah* should coincide with the pop. Never maintain constant pressure on the collar, since this will cause your pup to resist and pull away from you. The quick check/*no* is meant only to interrupt the unwanted behavior and get your pup's attention. Once you've got it, give the positive command immediately, following with cheerful, encouraging praise as the pup responds.

Initially you may feel awkward snapping and releasing the leash. With practice, however, this sequence of pop-command-praise will become spontaneous and relaxed, and you will use it naturally as a means of communicating with your puppy. It will get your pup's attention and establish you as the leader in her life. The following exercise, which simulates the pulling of a puppy on a lead, will help you get accustomed to the leash pop before you actually begin using it on your puppy. Spend several sessions practicing this with a helper until you are comfortable with the movement. Then you can gently introduce it to your pup.

1. Have your helper sit in a chair facing you, at a distance of one leash length.

2. Have him put his right hand through the loop of the leash, and then clasp both of his hands firmly together. The loop should be positioned around the right wrist.

3. Take the other end of the leash and hold it out straight. Grasp it a foot from the clip with your left hand (knuckles on top), and hold on to the clip with your right. Now make a quarter turn sideways to the right.

4. Instruct your helper to try to prevent you from drawing his hands toward you. Now, without jerking the leash, try pulling with your left hand. Do you feel the tension and resistance? The harder you try, the more he tends to pull away from you. This simulates a dog's actions on a taut leash and shows the futility of trying to force him into obedience. Relax.

5. Have your helper begin putting tension on the leash again. This time, instead of pulling the leash straight back, slacken the leash, "pop" it, and immediately release it again in one continuous motion with your left hand. His hands should jerk forward in your direction, and he should feel the effectiveness of the pop. It is attention-getting. Remember, strength is not the issue here. A

Practice leash corrections with a human helper before attempting them with your pup.

snappy check is all that you are looking for. Now synchronize the *nah* with the pop. Repeat this at least a dozen times per session.

Using Your Voice Correctly Before continuing on to the obedience exercises themselves, we would like to emphasize one more preliminary point: *clear communication with your pup requires the proper use of your voice.* Particularly in the beginning stages of your life together, your puppy will be much more conscious of your tone rather than of the specific words you use. Because of this, you must learn to vary your voice pitch in accord with the specific meaning you intend. We should take our cues from the primary canine sounds to which puppies are conditioned in the litter. Higher tones are associated with the sounds of littermates and elicit enthusiasm and playfulness. By contrast, when necessary the mother communicates her authority in low, guttural growls that the pups learn quickly to respect and obey. The general rule to draw from this is to use higher (though not silly) tones with praise, encouragement, and more active obedience exercises (*heel* and *come*), and lower voice tones with correction, discipline, and stationary obedience exercises (*sit, stay,* and *down*). When your pup experiences marked contrasts in the tone of your voice, she will respond more readily to your true intent, resulting in less frustration and irritation for you. This applies to both men and women. Each person should learn to vary his or her voice tone in communicating with a new puppy. Men, whose voices tend to be naturally deeper, will likely need to lighten their tone for praise and encouragement, as if they are speaking to a small child. With women it is typically just the opposite: since they have higher-pitched voices that naturally communicate effective praise and encouragement, they will need to be flexible enough to deepen their tone to communicate leadership or a correction. Interestingly, mothers with young children understand this principle instinctively.

Which brings us to two related areas of pet-human communication that often cause problems for owners: whining and nagging. Please, in your daily life with your pup as well as in training sessions, avoid any kind of whining or nagging. These only undermine your leadership, communicating weakness and indecisiveness, and your pup will learn to ignore you. The command is not *sitsitsitsit* or *pleease siiiiit*. It is *sit*. Give your command clearly—once. If your pup does not respond, use the three-step correction. This communicates an unmistakable set of expectations to your pup—you mean what you say and you are willing to back it up with action. Also, keep the tone of your voice calm and controlled, and avoid the temptation to yell or shout at your pup. The cardinal rule in puppy training is never to lose your temper. Aside from being emotionally unsettling for you, it may prove harmful to your pup. Besides, it is totally unnecessary. Your puppy has very sharp hearing and will respond well to a curt *no*. Save your loud, bellowing voice for a real emergency.

The Basic Exercises

If you follow the approach described in this book, by the time you begin working with your pup formally during the juvenile stage (after three months of age), she should be able to walk on-leash in a fairly relaxed manner and be accustomed to the training collar around her neck. Further, you will have already introduced her in a very general way to *sit, down,* and *come* exercises, and you will have spent ample time familiarizing her with being handled and touched. With this foundation to build on, the more structured obedience sessions can now follow naturally, without a great deal of stress.

Regardless of the method you use, motivating and rewarding particular behavior is an essential part of good training. There are any number of effective motivators and rewards for teaching new behavior: warm praise, food treats, a favorite toy such as a ball. In part it depends on the individual dog. For some pups food treats are a powerful motivator, especially when they are hungry. For others who are more play driven, a spirited retrieve can be something they will work eagerly for. What is of greater import than the particular way you motivate and reward is how it facilitates the pup's understanding at the same time as it builds up and strengthens the relationship.

That said, one guideline we would offer, especially when choosing food as a motivator/reward, is to use it to teach new behaviors and not to stop unwanted behavior. This is a common mistake that can actually reinforce the very behavior you are trying to end. For example, suppose your pup growls at a child and you quickly distract him with a treat, then reward him when he stops growling. What is the real message you've given him? While your intent was no doubt to reward him so that he wouldn't growl again, he's making the connection between growling and the treat. Guess what will happen if you continue such a strategy? Before you realize it, you'll have a Cujo wannabe on your hands.

A food treat is particularly effective in teaching behavior so long as the how, when, and where of delivering it reinforces what you intended. Once you accomplish this and the pup understands what you want, start cutting back on the treats gradually. All too often owners fall into the trap of overusing treats in a manner that focuses the pup's attention on the food instead of on them. If you don't eventually scale back, the dog will get hooked on the treat and won't respond to you without that incentive. This doesn't happen with praise, which is why it never needs to be phased out as a motivator. Sincere praise always focuses the puppy's attention on the owner, inspiring the pup to work out of a more personal connection, thus strengthening the relationship.

Because our approach to training emphasizes companionship, not competitive obedience, we use the puppy's name with the commands more often than do other techniques. We find that this helps focus a pup's attention and prepares her to do something. The only command we do not use in conjunction with the pup's name is *stay*, in which the idea is to do nothing. Saying the name first with an active command (e.g., "Blitz, come!") gets the pup's attention and focuses her on the upcoming command. We never use the name after the command.

When we begin the initial formal training sessions with one of our own pups, we start off with some informal leash work using the *let's go* command (chapter eleven) and then the *sit* command. This serves as a bridge from the preliminary puppy exercises to the formal commands by introducing the pup to the general idea of walking at the handler's side, receiving light corrections, following the handler's lead, and sitting after she stops. Demanding the precision of a formal heel during the first sessions would most likely involve too many corrections, so we put this off until later in the training process. Instead, we concentrate initially on *sit, stay,* and *come*. We like to keep the sessions short for puppies: no more than ten minutes at a time. However, as mentioned previously, we also like to turn brief opportunities throughout the day into teachable moments — often lasting no more than thirty seconds — such as sitting before a door or holding a *stay* before the pup eats her food. Similarly, you can easily incorporate a short training session in the context of a longer walk.

Sit By the time you start formal sessions with your pup, she will have already been introduced to the *sit* through the noncoercive methods we described in chapter eleven, so this is a command she should already have some familiarity with, albeit in a preliminary way. But make no mistake about it: a reliable sit in almost any circumstance is a crucial component of any formal training program. If you can get your dog to sit in a variety of contexts, you will have gone a long way toward securing the proper control intrinsic to a well-trained dog. This starts in puppyhood. From the introductory sit, your task now is twofold: to increase your pup's ability to sit whenever you want her to, and to teach her how to follow the command when she is walking on a leash. In time this will be linked with a formal heel, and you can work toward an automatic version, when your pup will learn to sit on her own every time you come to a stop. At this stage, however, any thought of these advanced techniques is premature; all you should concentrate on now is getting your pup to respond to your *sit* command on-leash in a variety of ways.

Some pups are able to make the connection from the noncoercive sit to the regular sit on-leash with little difficulty, while others require some help and preparation. It just depends on the individual puppy. Following are two methods of teaching the sit that we have found quite

A handler teaches the sit by bringing the pup to a stop at heel while gently touching the puppy's lower back.

*After your pup sits, get
her attention with
a "Watch me!"*

effective for pups, one starting from a stationary position, the other used in conjunction with the heel.

To teach *sit* from a stationary position, have your pup standing next to you on your left side, facing in the same direction you are. You can either stand or crouch, depending on the size of your pup and how jumpy she is. Take your right hand and position it between her collar and neck so that you can hold her still. Gently put your left hand on your pup's withers, and in a continuous stroking motion, move down the length of her back, over the tail to the hocks. As you tuck her into the *sit* position, lift up on the collar with your right hand and say, "Sit." Praise her calmly as you hold her in this position for several seconds, then release her with an "Okay." Repeat this procedure over several sessions until your pup appears completely at ease and familiar with it.

You can then begin to practice commanding her into a *sit* position from a stand while she wears a leash, snapping your fingers as you elevate your hand in front of you, saying, "Sit." Praise her warmly when she complies. If she doesn't respond, gently push her rear to the ground, following with praise. Then give a very quick "Stay!" and try keeping her in the *sit* position for five seconds. Release her with warm praise. You can then slowly but surely extend the process for greater length. Be sure to reinforce with praise or a food treat when she holds until your release.

Since you've already introduced the command at mealtimes, your pup should have a pretty good idea of what you are asking of her, but understand that you're liable to have to patiently put her in the sit as you vary the contexts in which you use the command. Trust the process and know that it is leading to a reliable sit that can be produced whenever the occasion demands it.

Preconditioned puppies are often able to learn to sit while walking on a leash without needing separate sessions in stationary sitting with a lead attached. As you are walking with your pup in a relaxed manner, move your right hand out in front of your pup's path where she can see it. (This will require that you bend forward somewhat as you walk.) Raise your right hand out in front of her as you say your dog's name and "Sit," and glide to a stop. Your pup will follow the movement of your hand with her head, causing her rear to sink naturally into a *sit* position. Praise her cheerfully and start walking again, changing directions frequently and repeating the process throughout the walk.

A helpful tip for conditioning your pup to sit in a straight, forward position early on is to have her move into the *sit* position from a 180-degree turn. When your pup maneuvers around you to follow your turn, it is natural for her to get into a straight *sit* position as you give the command. Even so, do not be concerned with perfectly straight sits early on in puppy training. Pups tend to be a little clumsy, and her positioning can be refined as the training continues. For now, your focus should be on getting your pup to sit when you ask her to.

If your pup ignores your *sit* command when you come to a stop, give her a gentle pop/*nah*, repeat the command, and praise her when she corrects herself. Do not simultaneously jerk the leash and repeat the command. *Nah/No* is your corrective word. You do not want your pup associating the word *sit* (or any other command) with a correction. If your puppy still does not go into a sit after the first leash check, repeat the correction, and as you give her the command once again, touch her rear quarters with your left hand and pull up slightly on the leash with your right. Pause momentarily, then begin again with a "Let's go" and repeat the *sit* sequence.

The intention behind this sitting while walking on-leash is to get your pup under control during the early phases of training. Pups tend to need movement to focus their attention. By alternating controlled walking with sitting throughout the first several lessons, and by striving to keep the climate of the training light and encouraging, you will find your pup quickly learning to follow your lead willingly. This will not only make teaching the other commands much easier but also make your daily walks much less of a struggle as you establish a consistent pattern of behavior that your pup becomes accustomed to.

Stay *Stay* is a control exercise to use with either the *sit* or *down* command. In puppy training, we begin to teach it in conjunction with the *sit* command and refine it once the pup has learned to sit reliably. The object of the exercise is simple and direct: the pup is not to move out of the commanded stance.

Begin in the starting position, with your pup sitting next to you on your right. Put the leash in your left hand and hold it vertically over your pup's head, ensuring that there is a slight amount of tension on the leash. With your right palm open, fingers together, bring your hand in front of your pup's face and say, "Stay," in a firm, deep voice. Remain beside your puppy for a few seconds to make sure that she is set in her position, then step in front of her, continuing to hold the leash taut. If your pup starts to move with you and breaks the stay, give an immediate leash check straight up with a *nah* and repeat the exercise. Initially, keep the time you expect your pup to stay very brief, five to ten seconds, and then return to the starting position. After several more seconds, praise her warmly.

When your pup begins to consistently stay in this preliminary manner, make things a bit more challenging. While you are standing in front of her, reinforce the *stay* command with your hand signal and walk halfway around your pup. Then return to your starting position and move halfway around her in the other direction. Practice until you are able to walk about her in a full circle. If she should break position, give her an immediate quick check, reinforcing the command with the hand signal.

Anticipation is the key to teaching the *sit-stay. Watch your pup like a hawk:* the moment she breaks, give her a leash check with a *no* and repeat the exercise. If your timing proves to be off and she ends up out of position, simply walk her back to her original stance and start over again, making sure to watch more closely the next time for any signs that she is about to break the command. With consistent practice, your pup will soon come to understand what you are asking, allowing you to loosen the leash and step farther away from her without her breaking position.

A proud puppy during a class session. Pups can easily progress from a sit-stay to a stand-stay.

Once your pup comprehends the sit-stay, it is important to apply it to common, everyday occurrences in your home. For example, dogs love to bolt through open doors. To avoid this potential problem, you should practice making your pup hold the sit-stay each time you lead her to a closed entryway. After parking her in the stay, open the door, making her wait for your permission before proceeding through the doorway. Consistently practicing this each day is a sensible way of training your pup to move with you in a controlled manner, and one day it might save her life by preventing her from running out into the street.

Another practical application of the sit-stay is to use it for introducing your pup to guests as well as to people you may meet outside. Often puppies get into the bad habit of jumping up on people because their owners do not practice a proper on-leash introduction, making their dogs sit-stay in front of the guest. This results in puppy unruliness that might make friends avoid coming to the house. We will address the specific problem of jumping up later in the book; for now, remember that the foundation for proper control of introductions is the sit-stay. The best way to prepare your pup for future challenges is to start with members of your household: "introduce" her to them during relaxed moments and make her hold the sit-stay. By practicing this in a progressive, controlled way, you can show your pup how to meet people politely.

Eye Contact Throughout this book we have stressed the point that your puppy must learn to look to you as the leader in your relationship. One of the primary means of developing this relationship is to include structured eye-contact exercises in your daily training sessions, which will build on the moments of spontaneous eye contact mentioned before. Just as the alpha wolf maintains order in the pack by utilizing such contact in many different situations, so must you with your pup. A puppy who learns early on to make eye contact with you willingly will not only acknowledge your leadership but also bond with you more deeply.

With your pup facing you in a sit-stay, snap your fingers in front of her face and draw her attention up to your eyes. As you do this, say your dog's name and "Watch" in an animated, cheerful voice. Do not bend over to look at her or go through all sorts of verbal gymnastics to get her attention. The idea is to get her to look up at you. If she is distracted, you may need to give a little upward flick on the leash to get her attention. However, when you do, be sure to hold the eye contact for no more than several seconds at the start, since direct stares can be intimidating to dogs. When she looks up at you, praise her warmly for several seconds and then return to her side.

In addition to training sessions, you can easily practice making eye contact with your pup in more relaxed moments. The point is to carry this out naturally and frequently. As you and your pup progress, the moments of eye contact will spontaneously become longer and more common, and you will experience their profound effect on the quality of your relationship.

Come We dislike labeling one exercise as more important than any of the others. In obedience training, all of the exercises are interrelated, fitting and working together as a whole to help you develop control of your pup in a wide variety of circumstances. Each has its proper place. Your puppy needs to achieve a knowledge of all of the five basic obedience skills, not just one or two.

Unfortunately, many owners single out the *recall* as the most important exercise, to the exclusion of the others. Certainly this is a crucial skill. By far the most persistent complaint we receive concerns owners' inability to get adult dogs to come when called, which can have dire consequences. Put simply, your dog needs to learn the recall, no matter what the circumstances or distractions. However, there is no "shortcut" to get to that level of reliability. You'll be fooling yourself if you think you can teach just the one command, since reliable recalls require the connectedness and consistency fostered by the other exercises. Owners who take the attitude of "I don't care about all this training; all I want from my puppy is for him to come when I call" use this self-deceptive smoke screen to avoid the time and responsibility necessary for developing a trained and well-adjusted companion. In our experience, rarely does a pup learn "just to come." The most effective way to teach *come* is through the early puppy conditioning we have described in chapter eleven, followed by a structured training program that covers all the exercises.

The goal in teaching the recall is to train your dog to come to you reliably and willingly, whenever and wherever you call. Unfortunately many owners often make serious training errors that have precisely the opposite effect on a puppy: they teach her *not* to come. Before we consider a positive approach to the recall, let us first examine several common mistakes and describe the effect they have on puppies.

The most basic error is when owners allow their pups to be off-leash in uncontrolled situations before they are prepared for it. A fundamental rule in training is for the handler to always be in a position to guide the pup's compliance and to not allow the dog to ignore what he or she is asking. Pups learn very quickly that they do not *have* to come when they are put in circumstances in which their owners have no control over them. With common attitudes such as "It's a nuisance to walk my pup on a leash" or "Dogs were meant to wander freely," owners are begging for trouble. They are actually placing the pup in the position of leader, since the puppy decides on her own whether she wishes to come or not. This fosters an attitude that is counterproductive to training.

A second error, often related to the first, occurs when owners get into the habit of repeating the *come* command over and over without enforcing it. Yelling, "Come, come, come," at your pup without backing up the first command with some form of controlled guidance or correction only conditions your pup to ignore you. She learns that she does not have to come.

Finally there is the mistake of calling a puppy over to discipline her. *Never* do this, under any circumstances: not for house-soiling, destructiveness, overbarking, roughhousing, or anything else. If you do, your pup will associate the punishment with the act of coming, not with what she is being disciplined for. The next time you call her, the real message she received will be painfully obvious. If you must discipline your pup or subject her to something unpleasant (e.g., a shot or medicine), get her calmly and without drama. That way you will always preserve positive associations with the recall.

The key to building a consistent and reliable response is for the pup to understand that the fruit of her coming is praise and all manner of good things. This requires patient practice. Putting your pup in a position to succeed is part of good training and builds in her a thoroughly positive attitude and spirit.

A Positive Approach After your pup has been initially conditioned to coming through the jingling of keys, informal round-robin recalls, or simple "retrieve" play sessions, you can teach a more structured recall using the following approach, which keeps the tone of the exercise happy and gives you control over your pup at all times.

The first step in the recall is to make sure that your pup understands the meaning of the word *come*. Start by putting your dog on a long line (parachute chord, clothesline, or such) and let her wander a bit away from you. As she moves, pick up the end of the line and in a pleasant, high voice say your dog's name and "Come," crouching over slightly and throwing your arms wide. Make sure that your body language is open and inviting. If she comes, praise her enthusiastically, guiding her gently into a sit as you taper off the praise. If she fails, you might apply a little pressure to the line to get her moving as you repeat the command, then encourage her with a pleasant voice. Another technique you can use in the event that she resists is to begin trotting in the opposite direction. This will trigger her inclination to chase after you, but it is also fueled by the pup not wanting you to get too far away from her. You can also start off using a food treat to motivate her recall, but be careful here. It is easy for the pup to become more focused on the tidbit than on you. If food rewards motivate your dog's recall, you should gradually phase them out so that they are more and more sporadic, until you're not using them at all. Obviously you will continue to use praise.

We used to teach *come* from a sit-stay; however, we have found that teaching it from a relaxed, moving position is more helpful for several reasons. First, you won't be counteracting the *stay* command, which can easily happen if you are calling the dog from a sit-stay. When you routinely summon a pup from this position, he learns to anticipate the recall and not hold the stay. As you move away from the puppy you'll suddenly hear the patter of footsteps behind you. The pup thinks he's doing you a favor by saving your breath! By recalling him from a moving position, you avoid this problem, which brings us to the second reason for practicing the recall in such a way: it more closely mirrors what happens in real life. When people call their dogs to come, the dogs are rarely in a sit. Ordinarily they are sniffing, walking around the yard, or otherwise distracted. Why not practice in a way that reflects this?

Another general tip for facilitating good recalls is to ensure that your facial expression matches your tone of voice. Your expression should be soft and encouraging. Show genuine pleasure when he comes to you so that he will want to come in the future.

Further Steps Once your pup is starting to come consistently, you can work on further refining her recall. One of the most frustrating scenes owners can experience is having their dogs race toward them when they call, only to veer off at the last second and go flying by, always just out of reach. Dogs can make a great game out of this and may keep you occupied for a long time. You avoid the problem by training your pup to always come toward you. The purpose of the following exercise is to teach your puppy to keep you (i.e., the person she is coming to) in front of her.

Begin by walking with your pup with a relaxed leash — not in a formal heel but close enough that you can easily change your direction, saying your dog's name and "Come" as you move backward. Hold your leash slack as your pup comes toward you. Praise her in an encouraging tone as you move, keeping her focused on coming to you. If she should start to widen her path as if to go past you, simply turn the other way, giving a slight tug on the leash, and continue to trot backward. You can keep this up through several turns until you finally bring the puppy into a sit. Puppies think that this exercise is great fun and usually respond to it with zest and animation. It is also effective in teaching them to come directly to you.

Only when you have thoroughly practiced with your puppy and achieved consistent and enthusiastic recalls are you ready to move on to more challenging situations that involve both distractions and recalling her from a sit-stay. Let's look at each.

Moving from an undistracted situation to one in which you have to compete with other claims on your pup's attention is part of the natural progression of obedience training. Remember to look at mistakes as opportunities to learn and not as failures.

Take a long line (twenty-five to forty feet) with you to a local park—this way you can easily practice with your pup to solidify the recall, but now in the presence of competing objects of interest. As before, start by attaching the line to your pup's collar and then casually let her explore the vicinity, taking her close enough to other dogs and people that she can be interested in them but not so close that they totally engage her. Be relaxed in her presence. When she is the entire length of the cord away from you and occupied with some distraction, turn away from her and call her name cheerfully with "Come," clapping your hands several times. If she does not respond immediately, give a quick attention-getting check on the cord and continue encouraging her, keeping the tone of your voice pleasant. Do not reel in your pup like a fish; tug and release. The purpose of the tug is simply to focus her attention and get her moving voluntarily toward you. Your voice and body language will then help her to form a positive association with the recall—a *come* stands for love and praise. If you are using food treats to help prompt her, you should reward her when she comes to you but also focus on your praise as something that can be deeply motivating. That way, as you begin phasing out the food treats, she will still respond happily.

You can now start to practice recalling your dog from a sit-stay in a manner that reinforces both the sit-stay and the come. The secret is to put your pup on a sit-stay with a long line attached, then move away from her for a distance. Do not call her yet. Instead, walk back to her and gently praise her sit-stay. Move away again in a different direction and repeat the sequence. Only when you have returned to her successfully three or four times should you call her to come. Praise her as she approaches you, then help her to finish in a sit by lifting your hand upward as she draws near. She will likely move into a *sit* position; if she does, place your left hand on her chest as you gently pet her with your right. By alternating a number of sit-stays with a recall, you'll be able to preserve the sit-stay in a clear way at the same time as you practice the occasional recall. Should she break the stay as you walk away from her, quietly go back and reposition her, then start moving away and returning to her again several times before you try calling her.

In addition to working with a long line, you can play a game of fetch to reinforce the recall.

Playing ball leads to a quick recall.

Be animated and encouraging in calling your pup back to you.

Satisfaction and praise are the rewards for a good retrieve.

In each of these exercises, your pup has the initial option of not responding to your command. What makes her quickly correct herself, however, is your guidance and encouraging praise. When you practice consistently, the recall becomes more and more ingrained in your pup, so that there is almost never a time when she will not come. By always keeping the recall positive and upbeat, you can gradually work on increasing the distance from which your pup will come reliably and willingly.

If a Mistake Happens Occasionally, accidents do happen. House or apartment doors are left open, kids let go of the pup's leash, or you simply get careless and assume that your pup will come to you in the park. Suddenly you find yourself with your puppy off-leash and not responding to your command. In such unforeseen circumstances, there are several emergency measures you can take. First, if it can be avoided, do not chase her. After four months of age, pups become much quicker and can usually dodge a single person out in the open by running around and making a great game of things. Instead, try moving quickly in the opposite direction. Dogs have a predatory instinct that manifests itself when something runs away from them, and often you can trigger this by pretending to "escape" from your pup. When she catches up with you, simply reach down and take hold of her collar. *Do not discipline her in any way.* Kneel down next to her and settle her quietly for several seconds, then clip on the lead and work with her briefly, taking her through some zippy *let's go, sit,* and *come* sequences on-leash.

If running away from her is not successful, try turning your back to her and sitting on the ground, acting very casual. Sometimes it is even helpful to lie down all the way on your back. This often provokes curiosity that will bring the pup toward you to investigate. As she approaches, praise her quietly but stay very still. When she is next to you, sniffing, gently put your hand on her collar and attach the leash, praising her softly. Again, follow up the episode with some brief obedience exercises.

To avoid accidents during your pup's first six months, we suggest you put the issue of off-leash recalls on a back burner when out-of-doors. Instead, work on ensuring that the foundation you are laying for the recall is consistent and positive, and simulate off-leash situations in such a manner that you always have a chance to control her execution of the command. Then, as your pup matures, you will be able to accomplish more.

Heel Once you have established a basic foundation in sit, stay, and come and are walking your pup in a fairly relaxed way with a loose leash, you can start to work toward a more formal heel. The object in heeling your puppy is to teach him to walk next to you on your left side, at your pace, with a loose leash. Heeling has importance independent of making walks enjoyable and pleasant for you. When a pup is out in front, pulling on the leash, the message he receives is that he is the alpha, the leader, and as he makes the decisions on the walk, choosing where to go and at what pace to move, he will start to apply that tendency to your entire relationship. The result will be an unruly puppy who fails to pay attention to you. On the other hand, the pup who learns how to walk by your side at your pace is following your lead, focusing on you. This sets a healthy tone for your relationship.

When teaching a new exercise, you should always start off in a quiet, undistracted area with enough space to move around. Backyards are

An older puppy heeling correctly and attentively at the handler's side.

usually suitable. If you live in a big city, start by practicing inside your apartment, since you do not want to be competing for your pup's attention with the sights and sounds of urban life. Begin by getting your pup to stand or sit next to you on your left side. Make sure her collar is on correctly, high up on her neck, and assume the starting position with the leash, being careful to keep it slack. You are now ready to proceed. In a pleasant tone of voice, say your pup's name with the command "Heel," immediately moving forward with your left foot, the one closest to your pup. Do not wait for the pup to begin walking. Simply move forward, tapping your left leg enthusiastically with your left hand. Since she is familiar with the leash, your pup should begin following right away. Cheerfully praise her. If she should fail to move, give a quick check with the leash and a *no* (releasing the pressure on the lead immediately), repeat the command, and praise her as she begins to go forward. Be animated. It is important for your pup to sense your enthusiasm and encouragement as she follows you.

As you proceed in the same direction, your pup will probably trot past you and begin pulling on the leash. *Do not jerk the puppy back to your side.*

Going through the paces in daily behavior exercises should be a positive and happy experience.

Instead, give a quick pop/*no* correction and immediately reverse your direction, tapping your leg reassuringly as you say, "Heel," again. Praise her warmly as she follows you. Remember, the pop is merely attention-getting, and the *no* is free of any anger or frustration. You are merely teaching your pup to walk by your side. Keep your hands low and your leash loose. By moving back and forth, using little pop-release checks when necessary, you will teach your pup to look to you to lead her, and she will watch to see when you are going to turn. You should praise her enthusiastically, conditioning her to focus on you throughout the session.

As you and your pup become more proficient at walking on-leash, you can vary your routine, practicing left- and right-hand turns, figure eights, and circle patterns. It is important to prepare puppies sufficiently for the turns. Several steps before you change direction, say your pup's name as you bend over slightly and slap your leg, getting her full attention. Then say, "Heel," turning as you allow her to follow along with you. If she scoots off in another direction, give the three-step correction and continue encouraging her, slapping your leg as you go. With consistent practice over several months, you will be amazed how quickly your pup learns to follow you, and equally how that response reflects her per-

When heeling on a turn, this young-adult dog learns to keep up with the handler, who slightly coaxes the dog with tension and release on the lead.

As your pup heels, you can forestall a collision by turning into the puppy and walking toward her while moving your left hand over her head.

ception of you as her leader. In time, you should vary the pace of your walk, going from quick to slow to normal speed. This breaks up the monotony of a constant pace and helps keep your pup tuned in to you.

Down The final exercise, *down*, often gives owners a lot of trouble because it requires a puppy to move into a controlled, submissive posture that implicitly acknowledges your authority. If you have a strong-willed puppy, the training can unleash a leadership struggle that results in some yipping and resistance. This is why we begin getting our puppies accustomed to moving into the *down* position voluntarily during the first weeks after adoption by conditioning them with the noncoercive methods described in chapter eleven. It defuses the potential resistance the pup may make to being placed in the down, so that when we come to formally work on the command later on, the puppy is already familiar with getting into the position. Even if your pup has not had the benefit of such early conditioning, it is essential for you to work firmly and patiently until she learns to accept the command, for once a pup knows down, the length of time she can spend with you in a controlled manner increases dramatically, which in turn helps to solidify the bond that is developing between you.

The best way to begin teaching down is to work on a comfortable surface, either carpeting or grass. If you choose not to use treats, start by kneeling beside your pup while she is positioned in a sit-stay. Place your left hand on the back of her shoulders as you pass your right under her front legs, clasping her left leg just below the elbow. As you gently lift her front legs up and out, say your dog's name and "Down." At the same time apply mild pressure on her shoulders with your left hand. Ease her into the *down* position, praising her reassuringly as soon as she is lying on her belly. Be sure to avoid pulling her legs out from under her, since this could easily frighten her. Once she is down, stroke her shoulders with your left hand to ensure that she does not immediately bounce back up, and after she is in the position for five to ten seconds, release her with an "Okay" and praise. Keep the down very brief in the beginning. If your puppy tries to get up, correct her immediately with a "No, down" as you apply downward pressure to her back with your hand, then praise her as she holds.

You can gently clasp your pup's forelegs and lift them up, easing her into a down.

Follow through, placing the puppy in the down.

With lots of repetition and practice, the pup soon learns the down.

A variation on this exercise for a mellow puppy is to kneel beside her while she is sitting, as before, only now place your right hand behind her right foreleg at the same time as you drape your left arm around her withers, putting your left hand behind her left foreleg. Lift up her legs and ease her into the down, saying her name and "Down" as above, following this with praise.

Practicing the guided down several times a day will quickly accustom your pup to the position, allowing you to begin weaning her from being *placed* into the down to moving into the down herself. To make this transition, you should stand next to your pup in the *heel* position, with her sitting beside you. Fold your leash into your left hand and rest it where the lead and training collar meet, underneath your pup's right ear. Now turn left 90 degrees so that you are facing your pup's right side. In one continuous, graceful motion, pass your right hand, palm down, in front of your pup as you say her name and "Down" in a firm, deepened voice, making sure to bend over at the waist. Many pups will follow the movement of your hand straight to the ground and progress into the down easily. If this is the case, immediately say, "Stay" (using the hand signal as well), and praise her reassuringly. After several seconds, release her with an "Okay." If your pup does not follow your hand movement down, your left hand is in perfect position to give a quick, forward pop with the leash as you say, "No, down." *Do not force her down; pop the leash and release.* If she corrects herself, praise her. If not, place her into the down manually.

A point to remember with this exercise is that sometimes when puppies go into the *down* position, they roll over on their backs and begin acting playful. If this should occur, stand up straight at once. By not feeding into the play mode, you will project a positive tone of leadership, and most pups will respond by straightening themselves up and focusing on the command.

Working Toward a Down-Stay Once your pup understands the down and is able to move into it on her own, gradually extend the length of time that she holds the position. *Down* achieves its true goal only when it matures into a sustained *down-stay*, because that is what enables your pup to remain calmly in your presence without becoming an annoying bundle of unfocused energy.

Be patient with this process. Because pups have short attention

The down-stay lays the foundation for obedience work and future safety. In one continuous and graceful motion, pass your right hand in front of your pup and say her name and "Down" in a firm, deep voice. Be sure to bend at the waist and knees.

Practicing the down-stay. At first, keep your left hand over your pup's back so you can quickly correct her from getting up. Then you can gradually move farther and farther back while holding her focus.

You can reinforce the down-stay by walking around your puppy while maintaining communication.

spans, initially they are able to stay down for only short periods of time. You need to work methodically, step-by-step, to increase your pup's abilities, without putting too much pressure on him. We suggest two approaches: First, during training sessions, gradually increase the length of the down-stay from ten to twenty to thirty seconds and up, keeping your left hand over the pup's back to start with, so that you can correct him swiftly should he break. When he is comfortable with this, make the exercise more challenging by standing erect, then moving around him in a circle. If he gets out of position, calmly use the three-step correction and try again. Being introduced to these types of mild disturbances and receiving gentle corrections for resulting errors will teach your pup to hold the down-stay for longer and longer periods of time. Now you can be more imaginative with distractions. For example, try stepping over your pup as he holds the position, or clapping your hands as you walk around him, or tossing a stone on the ground several feet in front of him. These exercises make the down-stay more reliable, teaching him to hold the position despite temptation.

Once the older puppy learns to hold a relaxed down-stay, make things more challenging by jumping over her.

The second approach is to look for natural opportunities to put your pup into the down-stay when he will be disposed to keeping still for longer periods of time, such as after walks and play sessions, when he is likely to be tired. Put him into position and then sit down and relax, reading the newspaper or watching television. Do not be concerned if he falls asleep; the point is to get him accustomed to remaining in the down-stay for an extended period of time. If he breaks the stay without permission, get up and correct him without making a big fuss about it, then return to what you are doing. Consistency on your part will show him that you are serious about the command and will habituate him to accepting the position. Finally, whenever you release your pup after a successful long down-stay, be sure to give him plenty of praise.

Future Options: The Question of Remote Training

As we have indicated previously, training is a process that unfolds dynamically throughout the life of a dog. To think of training as a set three-week program that cranks out a well-behaved dog—whom owners don't have to continue to work with—is alien to how we see things. Training takes place continually, and far from being a burden, it can add real depth to the relationship you enjoy with your pooch. Thus, it is entirely possible that as your pup gets a little older you may wish to expand on his training in any number of areas: formal and more advanced obedience training, agility training, search and rescue, gundog training, therapy training, obtaining a CGC certificate...the list goes on and on. Given what you hope to achieve with your pup, you may find the idea of training with a club or group, or with a specific trainer, very appealing.

That said, further teaching ultimately raises the question about the effectiveness and safety of new approaches that incorporate technology into the training of dogs, specifically the use of remote collars. Over the years many people have asked for our opinion on these devices and whether such collars should have a place in the trainer's toolbox (specifically our own). Admittedly, it would be difficult to find a more hotly debated issue in the training community than this one. Many professionals see the collars as exceedingly valuable training tools that offer dogs and their owners new levels of freedom and enjoyment. Others portray the devices as cruel and can be quite vocal about it. Often it's difficult to have a true conversation on the matter because both sides have such intense feelings. If we wish to come to a balanced view that is based on knowledge and understanding rather than on raw emotion, we must understand a bit about the history and evolution of these devices.

There was a time when we were decidedly uncomfortable with using remote collars in training except in the most serious cases, when behavioral modification was essential to saving the dog's life. The first electronic collars in the '60s and '70s offered only one level of intensity, which produced a very unpleasant shock to the dog. It was a crude yet seemingly effective tool in breaking behavior such as car- and livestockchasing as well as in training hunting dogs who could withstand the intensity of the stimulation. Its relevance to more routine obedience training was less apparent, since it was clearly an aversive tool, a genuine "shock" collar. Why use such a device when the only stimulation one could give was "Wow!"? By today's standards the progenitors of the modern remote collar were rough and one-dimensional.

As with most technology, however, where one tool begins at an initial, foundational level, it paves the way for progress that quickly transforms the tool into something more sophisticated and profoundly different. Think of the field of medicine: surgery was initially performed with knives and saws but has now evolved in breathtaking ways, with lasers and microsurgical tools serving the healing process. Ask a person who has had his cataracts removed through laser surgery, for example, what it has meant to his quality of life, and you will get some idea of what's at stake. Granted, surgeons must be trained to use these tools effectively. Still, where would we be without them?

This technological evolution also applies to remote collars (sometimes called e-collars), and as a result we've rethought our view of them. While historically we've been wary of using or recommending such collars, at the same time we've understood that the technology has been changing steadily and that some trainers have claimed marvelous results with them. Anyone who works professionally with dogs understands how satisfying it is to help owners reach a high level of trust and freedom with their pups, and this is what respectable trainers were reporting—in ways we found difficult to imagine: off-leash reliability in a relatively short time, greater inclusion of the dog in the owner's life, calm and consistent behavior, all amounting to transformed relationships. For us, however, seeing is believing. It was only when we witnessed for ourselves how this tool was being used by expert trainers— whose talent and creativity were helping others to understand the tool and use it effectively—that we suddenly "got it."

After attending several seminars and speaking at length with bona fide masters of this tool, we found the evidence compelling, and it's worth describing in some detail. Gone indeed were the days when the e-collar was a one-dimensional "shock" collar; instead, we saw how it had transformed into a multidimensional training tool, providing precision, reliability, and versatility to trainers, owners, and dogs alike. Unlike in the early days, today's remote collars have a wide range of stimulations, from very low (almost imperceptible) to levels that are strong enough to correct and gain attention in highly distracting circumstances. The handler can control the amount of stimulation in extremely subtle ways, primarily by associating a very mild stim with a command. In fact, the trainers we saw had their devices set to a slight tingle, and the dogs displayed no discomfort during the sessions. Indeed, to reassure ourselves, we asked to experience the normal-working-level stimulation on our own hands. It was barely perceptible and in no way painful.

More interesting to us, however, was how the dogs responded to the stim and the pedagogy the professionals used. The dogs seemed to understand very precisely the association of the stim with the various commands, and as we observed the trainers we saw repeatedly how they used a "tapping" technique that facilitated the association. They still employed body language and voice effectively, with plenty of positive reinforcement and quiet encouragement, but what made the biggest impression on us was how they used the stim as a direction instead of a correction — a way of "tapping the dog on the shoulder" to indicate what was required. The results were impressive indeed, a skillful blending of grace and technique that belied any trace of heavy-handedness. The dogs we observed seemed happy and nonstressed. What we witnessed demonstrated compellingly how remote collars could be used skillfully to train a dog in on- and off-leash obedience; the approach was cutting-edge in terms of training theory.

At this point we were forced to ask ourselves, if such training is really more effective at the same time as being less stressful than conventional training, if it leads to greater freedom between owner and dog, and if the dogs respond well to it, why shouldn't we incorporate it as a tool in our own approach? Not using remote collars simply because some folks might misunderstand or judge us poorly isn't sound reasoning. Having paid attention to the debate for years, we believe that the most vocal critics of remote collars are those who are ignorant of how they can be used and who have had little or no hands-on training with them. Once a person witnesses their positive use firsthand, the picture changes radically. In the past several years we have begun introducing remote collars in our adult training program, and the results have not only confirmed our hopes but exceeded them. More important, we have discovered that owners, once fully educated in their proper use, are able to implement them to great advantage as well. As a result, we can pass over control of their trained dogs to them with far greater effectiveness and continuity than we had in the past, improving an already successful training program. Remote collars have helped us become better trainers, and our clients better owners.

Do remote collars have the potential of being misused? Of course, as is the case with any training tool. But most trainers will acknowledge readily that an ignorant handler can transform even the most benign instrument or method into a pedagogical catastrophe. Whatever device one uses to train a dog, the crucial tools are guidance and understanding. These are the motivating factors that have preoccupied us these many years and that continue to inspire us.

So why discuss the remote collar in the context of a puppy book? Quite simply, to educate you about it and to prepare you in case you decide to use it as your puppy matures. We certainly have no desire to explain this approach as a do-it-yourself method that any owner can master on his or her own. Nor do we recommend going out to the local pet store to purchase a unit that you can slap on your dog to start training. That is total folly. To use the remote collar effectively and safely, you should learn the technique in collaboration with a skilled professional who is familiar with the latest training methodology. The trainer will also steer you toward the best equipment. If you come upon trainers who use remote collars, find out how they are implementing them and what sort of experience they have had with the devices. When you observe such a professional working, it should be apparent that the teaching approach is largely directive and positive (though not *purely positive!*) and that the collar is used in conjunction with a number of other training tools and techniques. The session should not be primarily aversive. What you are looking for is a balanced approach to training that serves the relationship you are establishing with your dog. Working with a remote collar certainly does not replace the importance of building a bond with your animal, of being able to read his body language and adapt quickly in teaching particular skills, and of motivating him and being patient with the training process. Nor is it a magic wand that automatically makes your dog obey your every command. The remote collar is simply a subtle and powerful tool that can help you realize the hopes you have for your companion with a minimum of stress.

Looking Back

Throughout this book we have continually highlighted the importance of becoming the alpha figure, or pack leader, in your puppy's life, and we have presented positive elements involved in that achievement. All puppies require the consistent, responsible guidance of their owners in order to mature into balanced, well-adjusted companion dogs. What makes the training process such a necessary part of a healthy dog-owner relationship is that it confirms your position as leader at the same time as it provides your pup with the practical skills necessary to live happily with you. *Training is a humane form of dominance.* In following your directives, your pup implicitly recognizes and submits to your leadership. This goes a long way toward preventing future problems.

16

Training and Play: Enjoying Your Pup

All work and no play makes Fido a dull dog and your relationship something that lacks sparkle. Training takes place over the entire life span of the dog: your companion is always learning, so the challenge is to keep him motivated and interested as he moves through each stage of his life. An important element in this process is linking play with training. Fun can be incorporated into your pup's lessons from his earliest days through adulthood, as a conclusion to a session or as something done independently. Since dogs are creatures of play, spending fun time with your pup helps deepen the relationship you share. Sometimes owners are so fixated on teaching their puppy the obedience exercises that they put too much pressure on the pup and themselves and lose sight of the broader picture: that having a dog can fill their lives with joy and that they can tap into this naturally every day. Following are some ideas for incorporating play into your training both as a pleasant conclusion to a formal session and as a positive stand-alone activity.

Retrieving

One of our favorite games to play with a pup is retrieving. While some breeds (and individual dogs) are more naturally gifted with retrieving ability, we have found that most pups can be coached into enjoying this game, particularly if you start early enough. Retrieving plugs into a dog's innate drive, and taking the time to teach the skill pays big dividends in exercise and enjoyment.

Beyond the basic commands, exercises such as walking the bridge allow pups to show off their learning accomplishments. With the pup on-leash, we coax her to jump onto the top of a low half-crate.

Teaching a Retrieve

With an eight- to twelve-week-old pup, the first retrieves we attempt are with something small, soft, and lightweight. A rolled-up ball of paper, a knotted rag, a bundled sock…these are ideal items to start with: they are light, so they can't be tossed very far, and the puppy can easily pick them up. Remember that with a youngish pup, it isn't necessary that he knows sit and stay to start out with. You can easily restrain your puppy as you toss the object. Hold him for a few seconds, then release him as you say, "Fetch" or "Get it." Make sure you don't throw the object too far. If the pup trots and picks up the item and turns, clap your hands lightly and crouch low, calling his name and praising him when he comes to you. If he doesn't seem to get it right away, try engaging him by using the object as a tease, rubbing it in front of him playfully and then tossing it a short distance. Find an appropriately restricted area such as a hallway or a small backyard that will help your pup stay focused and keep him from taking off with the item. Make the first sessions very brief and fun. You should start off early with this play, because at eight to twelve weeks your pup is inclined to stay around you, which in turn makes for a smooth process. As the pup grows you can change the retrieval item to a ball or a small bumper, as he'll be more comfortable carrying a slightly heavier object that is tossed farther away.

If you begin retrieving later, at fourteen to sixteen weeks, you're liable to find the process a bit challenging, with the pup more interested in playing keep-away or running with the item in the opposite direction than in bringing it back to you. Regardless, always be patient and trust in the process. Consider using a light check cord or long line that trails behind the pup, allowing you to guide him back, if necessary. This will keep things upbeat and positive by preventing your pup from manipulating the situation. Another piece of advice: In the early stages, always stay low to the ground when you are calling the puppy back. Pups can find a large figure intimidating to approach, whereas if you're crouched and tapping the floor playfully, the puppy will be much more disposed to come back. Keep your praise warm and put a big smile on your face. Your pup needs to learn that this is really something fun.

If the puppy starts trotting away with the object and you don't have a check cord or long line that you can tug, try running in the opposite direction and see if he follows you. As we've stated previously, you can even lie down on the ground—something that evokes the pup's curiosity. When he comes to investigate, gently hold him and get back in the crouch.

With this sort of foundation, you can progress to further retrieves as the pup grows, using an indestructible foam ball, for example, which most dogs love. However, be careful to use an object that is large enough that your dog will not accidentally swallow it. A ball with a string attached can be helpful in this regard. Also, always exercise in a way that is appropriate for your pup's age. Once the puppy is more mature—say, eight to nine months—a ball launcher (available at most pet stores) can be handy to send the object farther than you can throw it. Dogs who play fetch in this manner from their youngest days not only have a blast but become more and more reliable in their recall in a totally natural way.

Back and Forth

Another simple game for a young pup that reinforces the recall while allowing human and pup to have a great time is "back and forth." This is much more straightforward than retrieving, but it is a terrific way to involve two people and a puppy in a play session at the same time. Start with the two humans crouching, facing each other at approximately twenty feet apart. One person should hold on to the puppy, while the other faces the pup. Have the second person call the pup enthusiastically in a light voice, clapping hands and giving encouragement. At the same time, the human holding the pup should delay releasing her for about ten seconds, in order to allow the puppy to get excited. With the other person continuing to call, the pup will ordinarily struggle to break free and move toward that person. When she reaches her target, give plenty of praise and petting to the pup, and then reverse the rolls. This is a short game that can go on for five to ten minutes, reinforcing both the recall and the bond between owner and pup.

Other Forms of Play

Use your imagination to develop other games you can share with your pup, but always remember to keep the game or activity age-appropriate. For example, many athletic dogs love chasing a Frisbee. However, until a pup is somewhat mature (six to eight months of age), it is best to keep him from jumping, because this puts strain on his young muscles and joints. That said, we have found that using other pieces of agility equipment such as tunnels and ramps — items that can easily be incorporated into light play sessions — can be stimulating for our pups.

Finally, how can we not mention hide-and-seek, which can be great during a hike in the woods, provided your pup knows sit-stay. Simply put your pup in position, then trot ahead around a bend and hide behind a tree. Call the puppy and let him find you, giving him plenty of praise and encouragement when he does. You'll see how clever he thinks he has been, and it really helps deepen your bond.

As you can imagine, the possibilities are endless. What we want to underscore is simply the importance of having fun with your dog in a manner that stimulates his mind and reinforces the bond of relationship. Playing with your dog keeps training from getting stale and creates a positive attitude that you will always be able to build on — something genuinely life-giving for both you and your dog.

Moving out onto the low bridge with energy and encouragement.

Playground obstacles pose an easy challenge and build self-confidence. Walk your pup in a heel position, then lead her up the ramp, praising her.

A relaxed pause at the top of the slope.

After your pup accomplishes the first climb, you can carefully but confidently lead her in reverse, back up the slope.

Finally, an easy run down the other side.

A short four-foot tunnel is bright and simple; here, an older pup is led through on a long leash.

Running through a very long and darkened tunnel is an advanced accomplishment. With the help and encouragement of two people and the come *command, it's an exciting and positive experience.*

17

Discipline and Common Puppy Problems

No matter how well-behaved your puppy is, it is entirely normal for occasions to arise when discipline is necessary to correct bad behavior. Much like children, pups — aside from simply not knowing any better — go through bratty episodes when they vie with you for leadership, testing to see just how much they can assert themselves. In such circumstances, you must respond correctly as a convincing pack leader, letting your puppy know in a straightforward manner the error of his ways. Too often new owners let bad behavior go unchecked, unintentionally allowing it to evolve into something more serious. This usually happens because they are uncertain as to what constitutes legitimate discipline for a pup and are afraid of being abusive in any way. The unfortunate result is a spoiled, willful puppy.

It is also possible to err in the opposite direction. When owners administer discipline incorrectly, such as punishing a puppy long after the fact (as commonly occurs in episodes of house-soiling or chewing, when the pup does not understand the reason for the correction) or by using ill-advised techniques such as a rolled-up newspaper or a harsh slap across the rear, puppies can end up manifesting shy, skittish behavior.

Especially with puppies, you must always walk a fine line between too much and too little. What makes discipline such a difficult topic to address is that it varies according to the circumstances. No book can tell you the precise correction to use in each particular situation; we can offer only guidelines, which you must then apply to your own puppy. As we have emphasized, each pup is an individual, and what may be appropriate for one puppy may be excessive for another. The real starting point for understanding discipline is for you to know your puppy, to be able to "read" his body language and get a feel for how he responds to correction. Then you can proceed intelligently, using only as much force as necessary to make your point, without losing self-control.

This is why we recommend disciplinary techniques that mimic those your pup would receive in a natural setting, particularly from his mother or a senior pack member. These harmonize with his makeup as a canine while effectively communicating your displeasure. For example, you will discover from your eye-contact sessions that your pup becomes highly sensitive to the message you send to him with your eyes. Usually this will be kind and encouraging; however, there will be instances when your assertive glare will stop his behavior cold, particularly when it is accompanied with a deep, clear *no*. Avoid loud and out-of-control histrionics—"You bad dog! Stop that right now!"—which lack any sort of true leadership and compromise your authority. We draw inspiration from the example of the alpha wolf, who regularly maintains pack order through a threatening growl and stare.

There are also times when a puppy's behavior merits stronger correction than simply a penetrating look or a strong verbal rebuke. Particularly if you have a pup who is dominant and headstrong, you may find that he is unaffected by eye contact and voice tone. For your puppy to get the point, you must express your authority with physical discipline that immediately follows his bad behavior. The timing of the correction is crucial, as dogs live in the moment and will not understand discipline that happens well after an infraction. The correction must coincide with the transgression. For these occasions, we prefer holding the scruff or sides of the neck, which resembles what the mother does to her pups to keep order in the litter. She doesn't shake the pup but holds him in place until he relaxes and submits. Following this example with an eight- to twelve-week-old pup, we grasp the scruff of his neck and hold it firmly as we apply mild pressure with a clipped *no* and wait for him to relax. If the pup is older, we grasp the sides of the neck with both hands and lift him off his two front feet, making eye contact and holding him in place as we say *no*. If your pup has advanced in his obedience work enough to understand *down*, follow up your discipline immediately with a down-stay, since that position expresses submission and effectively reinforces your dominance. Also remember never to use your pup's name in conjunction with a correction or discipline. It is much more helpful to keep his name associated with something positive.

A firm grab by the scruff mimics the mother pinning her pup to the ground.

A strong correction: Grab the scruff of the neck with both hands, make eye contact, and hold your pup in place as you say no.

Ordinarily, these disciplinary techniques are quite effective for puppies raised within a well-rounded program of conditioning and training. When applied correctly, they communicate your authority in a humane and convincing way and will help you avoid the need for sterner techniques later on. A word of caution: occasionally a five- or six-month-old puppy from one of the more dominant breeds (e.g., German shepherd, rottweiler, Akita, Doberman pinscher) may misbehave in a manner that merits stronger measures. For example, out of the blue your self-confident, five-month-old male German shepherd may growl at a guest you have invited into your house. In a situation like this — involving either the threat or the actual manifestation of aggression — you should seriously consider using a firm cuff underneath the chin with your open hand. We advise this because we have seen only too frequently the results of ineffective corrections involving aggression: the behavior escalates and real problems occur. Better to nip it in the bud.

To make this correction effectively, you must anchor your dog in a sitting position with your left hand holding his collar. As you make eye contact, cuff the underside of his mouth with your open right hand, rapping him sharply several times as you say, "No!" The discipline should be firm enough to elicit a short yelp, and it is best to follow it up immediately with an obedience command or sequence that reinforces your authority. After that, over the course of several weeks, you should stage mock scenarios that give your pup the chance to learn how he is supposed to act in such situations. By reinforcing correct behavior with generous praise, you establish a healthy pattern for him to follow that curtails aggressive actions.

Remember, use this correction only with an older puppy and only in the rarest of circumstances. Don't use the technique if the puppy isn't emotionally strong enough to handle it. If this forceful step does not help, or if your pup's aggressive behavior starts to become a pattern, be proactive and seek professional help from a qualified trainer.

Finally, there are a number of specific problems common to puppyhood that all new owners must learn to deal with. All puppies make mistakes. No amount of preventive thinking can possibly cover all the potential problems involved in raising your pup. Because he is still young and immature, your puppy will, at times, behave in ways that annoy and irritate you. When these inevitabilities occur, you must be careful to respond with understanding and balance, avoiding either a passive "he'll eventually grow out of it" attitude or a "put the baby to sleep with a sledgehammer" type of solution. Both of these extremes only make matters worse. Instead, by following a more moderate course, blending prevention with correction, you can change unwanted behavior in a manner that is properly suited to your puppy's young age.

Here it is important to distinguish puppy problems from the more serious behavior issues characteristic of older dogs. Unlike deeply ingrained neurotic behavior that requires professional help to treat, most puppy problems are entirely normal. That is, they are the result of your pup being a young canine and acting inappropriately within a domestic context. For example, it is perfectly natural for a dog to bark, chew, bite, play, dig, jump, and urinate — this is the definition of being a dog. The difficulty comes when these activities are not channeled to fit our domestic situation. Your pup has no innate idea how to behave in your household; he will simply do what comes naturally. Since you are the one who introduced your puppy into your home, it is your responsibility to teach him how to act and to help him learn from his experiences. This is much easier to do while he is a puppy, before issues become more serious. In the following sections, we will consider a number of typical puppy problems and offer you some effective and humane suggestions for resolving them.

Mouthing

As we have seen, puppies use their mouths to explore and investigate everything, especially each other. If you watch a six-week-old litter of pups at play, you will observe them mouthing and nipping each other continually, chomping on ears, neck, muzzle, legs, or tail, learning how hard they can bite down before their playmate protests. Such behavior becomes a natural way for them to communicate and express themselves. It is easy to understand, then, why your pup would direct this same sort of behavior toward you once she arrives home. Separated from her littermates, she now focuses her attention on you, so it is only logical for her to express this by mouthing your fingers, arms, and feet. At first this might seem like cute, harmless behavior, but your pup's sharp milk teeth will quickly convince you otherwise. Furthermore, if you ignore it, the mouthing will only get worse, becoming a normal way of behaving toward friends and visitors. Before this becomes a bad habit, here are several techniques to stop the problem.

1. For young pups, an effective technique that gently discourages mouthing is to let the puppies experience an unpleasant result from the behavior without any show of anger on your part. Begin by petting your pup around her neck and chest. As she begins to mouth your hand, gently put your index finger down her throat, just enough to elicit a gag reflex. (Anyone with long fingernails should not attempt this.) When your pup gags, remove your finger and open your hand for her to lick, praising her if she does so. If you practice this consistently, your pup will quickly associate the unpleasant gagging with the mouthing of your hand, and the behavior will stop.

2. For a pup who is a bit older, you should kneel on the floor, facing her. Gently pet her around the neck and head. If she starts to mouth you, put your dominant hand around her muzzle while placing your nondominant hand on her rear. Swing her around so

Mouthing should be controlled from a pup's earliest days.

that you can contain her body between your legs. Now put your nondominant hand behind your pup's head to prevent her from pulling it free. Say, "No," quietly. Do not squeeze the muzzle; simply keep your hand around it so that she cannot break loose. If you do this correctly she may struggle, but she won't be able to escape and after some moments will suddenly relax, perhaps with a sigh. At this point say, "Good," in a calm voice and slide your hand to the side, off your pup's muzzle. If she tries to mouth or nip at you again, repeat the procedure.

3. Another technique that discourages mouthing is similar to the first suggestion, in that it lets your pup experience an unpleasant result from the behavior. Begin as in the first example by petting your pup around her neck and chest. As she begins to mouth, squeeze lemon concentrate from a plastic lemon into her mouth. A quick squirt will create an interruption that is harmless, albeit unpleasant. Then simply put some of the lemon juice on your hand and resume petting your pup. The scent will project the concept of *undesirable*, and the puppy will quickly learn to leave your hands alone.

4. The massage/dominance exercises we discussed in chapter fourteen are also helpful in teaching your pup to accept being handled and manipulated without an oral response. For corrections, you should either hold the pup down briefly by the scruff or use one of the techniques described above. Always remain calm and assertive.

5. Finally, avoid all tug-of-war games with your puppy. They condition her to be mouth-oriented and unrestrained in her bite.

Chewing

Chewing is the flip side of mouthing: your pup focuses his oral attention on all manner of household objects and personal items, gladly gnawing on whatever is within reach. Puppies are amazingly resourceful; if something can be chewed, your pup will chew it, and there are several very good reasons for this. Puppies have a physical need to chew that is associated with the teething process. This begins around three months, with the permanent teeth pushing up underneath the puppy teeth, and peaks between six and ten months, when the permanent teeth are set solidly in the jaw. During this period, if your pup does not have something to chew on, he will actively try to find something. This exercise also occupies your pup's attention, relieving boredom and normal puppy tension. A pup can keep himself occupied for hours if he has an object to gnaw on. Hence, rather than waiting for a full-scale problem to develop, you should control your pup's natural inclination to chew by following these guidelines:

1. The first priority in controlling destructive chewing is prevention. Use common sense. Before you even bring your new pup home, make sure that shoes, socks, books, and other personal items are picked up off the floor, and store valuable objects up and away where they cannot be damaged. Check that electric cords are safely out of reach and plug up electric outlets you are not using.

2. Once you have your pup, you must always be aware of where he is and what he is doing. Take the same attitude you would if you were caring for a baby.

3. Whenever you leave your pup unattended for any reason, short or long absences alike, confine him safely in a crate or in a "puppy-proofed" area. It is astonishing how many clients complain about puppy chewing when they insist on giving their pups free rein of the house while they are away. This is foolish, sentimental thinking. It is completely unrealistic to expect a young puppy not to chew if he is left unconfined and alone in the home.

4. There should be nothing in the confined area that is easy to chew on, except for one permissible object that belongs to him, such as a nylon bone. Make this item the focus of all your pup's chewing. To get him accustomed to it, introduce it right from the start in play sessions, and use it as a replacement object after he has been corrected for chewing on something inappropriate (see guideline 6). We prefer meat-scented nylon bones because they are long-lasting, safe, and nonabrasive to the teeth, as are natural hard bones. While pups love rawhide bones and squeak toys, these are too easy to destroy, and older pups occasionally ingest large pieces of them, which can be quite dangerous. Also avoid traditional favorites such as old shoes or knotted-up socks. Once pups learn that chewing on leather or cotton is acceptable, they are unable to distinguish old articles from new ones. To your pup, a shoe is a shoe.

5. Before leaving your puppy alone for an extended period of time, roll the nylon bone between your palms for several minutes so

that your scent is firmly on it, then present it to your pup as you leave. Keep your departure low-key and nondemonstrative, since highly emotional farewells can lead to separation anxiety that your pup will try to relieve in any way he can — through destructive behavior, if that is a possibility, or through nonstop barking and whining. Leaving a radio tuned to a classical music station can also provide a calming influence.

6. Beyond mere prevention, you should also begin actively conditioning your pup to ignore forbidden objects and to focus his chewing solely on the nylon bone. Initially this means holding him down by the scruff or sides of the neck with a *no* whenever you catch him chewing on something inappropriate, then presenting him with the nylon bone instead. If he accepts it, follow with encouraging praise.

7. As your pup grows, concoct situations in which he must learn to ignore different objects placed temptingly on the floor while you are in the same room with him. Make sure his nylon bone is one of the objects. After you put your pup in a down-stay, pretend to read the newspaper, keeping a close watch on him out of the corner of your eye. If he begins to edge over to one of the forbidden items, wait until he actually starts to put his mouth on it, then correct him with a firm *no*, pointing out his bone instead. If he repeats the mistake, attach a light cotton line to his collar and extend it toward you. Should he break his down-stay and start to grab something inappropriate, give him a brief tug on the line with a *no*. Then present him with his bone again. Several such sessions should teach him to ignore the various articles and play with only the bone *while you are in the room*. At this stage you can begin to practice leaving the space for very short intervals, so that should he go back to chewing on a forbidden object, you can quickly return and catch him in the act — the only justifiable occasion for a correction. The object of this exercise is to gradually prepare your pup for the day when he will be trusted alone in the house while you are away.

8. Make sure your puppy receives plenty of exercise each day. Proper exercise helps curtail boredom and high energy levels, two significant factors in destructive behavior.

A final, practical point: if you ever have to forcibly remove an object from your pup's mouth, place your hand across the top of his muzzle behind the teeth, thumb on one side and fingers on the other, and pull down the bottom jaw with the other hand. Praise the pup as he releases the object.

Jumping Up

Most puppies have the annoying habit of greeting people by jumping up on them, which is actually an attempt to reach the individual's face. For puppies, the facial area of both dogs and humans is the chief point of contact, the primary reference in all social encounters. This stems from behavior learned around the time of weaning; remember how wolf pups jump up and lick at the muzzles of older pack members to solicit food, which the adults then regurgitate for them. After weaning, this face-licking continues with a more generalized meaning, becoming the ordinary way subordinate wolves greet those of higher rank.

Regardless of how natural this behavior is, however, when it occurs in human society, it quickly becomes an annoying and potentially dangerous habit. While a small pup jumping up might seem harmless enough, it transforms into something more serious once that pup is fully grown. Furthermore, most visitors to your house will not appreciate your pup's paws on their clothing, and dogs in the habit of jumping can easily frighten young children or knock over an unprepared elderly person. Our advice is to stop the behavior as soon as it begins by following these guidelines:

1. Resolve to discourage all occasions of jumping up. It is not fair to your pup to allow him to leap on you, then to correct him for doing it to others. This is bound to confuse him. Keep your expectations consistent.

2. Whenever your pup attempts to jump on you, simply grasp both of his front paws securely, holding them up long enough for him to become uncomfortable with the position. Show no anger. Most pups like to be up for only a very short time; when your dog starts to protest, continue holding on to him for several more seconds, increasing his discomfort. Then put him down gently, helping him into a sit. When he experiences this response consistently, he will avoid jumping up on you.

When your pup jumps up, grasp both paws securely and hold them until she becomes uncomfortable.

3. Another possibility is to put the palm of your hand flat out in front of your pup's face when you sense he is about to jump. This blocks the jump and disposes him to respond to a *sit* command.
4. Since jumping up usually occurs during greetings, teach your pup an alternative manner of greeting both you and other people. We recommend crouching down to his level when he comes to meet you, then guiding him into a sit and petting him calmly for several seconds. For greeting guests, practice bringing your pup to people on-leash, leading him into a sit-stay several feet before he reaches the person. Then have the individual approach. If your pup tries to jump toward the visitor, give a quick sideways leash correction as you move to the right. Circle him around on heel and repeat. When he allows the individual to pet him and does not jump, praise him cheerfully.

Possessiveness

When puppies start eating food and playing with toys, around four weeks of age, it is quite common for them to show the first signs of possessive behavior. For example, as the litter eats from a common dish, a dominant pup may suddenly growl and snap at her neighbor, trying to scare him away from his share of the food. Often, the other pup will growl right back, learning that he must stand his ground if he is to get his own portion. The same dynamics occur during play sessions: a puppy might be batting around a particular toy when a littermate tries to take it away from her. The first pup growls threateningly, and if she happens to scare the challenger off, she learns an important lesson about dominance and pack life. Thus, what we call *possessive behavior* begins quite early as a normal part of puppy development.

As a pup grows older, however, the situation changes radically; possessiveness can easily evolve into aggression if it is not checked right from the start. Never procrastinate with this. Having your full-grown dog growl menacingly at you because you approached him too closely while he was eating or because you were trying to take something away from him is a very unsettling experience. Through a gradual process of desensitizing—by training your pup to let you pick up his food or take any object out of his mouth—you assert your alpha stature in a healthy way before the behavior has a chance to develop into something serious. Here are three simple steps to follow with your pup to condition him away from possessive behavior:

1. At his feeding time, have your pup on-leash and instruct him to sit. Place the dish down in front of him as he waits. Lightly correct him if he makes a move toward the bowl. Once he succeeds in waiting patiently for five to ten seconds, let him begin his meal. After several more seconds, command him to sit again, gently guiding him into position. Follow with a stay, keeping your pup in place with the leash. Pick up the dish and wait ten seconds. If your pup has been patient, place the food back in front of him and release him with a "Good boy. Okay." Treat any growling with a quick leash pop and a *no*, and move him away from the food. After any correction, make sure you do not return the food until you have made him sit.
2. Teach your pup to take a piece of dog biscuit gently from your hand. First instruct him to sit. After praising him, offer a small chunk of biscuit by first moving the back of your hand in front of his mouth. When your pup is relaxed, turn your hand around, making sure he takes the biscuit gently. Praise him warmly. This simple exercise teaches a pup self-control around food.

3. Each day, practice giving your pup the nylon bone (or another favorite toy), then taking it away from him, praising him as you do so. If he resists, utter a clipped, "No, leave it," praising him if he releases. If he still does not let go, give him a brief leash pop with a verbal reprimand and repeat the process. Then let him play with the bone.

Should you see any serious escalation in aggressive, possessive behavior, you should contact a professional to help you address the problem while the pup is still young.

Submissive Urination

We have noted how puppies, having been originally cleansed by their mother while they were on their backs, can subsequently demonstrate submission to adults by moving into a similar position, involuntarily releasing a small amount of urine as they do. In canine terms, this reflexive act acknowledges authority and has a placating effect on the higher-ranking wolf or dog, defusing possible aggression.

Because of its deep, instinctive roots, this behavior is often transferred into a puppy's new pack. In a domestic situation, submissive urination reflects the same recognition of authority, only now it is directed toward a human alpha. It can also occur during moments of extreme excitement. Needless to say, if the behavior happens repeatedly, it becomes an unwelcome problem that must be handled with sensitivity and understanding. Here are some guidelines to avoid future problems:

1. Submissive urination must be clearly distinguished from house-soiling. The puppy does not intend to urinate, only to show submission; therefore he must never be reprimanded for this behavior. Punishment will only encourage a more pronounced display of submission.
2. It is vital to teach a submissive puppy the obedience commands in a positive, confidence-building manner. Whenever possible, use noncoercive techniques that avoid triggering submission through dominating physical contact (see chapter eleven). The pup needs to experience praise and encouragement in a manner that draws him out of himself.
3. Avoid highly emotional greetings as well as situations in which you tower over your pup. Whenever you arrive home, ignore your

dog for five minutes. Then, when you do greet him, crouch down to his level, guiding him into a sit. If possible, do this on a noncarpeted surface such as grass, tile, or linoleum in case an "accident" does occur.

4. Stage controlled introductions to other people by bringing your pup up to them on-leash and making him sit in front of them. It is difficult for a pup to urinate while sitting, and the position is ideal for controlling excitement.

Car Sickness

When a dog is able to ride well in the car, it significantly increases the time she is able to spend with her owner, making for a more flexible and enjoyable relationship. By conditioning your puppy to ride in your car at an early age, you avoid the headache of car sickness later on. Neglecting to work with a pup on automobile etiquette makes practical matters — such as trips to the veterinarian and ordinary outings for recreation and exercise — a major project. Start taking your pup for daily rides soon after she comes home, following these general guidelines:

1. Your pup should learn to ride in the back of the car. For safety purposes, use a crate, safety harness, or car barrier to protect both you and her from sudden stops.
2. Begin the conditioning process by taking your pup on a very short trip (up and down the block, for example) every day for a week. Make sure your puppy hasn't eaten for two to four hours, and avoid a route with curves. Keep the trip upbeat and happy, and follow up with a play session so that your pup associates the car with something she likes.
3. Do not scold the pup for whining, and ignore any vomiting. Clean the mess when you get back home, and try again the next day, making the trip even shorter. If necessary, limit the ride to going up and down the driveway.
4. When your pup shows no signs of nausea, begin increasing the distance of the trip. Always be sure to praise your pup at the end of the ride.
5. Though it is fine to crack the rear windows for ventilation, do not allow your puppy to put her head out the window. This common

behavior is dangerous, since your pup could be hit by a flying pebble or other foreign object. Also, be sure never to leave a puppy or adult dog unattended in a car out in the sun, since canines are more sensitive to heat prostration and heat-related death than we are.

Stool Eating

Coprophagy, or stool eating, is one of the more distasteful habits a young puppy can engage in. Though utterly incomprehensible to most owners, there are usually very specific reasons for the behavior. When addressed quickly, stool eating can be resolved before it becomes chronic. There is no need to panic. Treated sensibly, the problem can be overcome without a lot of difficulty.

To understand why stool eating occurs at all, it is helpful to consider a pup's first experiences in the litter. When puppies are with their littermates before weaning, their mother consumes all of their waste material. This is normal maternal behavior, essential for keeping the litter healthy. After weaning, much like little children, pups become inquisitive. They naturally investigate their own feces, smelling, licking, and even consuming them. This is why breeders and owners must be diligent about picking up stools. Keeping floors and yards clean helps control the problem right from the start.

Once a puppy is in his new home, stool eating can indicate one of several things. Often it points to a dietary deficiency. The pup is not digesting his food properly and subsequently smells undigested protein in the stools. This can be caused by poor food or an internal problem requiring the attention of a veterinarian. It can also be related to boredom. If a puppy is alone in a fenced-in backyard, for example, he may entertain himself with old stools. This is especially the case in colder weather, when frozen stools seem to be objects of particular fascination.

To treat coprophagy effectively, you can follow several specific guidelines:

1. Make sure that the food you are feeding your pup is a high-quality brand — one that is both palatable and nutritious. Be on the lookout for signs of poor digestion — large stool content or loose stools. You may wish to consult your veterinarian about this.

2. Be conscientious about picking up your pup's stools. While some professionals recommend mixing digestive enzymes or meat tenderizer with your pup's food (they supposedly give the stool an unappetizing scent) or spraying Listerine or Tabasco sauce on an old stool (same idea), it is just as easy to take away the source of the problem. If your pup has a yard to play in, pick up stools regularly or, if possible, as soon as he eliminates.

3. When you are walking with your pup in the neighborhood, do so on-leash and do not let him smell the droppings of other animals. Give him a quick leash pop to direct his attention elsewhere. With consistent corrections, he will learn to ignore the stools.

18

General Care of Your Puppy

Throughout this book, we have emphasized that raising a puppy involves much more than good intentions and sentimental feelings. Because your pup is entirely dependent upon you for her welfare, you must learn to see your role comprehensively, in every aspect of her life. Real companionship presumes a commitment to care for all of your pup's physical and social needs. Thus, in addition to her basic training and upbringing, you are also responsible for her physical condition: providing proper diet, conscientious grooming, and regular, vigorous exercise. Since these factors are essential to a pup's health and well-being, we will discuss each topic in the following sections.

Feeding Your Puppy Properly

With all of the advertising hype surrounding pet foods and with an abundance of commercial brands available, it is little wonder many new puppy owners are confused about how and what to feed their pups. Though it is outside the scope of this book to discuss specific brands, the basic underlying principle in deciding what to feed your puppy is this: the possibility of a long, enjoyable life begins with a pup's first exposure to food. The adage "Garbage in, garbage out" is true when it comes to what you feed your dog. If good nutrition is not provided from a pup's earliest days, preventable health problems can often develop later in life, when the situation is too late to correct. As a first step, choose a good puppy food that meets all of the nutritional needs of a growing pup. Puppies need more proteins, fats, and calories than adult dogs to meet the high demands of their growing bodies. In order to help you make responsible choices regarding diet and feeding, we will address some common questions that many new owners have.

What Is Puppy Food? Because puppyhood is a time of rapid growth and intensive development, puppies require approximately double the daily amount of nutrients per pound of body weight than do fully grown dogs. In addition, their need for specific nutrients differs from adults': these nutrients cannot be obtained from adult "maintenance" food no matter how much a pup eats. While it is true that there are some "active" adult formulas that meet the dietary needs of puppies as well, generally we don't recommend feeding puppies the same type of food as fully grown dogs. To meet a pup's special nutritional requirements, many dog-food manufacturers produce specially formulated puppy foods for the first six to twelve months of a pup's life. There are also size-specific puppy foods (i.e., for small, medium, and large breeds) that have differing nutritional values. For example, large- and giant-breed pups should be given food that contains less phosphorus and calcium to promote slower and more gradual growth, since this may decrease the possibility of orthopedic diseases later on. However, generally speaking, good puppy foods are nutritionally complete and balanced to give a pup the ideal amounts of protein (usually between 28 and 30 percent); fat (between 14 and 20 percent); vitamins and minerals especially required for proper bone development; and DHA, an important omega-3 fatty acid that is a building block of the brain as well as a vital element in the development of sight and the central nervous system. Normally, choosing a high-quality, balanced puppy food makes it unnecessary for you to supplement your pup's diet.

How Long Should My Pup Stay on Puppy Food? Manufacturers generally recommend puppy food for the entire first year of a pup's life, but some pups may have to switch to adult food earlier. A pup who is growing too quickly can possibly develop panosteitis (long-bone disease) or other orthopedic problems. For this reason, always discuss your pup's diet with your veterinarian.

What Type of Puppy Food Should I Use? There are three basic forms of commercially produced dog foods available: moist (canned), semimoist (sealed pack), and dry kibble, and each form has its pros and cons. Look at the labels. Our preference for the major part of a pup's diet is to use a premium dry puppy food that has a named animal protein source as one of its first two ingredients and that includes a highly digestible grain such as rice or barley. We avoid corn and soy, which are difficult for dogs to process. Chosen wisely, dry food is economical, convenient, good for keeping your pup's teeth clean, and relatively digestible and palatable.

Canned dog food is also highly digestible and palatable; however, it is expensive. It contains about 75 percent water, meaning your pup will have to eat much more of it to get the same amount of nutritional value that she would with kibble. Because it is soft, it also lacks the dental benefits of hard food. Instead of relying exclusively on a diet of canned dog food, we recommend mixing small amounts with dry kibble to enhance the kibble's palatability. Also, some companies market very high-quality, balanced raw-meat foods in frozen packs. This can be used along with kibble instead of canned food.

Semimoist foods are also highly digestible, palatable, and convenient. They come in premeasured portions and do not require refrigeration. But like canned meat, they are expensive and lack the dental benefits of kibble. Also, since they contain large amounts of sugar, salt, and preservatives, semimoist foods can lead to problems with hyperactivity and obesity. We advise you not to use them regularly.

How Do I Select a Particular Brand? When considering this issue, look for a puppy food from a company with a serious background in research and testing, whose labels meet or preferably exceed the standards established by the National Research Council (NRC) and the Association of American Feed Control Officials (AAFCO). Avoid generic or store-brand pet foods: though inexpensive, they contain meat byproducts, corn, sweeteners, and artificial preservatives and colors, and they may prove costlier in the long run because of the medical problems associated with poor diet. Veterinary studies have shown these products to be of inconsistent quality, with low food value and poor digestibility. Consult your breeder and veterinarian about several wholesome possibilities for your pup. Another good resource for pet nutrition is the *Whole Dog Journal,* which annually publishes its list of approved foods and helpful guidelines for feeding your dog. Finally, judge the results. If your pup thrives with a particular food, showing a plush coat and firm stools, then stick with it. You may have to purchase the food at a feed or pet-supply store, where you can find the higher-quality dry foods. Supermarkets usually carry decent canned foods.

How Often Should I Feed My Pup? For the first four to six months, a puppy should get three meals a day. Eventually she will be able to consume more food at each interval, at which time she can go down to two meals a day. For most dogs, it is preferable to continue this twice-daily feeding throughout adulthood, since it is healthier to digest two smaller meals than one larger one. If your young pup is home alone during the day and hasn't moved to the two-meal system, whoever walks the puppy at midday should feed her beforehand.

What Other General Feeding Recommendations Would You Offer? Feed your pup either in her crate or in a quiet, distraction-free area at the same time every day. Serve the kibble with a small amount of canned or fresh-frozen thawed meat for dogs, moistened with warm water. In place of meat, you may use cottage cheese or a cooked egg, and twice a week you could include a tablespoon of yogurt, which helps to restore intestinal flora. Give your pup fifteen minutes to finish her food; if she is not interested, pick it up without a fuss and refrigerate it. Later, warm up the leftover meal for the next feeding time — cold food can cause diarrhea.

Feeding should be a fairly straightforward process, one in which you train your pup and not vice versa. If your puppy goes on a hunger strike for a meal or two, wait her out. Many owners make the mistake of adding sizable amounts of meat and "people food" to get their pups to eat. Aside from disrupting the nutritional balance of the meal, this also produces puppies who are spoiled, finicky eaters. They learn to continually hold out for something better. Keep your feeding consistent — a premium, balanced kibble with a little canned meat is quite sufficient in most circumstances. Naturally, if your pup appears sick or does not eat for several days, take her to your veterinarian for an examination.

One other suggestion: never feed your pup from the table. Puppies fed in such a way, aside from becoming nuisances, tend to lose interest in their own food. Before you have your dinner, make sure your pup has already eaten and then train her to hold a down-stay a reasonable distance from the dinner table while you eat.

How Much Should I Feed My Pup? This will vary according to the particular breed and the individual dog. The recommendations on the bag or can are only general averages and must be adjusted by your own observation and understanding of your pup. However, beware of overfeeding; it is always better to keep your pup on the lean side than to let her get too heavy, since excessive weight in puppies can lead to serious future health problems. Conversely, if you can see your dog's ribs, either she needs more body fat and her food should be increased or you should have a fecal sample checked for possible parasites.

Should My Pup Always Have Water Available? While puppies need lots of water, we find it is preferable to offer it to them frequently rather than allowing them unlimited access to it. Puppies tend to gulp large amounts of water at once, causing house-training problems. Later, as the puppy gets bigger and is reliably house-trained, you can have water available at all times.

Grooming Your Puppy

Grooming is more than keeping your dog clean and attractive. It is an overall monitoring of your dog's physical health and appearance, and an aid in teaching her to be handled. Though many long-haired breeds require more time for brushing and coat maintenance than their short-haired counterparts, even tight-coated breeds require some brushing. Besides removing dead hair, dandruff, and dirt, brushing stimulates natural oils in a dog's hair and spreads them throughout her coat, giving it a healthy, well-cared-for sheen. All dogs benefit from this.

In addition to coat care, regular grooming allows you to check for fleas and ticks, dry or irritated skin, dirty ears that can easily become infected, eyes inflamed or irritated by foreign particles, tooth problems, and toenails in need of trimming. By examining your dog regularly, you will spot problems before they have a chance to develop into something more serious. Grooming helps keep your pup alert and healthy and saves on veterinary bills.

Starting Early Without a doubt, it is best to start grooming your pup as soon as you get her: people who delay this crucial step often have difficulties later on, particularly with nail clipping and ear cleaning. We begin routine grooming sessions as early as three weeks of age, so that by the time the puppies go off to their new homes they are fully acquainted with the process. This makes subsequent grooming by the owner a relatively simple procedure — one the pup learns to enjoy.

Brushing and Coat Care Because of the vast differences in grooming techniques for different breeds, we recommend that you check with your breeder or local professional groomer for specific tips on how to groom your puppy. Some breeds with long hair or dense, wiry coats require complex grooming procedures, and owners of these breeds should not attempt to clip or groom before they have received specific instruction. In general, however, most owners should have a metal

An assortment of grooming tools and materials is required for any puppy owner.

Most brushing should be done in the direction of the coat. Press down just enough to clean and massage the skin.

comb and a grooming brush appropriate to their pup's coat. For example, short-coated dogs (e.g., Doberman, beagle, boxer, Great Dane) need to be groomed with a bristle brush; breeds with double-textured coats (e.g., German shepherd, husky, chow chow) should be brushed with both a grooming rake and slicker brush; and breeds with long hair (e.g., Afghan, shih tzu, Maltese, Yorkshire terrier) do best with a combination of slicker and pin brushes, as well as a comb for final feathering.

We recommend daily brushing for a puppy, with sessions kept short and pleasant. Brush her either on the floor or on a steady table, as you prefer, and use a nonskid grooming mat or carpet to help keep her in position. Place the puppy on her side or in a sit and begin brushing gently. If the pup starts to struggle and give you a hard time, a firm shake with a "No, stay!" will help get her under control; follow immediately with praise.

The technique for brushing depends in part upon the coat type. In general, you should start by brushing the hair in the opposite direction, then conclude by brushing in the direction of growth. If your pup has long hair, be sure to ask your breeder about the best technique for your dog.

As you brush, speak to your pup in a soft, reassuring manner, and praise her when you finish. One bit of caution: if you use a grooming table, make sure you never leave your pup unattended. She might get curious and fall off the edge, breaking her leg or hurting herself in some other way. Keep one hand on her at all times.

Clipping Nails A dog's nails should be kept short by regular trimming. When nails are too long they cause the toes to spread and put unnecessary stress on the pasterns (wrist joints), making it difficult to walk. Also, long nails scratch people, furniture, and floors.

Though many owners are reluctant to try clipping nails themselves, if you start when you first get your pup and initially clip off only the tips, your dog will become comfortable with the process, and you will acquire more confidence in your own skills. You may want to have your

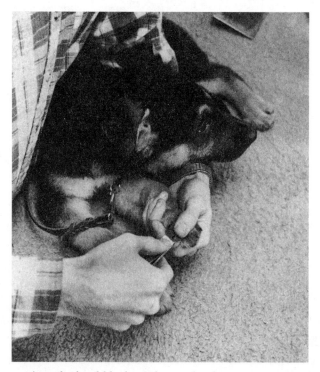

Your pup's nails should be kept short. Clip the tips once a week.

veterinarian or groomer show you the procedure firsthand. Another effective alternative is using a high-speed rotary tool that grinds the nail down in a way that keeps you from cutting into the quick. These tools are available online and in most pet stores.

We recommend clipping the nails once a week using professional clippers made for this purpose. Start off with two people, one to hold the puppy in place while the other does the clipping. After several sessions, the pup will become used to the procedure and only one person will be necessary.

To clip the nail, hold the paw with your hand and steady each toe individually by grasping it with your thumb and index finger. This allows you to control how much of the nail you take off with the clippers. Try not to cut into the quick, or the vein that runs partway up the nail. The quick is easy to see if your pup's nails are translucent, and you should clip just in front of it. However, if the nails are dark, the quick will be hidden and you must be more careful. This is why we suggest clipping off just the tips once a week. If you should accidentally clip the quick and cause a little bleeding, do not panic. Simply apply a little styptic powder or alum.

Cleaning Ears and Eyes We clean our dogs' ears once a week, using an otic cleanser such as Ear-Rite, available from your veterinarian or local pet-supply store. Place a generous amount into each ear, then massage the base of the ears for thirty seconds. After letting your pup shake the solution out, carefully wipe the visible portion of the ear around the canal with a cotton ball to remove residual wax. Do not probe too deeply into the ear canal, and avoid using Q-tips. A gentle swabbing is sufficient. If you notice your puppy shaking her head violently, scratching at her ears repeatedly, or having a foul smell coming from her ears, consult your veterinarian.

It is easy to check your pup's eyes every day for routine buildup of mucus and foreign particles that collect on the inside corners. When there is a buildup, take a small cotton ball moistened with warm water and dab the eye corners, freeing the discharge. Never dab the cotton over the eyes, since fibers can scratch the eyeball. A recurring buildup of yellowish mucus or crusty foreign matter may indicate an infection and should be checked by your veterinarian.

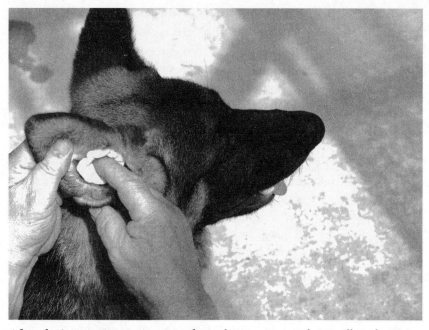

After placing a generous amount of otic cleanser into each ear, allow the pup to shake out, then wipe around the visible portion of the ears with a cotton ball or pad. Never use a Q-tip in the ear canal.

Bathing How often should you bathe your dog? It is generally not necessary to bathe most dogs on a regular basis, since dogs do not perspire as we do, and frequent bathing washes away natural oils that keep their hair shiny. Unless a dog is filthy or has rolled in something noxious, a bath twice a year is usually adequate. On those occasions, be sure to groom your dog before the bath and remove any tangles or mats. For shampoo, we suggest a pH-balanced product for dogs instead of a human version. Since dogs have more alkaline skin than people, human shampoos can cause itching or scaling. After the bath, make sure you thoroughly rinse out all of the shampoo and let your pup shake herself several times. When you are finished toweling her off, keep her out of drafts until she is completely dry.

Exercise

How much exercise does a dog need? All dogs require a daily vigorous workout for good health and sound behavior. The intensity, however, depends on the individual dog's breed. For example, daily requirements for an Irish setter are entirely different from those of a pug. Before you get a new puppy, make sure you have a realistic grasp of the amount of daily exercise needed for her breed. High-energy dogs who do not work out enough often develop problem behavior and give their owners fits.

In general, a four-month-old puppy should be tired out from exercise twice a day. Be creative and responsible in this: exercise involves more than walks for elimination. Do not work out your pup by allowing her to run free throughout the neighborhood—a sure recipe for problems. Along with walks and hikes, play fetch with her in a fenced-in yard or an enclosed area near your home. If you jog, beware of taking your pup with you at too early an age, since the stress on her joints might lead to problems. Wait until she is at least six months of age. Swimming is another great activity for dogs; if you provide this opportunity for them when they are young, they learn to enjoy it immensely.

Also, daily obedience training is important exercise for a pup; the energy and concentration demanded in a training session help to tire her out. Make the sessions snappy and interesting, and strive to keep your pup focused on you. Remember, there are many different ways to responsibly provide your pup with exercise, and the bonus is that all of them improve the quality of life for you and your dog.

19

Troika: When the Relationship Transforms

Dogs began a life of domestication as slaves rather than allies, and the warm relationship that has since developed and indeed was in existence in early dynastic times in Egypt developed gradually, together with mutual understanding and regard. It is a truism to say that the dog is largely what his master makes of him: he can be savage and dangerous, untrustworthy, cringing, and fearful; or he can be faithful and loyal, courageous, and the best of companions and allies.

— Richard and Alice Fiennes,
The Natural History of Dogs

If we have gone to some lengths throughout this book to explore the various elements of a successful relationship with a puppy, it is because *your* effort is crucial in the relationship. When you take the time and energy necessary to raise a puppy correctly, wonderful things happen. The dog becomes a friend.

In the following pages, we present three stories (a *troika*) — about two German shepherds and a Bernese mountain dog — to exemplify what we have discussed. Similarly inspiring examples can be found in any breed. Our intention is to encourage you and to illustrate the underlying message of this book: that when owners take their dogs seriously as companions, when they take the time to raise them with intelligence, love, and effort, friendships develop that are unique and transforming. Such relationships take the dog-human bond beyond the boundaries of what most people expect and significantly improve the quality of human life.

Moritz

Think "dog" and what spontaneously arises in the mind is most often the loyalty and devotion they express toward us, sometimes in the most remarkable of circumstances. Innumerable tales of rescue, comfort, and healing confirm that their connection with us is more than human projection; it's a grace we could never merit.

—Dogs & Devotion

Barry Schieber hadn't planned on coming back from Europe with a puppy in the summer of 2000. Nor had he planned on discovering while traveling that he had an operable form of bladder cancer that required emergency surgery. Yet, as often happens in life, unanticipated events conspired to become part of a broader mystery that took his future in new and stimulating directions. Happily, Barry's story has resulted in a unique partnership that reveals how the human-dog relationship can bring an abundance of joy in unexpected ways. To understand this is to journey into the remarkable tale of Moritz, a Bernese mountain dog whom Barry adopted in Switzerland ten years ago and who has become the principal subject of a number of Schieber's heartwarming books.

It was while Barry was recovering from his surgery in Switzerland that some friends from California stopped by who happened to be in the country at the same time. In the course of their visit Barry innocently asked how their dog Heidi was doing. The woman's eyes teared up at his question, as she and her husband had lost Heidi to torsion only a month earlier. "Heidi was such a wonderful dog," the woman said. "If we ever get a new dog it would have to be another Berner." Heidi was a Bernese mountain dog, a noble breed whose origins are in the Swiss Alps and whose name comes from the surrounding canton of Bern (hence the moniker *Berner*). Originally they were kept as farm dogs and accompanied herders and dairymen during their work. They were also used as draft animals and watchdogs. But today, there is no doubt that the Bernese mountain dog, with its striking tricolor coat and playful disposition, is known as one of the most beautiful breeds around, with a reputation for being a wonderful family dog—albeit a very *large* family dog (Berners typically weigh well over a hundred pounds).

Perhaps a seed was planted from that conversation, because a short time later Barry happened to be taking a stroll around a lake when he came upon a man walking a Bernese mountain dog. When Barry complimented the man on his beautiful dog, a lively conversation ensued. The man said he had obtained the animal from one of the greatest breeders in all of Switzerland. "As a matter of fact," he went on, "they just had a litter of puppies. Perhaps you should call them," which is just what Barry did. Three puppies were still available in the litter, so Barry took a ride to meet the breeders, a young couple who lived in the ancient pilgrimage spot of Flüeli-Ranft, where the patron saint of Switzerland, Brother Klaus, is buried near the Lake of Lucerne. Barry now remembers that all the puppies were friendly, obviously well-socialized by their breeders, and their mother, Deika, was both sweet and beautiful. Not having planned on a pup and never having had a dog before, Barry wasn't sure whether he should make a snap decision. So Pia, the breeder, said, "Go and think about it and then come back."

Over the next few days Barry turned things over in his mind, and the choice became clear to him. "For once in my life I'm going to make a decision with my heart," he said. But he also pledged to himself that if he went ahead with this step, he'd give his best to the pup, come what may. Although Barry didn't know it in advance, this heartfelt decision would change his life in important ways, enriching it in a manner he would understand only gradually through the experiences they shared together.

When Barry returned to Flüeli-Ranft, the pups were playing out in the yard. As he approached and watched, one of them came over and started to untie his shoelace. "So, how would you like to live in Montana?" Barry asked as he lifted the pup and cradled him in his arms. He had already decided on a name, Moritz, and after spending some time with the pup, he made arrangements with Pia to pick up Moritz shortly before his return to the United States. This fit the breeder's timetable exactly, as she explained that their practice was to keep litters until twelve weeks of age and handle all the preliminary socializing themselves. They wanted to ensure that their pups were exposed to all manner of experiences on a daily basis, a positive sign that they were serious breeders. Pia assured Barry that this would not negatively impact the pup's ability to bond with him, since the breeders would be actively socializing the whole litter every day. As Barry played with Moritz, he casually asked Pia how she was ever able to give them up. Her response stuck in his mind—a reflection of the quality of breeder he had stumbled upon: "I pour all the love I have into these pups, and then they in turn pour that love out onto all those whose lives they touch." That is a thought that resonates with our own experience as breeders.

The trip home and the transition into a new life in Montana was seamless. Barry said it took all of a few hours for Moritz to bond with him, and from their very first day together Moritz manifested a calmness and evenness of spirit that Barry found striking. Perhaps it was in part due to the fact that Montana and Switzerland are somewhat similar in topography, but from the start Moritz seemed to feel entirely at home wherever he happened to be.

Barry with his new Berner pup, Moritz.

Barry enrolled Moritz in a puppy class that turned out to be more of a puppy free-for-all, valuable for socializing with other pups but weak in any formal training structure. Moritz was always fairly calm and sociable with the other pups, but he also had the ability to disengage and walk away whenever the play turned too rough or whenever he was upset with another pup. It was an interesting mixture of tolerance and aloofness, but it reflected something deep in him. Barry refers to it as Moritz's "instinctive diplomatic skills," and the owner found that his dog's example left a deep impression on him. Since Moritz was growing so quickly and was bigger than most of the other pups, he could have been the bully and thrown his weight around. But instead Moritz chose to disengage, not in any sort of weak way but simply through lack of interest. It was an example to Barry, a lesson that inspired and reinforced his own values. He also came to realize that such daily occurrences with our pets are opportunities to train our minds and hearts, precious chances to expand our consciousness and live with greater joy. The only prerequisite is that we show up — that we be awake.

After about a month of bringing Moritz to puppy classes, Barry began working on the obedience exercises himself, and he found his dog to be a very quick study. Not only did Moritz learn the basic exercises without much difficulty, but since they lived in a fairly rural locale, Barry was often able to have his pup safely off-leash from an early age. Barry took Moritz with him everywhere, and Moritz always elicited the same response from the people he encountered: "What a beautiful, calm puppy." It was these remarks that helped Barry realize there was something unique and distinctive about his dog that could be shared with those in need.

Barry knew a bit about therapy dogs — animals who are certified to visit in hospitals — and it seemed to him that Moritz would be a perfect fit for such work. More than anything, it was Moritz's naturally calm disposition, coupled with more elusive traits that his owner describes as "intuitive and empathetic," that led Barry to consider this option. His feelings were confirmed by others often enough that he decided to act. Barry and Moritz attended a workshop through the Delta Society and studied a video detailing what was necessary to qualify for hospital work as a pet therapy dog. After a period of preparing and practicing for certification, Moritz took his test, which included a number of spontaneous distractions to determine his ability to deal with the unpredictability of a hospital environment. Moritz was the largest of the candidates, and he was tested for his reaction to loud noises, other dogs, and simulated patients. He easily passed the exam and was approved and certified as a pet therapy dog through the Delta Society, and Moritz and Barry were able to begin visiting hospitals on a weekly basis.

Many of those visits proved to be intense because of the impact Moritz had on the various patients — young children or older men and women, it did not really seem to matter: Moritz's gentle presence simply allowed each of them to take the focus off his or her suffering for a time and offered each a sense of respite. It is impossible to distill into one brief story the varied epiphanies of healing and comfort that patients both young and old experienced over years of Moritz's weekly visits to hospitals. These certainly didn't involve miraculous cures, but what they did reveal was Moritz's ability simply to be with patients in a way that consoled them and helped them heal. The "magic" was in the pure naturalness of the moment, so subtle you almost wouldn't notice it...until you witnessed its effects on the patient.

Moritz giving comfort to young Bella at the hospital.

Barry was so moved by these incidents that in time he started to write down his impressions after each visit and send them to his friends as a way of processing the events. In turn, his friends encouraged him to put his stories together in book form so that they could inspire others who faced similar circumstances or who were interested in the bond between human and dog. This resulted in the memoir *Nose to Nose*, which chronicles Moritz's encounters with various patients. Barry published the work through Silent Moon Books, a company he founded to promote issues he feels passionate about, such as pet therapy. Thus began something that Barry never anticipated when he first met the tiny puppy in Switzerland: a means to share with a much larger audience the significance of Moritz's ministry. The proceeds from the books also gave Barry a way to support various animal welfare projects. In particular, he directed the bulk of his efforts toward children, publishing a number of beautifully illustrated stories that are told from the perspective of Moritz. The tales are presented in a way that children can relate to, and collectively they communicate Moritz's gifts in a number of different contexts. The result is a portrait of Moritz that is compelling without being sentimental.

What is truly alive is never static. As the relationship between Barry and his dog has deepened over the years through extensive travel and companionship, so has the scope of the ways in which Moritz touches people. Going beyond the purely therapeutic dimension of visiting hospitals, Moritz has also been a presence at the Special Olympics; schools and libraries; a courtroom to support a child in an abuse case; and even the weekly meditation session Barry teaches in Montana. In fact, a story Barry tells in his book *Moments of Wonder* involves the aftermath of a meditation period. One of the participants began to cry because of thoughts that surfaced during the meditation. From his down-stay, Moritz got up and went over to the woman and stretched into a bow, then quietly looked into her eyes. The woman looked back, then reached out to him and pulled him close to her, petting him gratefully. His gentle presence helped release all her tension, and she left the class totally refreshed and renewed.

Of course, over the years Moritz has also been Barry's constant companion on frequent hikes into the wilderness, and there the owner sees another dimension of Moritz, one that isn't as visible when he is within city limits. Walking down a trail or moving through the hills, Moritz is full of life, totally alert. It is clear that he is completely aware of the possibility of another animal such as a bear or mountain lion suddenly appearing, and so he is on duty in a manner that impacts Barry as well. It is the quality of Moritz's attention, his "being in the moment," that exemplifies what many dogs bring to us if only we would notice. They keep us in the now in ways that are as ordinary as they are transforming. By taking us out of ourselves and helping us focus on what is right in front of us, dogs root us in reality. For humans, who so often get stuck in their heads, that is no small grace. It is something that never ceases to leave Barry in a state of wonder and gratitude.

Barry went with his heart when he chose to adopt Moritz, but it was a decision that was also informed by his will and intelligence. By following through on his promise to do his best these many years, both dog and owner have reaped the benefits of companionship. The result is a happy dog and a happy human being.

Both Barry and Moritz feel at home in the mountains.

Runge

The front door of the country house opens slowly, and a massive, richly colored German shepherd bolts across the front lawn toward the driveway, vigorously barking out his alarm. Despite the light layer of crystallized snow on the ground, the dog's gait is swift and sure, and as he pulls up effortlessly ten feet in front of us, his deep barking echoes from the ash, sugar maple, and locust trees that surround the property.

He stands tall, imposing.

His tail is erect, wagging ever so slightly, and his hackles are raised; his ears are straight and confident. He holds his position and continues to bark.

We try to appear calm and relaxed. We call his name, crouch low, and beckon him to come over. *"Runge, don't you remember?"* He ignores our greetings, absorbed as he is in a more important task: letting his master know that we have arrived.

A voice from the house calls out, "It's okay, Runge; they're friends."

Runge's loud barking gradually stops as his master, the artist Maurice Sendak, emerges from the house. While Maurice takes the front walkway to greet us, Runge waits patiently, continuing to eye us keenly and sniffing deeply, with his nose in the air. He lowers his hackles. After several moments his tail begins to wag in a more relaxed manner, betraying the first signs of recognition. It has been more than two years since Runge last saw us at New Skete, so his initial lack of recollection is perfectly understandable. Two years is a long time in canine chronology.

When Maurice finally reaches us, all trace of territorial posturing in Runge vanishes. Acting as though he is embarrassed by his former bravado, he joins fully in Maurice's warm greeting, circling around the four of us happily, wagging his elegant, bushy tail back and forth. Mercifully, he does not jump. Instead, he leans affectionately into us with his side and rump, enticing us to pet him.

"He's beautiful, isn't he?" says Maurice, vigorously rubbing the top of Runge's large head. As Maurice's hand passes gently down the neck and topline, Runge stands still. He is wonderfully proportioned, almost regal. He is a deep black-and-tan shepherd, big-boned, with a lush, full coat that makes him appear even larger than he is. Gray hairs surround the top of his muzzle, complementing his mature bearing.

For several moments, Maurice massages his fingers into the croup area above the tail, causing Runge to groan in pleasure. Twisting his head upward to meet Maurice's eyes, he holds eye contact for several seconds, then playfully dances off to the side as if encouraging us to follow him. "Come, come," says Maurice, ushering us toward the house. As Runge prances enthusiastically back and forth ahead of us, we follow him admiringly up the front walkway.

At five and a half years and ninety-eight pounds, Runge is a long way from the lively, twelve-week-old puppy Maurice came to get at New Skete. His poise, balance, and spirit confirm what was then only a promise, and watching him fully grown rekindles a sense of wonder at life's beauteous progression: nature melding with human care and responsibility. The fruit of that marriage today commands our respect and admiration. To understand Runge's progression, we must first examine his background.

Maurice is no stranger to dogs. As anyone who is familiar with his many illustrated books for children and adults knows, he has always had a profound interest in animals, dogs in particular. Indeed, a number of the dogs he has cared for throughout his adult life have been featured prominently in his books: Jennie, the spunky Sealyham terrier who appears in *Where the Wild Things Are* and who is the central character in *Higglety Pigglety Pop!*; Io, a golden retriever featured in *Some Swell Pup* and *Dear Mili*; and Erda, Aggie, and Runge, the German shepherds seen in *Outside Over There* and *Dear Mili*. His particular fascination with and love for German shepherds developed after reading J. R. Ackerley's deceptively charming tale *My Dog Tulip*. The story of Ackerley's extraordinary relationship with his German shepherd, Tulip (in real life, Queenie), moved Maurice so deeply that it prompted him to get his first shepherd, Erda. Years later, after his first two shepherds, Erda and Aggie, had died, he contacted New Skete about the possibility of getting a new puppy. Enter Runge.

Runge was born the morning of August 6, 1984, the Feast of the Transfiguration on our church calendar. He was the third of eight puppies from a breeding of New Skete's Natasha and Ch. Brimhall's Supercharger. From the first day, he was the largest in the litter, a very masculine puppy with a calm, confident temperament that never showed a lot of stress, and was quite playful. The early notes we made on him at five weeks focused on his balance and affection. "Though the biggest puppy in the litter, purple collar male [Runge] does not bully and interacts well with the other pups. Approaches people readily as well." On the puppy tests given at seven weeks, he manifested intelligence, curiosity, and sociability, and throughout the fear period (eight to ten weeks), we noted no obvious personality change. Basically he was an unflappable puppy, inquisitive yet not hyperactive. Because of that stability, we decided to place him with Maurice, believing that Runge would be able to fit into the fairly quiet, solitary lifestyle of an artist and still hold his own on social occasions.

Their first meeting was somewhat prophetic. Runge was already twelve weeks old when Maurice was finally able to come and get him. Prior work commitments abroad had made it impossible for Maurice to arrive any sooner, so Runge had to spend a month more than was usual in the puppy kennel. As we anticipated, he handled the month without difficulty, showing no signs of shyness, which might have been the case with some pups. In fact, when we finally brought him into our dining room to meet Maurice for the first time, he confidently marched right up to him and began pawing at Maurice's pants leg and hands — a bit of the "you did not choose me; I chose you" attitude. Later, after they had been playing together for a while, Maurice had to leave the room briefly to get something from his car. As he stepped over the puppy gate that we had set up to block off the room, Runge tried valiantly to follow him. He put his front paws on top of the divider and started whining impatiently, as if to say, "What about me?" The gesture captivated Maurice. He had asked for a pup showing poise and self-confidence, with a balanced temperament that could harmonize with his life as an artist. Since Maurice was a bachelor who worked at home, they would be spending a lot of time together, and Runge would need to adapt to a carefully structured, disciplined way of life. This seemed like a good start.

Over the years, Maurice has kept in close touch with us, periodically spending several days at the monastery for retreat and bringing Runge with him whenever possible. He also enrolled his dog in our three-week training program when Runge was eight months old, and was quite conscientious and disciplined about reinforcing that schooling afterward. This contact has given us the chance to observe Runge's development firsthand, over a long period of time, and to work with owner and dog on various dimensions of the whole relationship: training, handling, and management. We have seen not only the steady maturing of the dog but the maturing of a rich relationship as well. Maurice approaches Runge with the sensitivity of an artist, of one trained to see beneath the surface of things, and so brings a unique perspective to the dog-human dynamic. For him, the dog becomes muse not only to his creative work as an artist but to his self-understanding as well. Our desire to speak to him about this is why we now find ourselves at his home in Connecticut.

We are brought into a spacious, naturally lit living room that is comfortably reflective of Maurice's work and interests. Mickey Mouse artifacts, children's toys, and stuffed Wild Things are placed throughout the room on chairs, desks, and shelves, mingling naturally with beautiful posters by Toulouse-Lautrec and Winsor McCay. Books on art and music fill the shelves, and on the desk there is a haunting picture of Maurice walking down a nearby road with three dogs from his past: Erda, Io, and Aggie. A leather leash hangs on the knob of a set of doors that opens out onto a rolling backyard. While we chat informally, Runge stares attentively out the window at a group of mourning doves feeding in the backyard. His eyes blink repeatedly and his nostrils flare as he scrupulously studies their hopping around the ground for seed. He seems familiar with them, which is why he does not bark; nevertheless, they completely absorb his interest. His attentiveness befits his namesake, the German artist Philipp Otto Runge, a visionary painter of the early nineteenth century who, Maurice explains, blended an intense observation of nature with an intuitive awareness of the divine presence within it.

We call Runge away from his gazing, and he hops up onto the couch next to one of the monks, who shoots a quizzical look at Maurice.

"It's okay. In this house, couches are for dogs." Maurice chuckles, and almost simultaneously Runge leans his head affectionately into the monk with a pleased grin on his face. Rolling over on his back playfully, he paws at the monk, who returns the gesture with a couple of teasing pats of his own, and Runge begins to make a game out of it. He is totally at ease. After a while, Maurice goes into the kitchen to check on the coffee, and Runge quickly rights himself and follows him, returning just as quickly when his owner reenters with the drinks.

Maurice Sendak and Runge.

While we sit around the table to talk, Runge hops back on the couch and props his head on one of the cushions to watch us. He listens attentively, almost as if to witness that everything we talk about is true. He need not worry. In the ensuing conversation, Maurice becomes the real witness, continually expounding on a relationship that has grown and developed in many different ways.

Maurice, you speak of Runge as if he were not only a friend but a teacher as well. Most people don't think of their dogs this way. Why has this been the case for you?

Well, it's been a combination of things. Runge is the latest so far in a long line of dogs I've had, and I've been learning and getting better with each one. I've been best with him. I learned on Jennie, she suffered a lot, and then on Erda, and Io, and on Aggie. Each of these has been a relationship that is privately intense, unlike relationships with most friends. You wouldn't dare reveal to your friends what you reveal to your dog. With our dogs we wear no masks. A dog is so ruthlessly and unashamedly honest in the demands it makes of you; it is entirely dependent, and that need can provoke some surprisingly strong reactions from us. And so, in seeing myself through him, I see how many unpleasant aspects of my nature have to be repressed simply because I love him. Because of the way he has developed, I've had to try to give up certain bad habits, out of real respect for him. It would be totally inappropriate to behave in those ways. And, of course, I benefit from that repression, or self-discipline.

You say, "It would be totally inappropriate to behave in those ways." In what ways?

Well, losing my temper, for example, which is only too easy for me. I have a violent temper that, at times, I've taken out on him. Yet, in spite of this, he's been the healthiest dog I've ever had. My anger doesn't really faze him, and because of his strength and loyalty, I've come to see how inappropriate such behavior is.

His stability prompts you to change?

To work on that and to change myself, yes, absolutely. It seems to me that the way you relate to your dog is a subtext to the way you relate to everything and everybody. Since dogs are so transparent, they mirror you back to yourself, and the challenge for us is to take that seriously. Unless you're totally crazy, you can't use the reflection to make a case against the dog. It has to be you.... So the value of the dog who is balanced and well trained is that he helps you develop as a human being.

So the relationship with your dogs has been the fertile ground for a new level of consciousness?

Precisely. To put it almost too simplistically, it is like reliving your childhood with each dog—each time slightly improving because you see the mistakes you've made with each pup. When you see the dog cowering away from you, just as you likely did with your own parents, it forces you to look at yourself. Runge doesn't shrink away from me because I simply could not bear that. So I've had to learn to prevent that from happening. That means repressing all sorts of feelings inside yourself. It's as though you have a blueprint inside, not a good one either, and you tend to act out unconsciously on that blueprint. But with each dog, as you improve, the dog improves, because your self-training is better. You're emotionally calmer, more conscious. So, in that sense, Runge has benefited from all the other dogs.

What you're really saying is that the dog speaks the truth to us about ourselves. Yet most of us don't want to face that. Why haven't you been able to ignore it?

First, because I don't know how to — but, luckily, as an artist, that is a gold mine. Despite the fact that these experiences can be extremely painful emotionally, personally they are the pure gold I mine in all my work. Which is why, in another way, he's the miner — he digs for me, unwittingly. He brings up the ore that I use in my work. By living with him I experience these very primitive feelings in myself all the time, and either I use them against him when I'm bad or I repress them and deal with them when I'm good, or, best of all, I get them on paper, which is why he's in the picture. He's the miner, he's the digger; he brings it up. Nobody else does this in the same way. People can't, because socially I can control those situations. Most of us can. We don't reveal that deeper side to each other. We talk about it . . . but when you are alone with the animal, I'll tell you — like I suspect happens with mothers and their babies — things happen which are quite uncontrollable and terrifying. Socially unacceptable behavior occurs because you are now dealing with a nonverbal creature and reliving, perhaps, a nonverbal moment from your own past.

The dog can't tell anyone!

The dog can't tell. And a baby can't tell. Babbling won't help and barking won't make a bit of difference. Language is terrible in the way it is contrived to mislead you. Runge doesn't have language, and so he can't deceive. A baby can't either. A baby, if you hold him the wrong way, will scream because he knows he is in danger, and he screams to be put in arms that are safe. The mother takes him, and he is immediately pacified. Why? Because he is now safe and knows how to tell you directly and emphatically. So does the dog. I mean, the dog that flinches from you . . . that hurts. It's no joke.

Runge moves off the couch and saunters over to Maurice, who brushes his hand along the dog's neck for a few moments. He then quietly says to Runge, "Okay, that's a good boy, go on back to the couch." Runge obeys without complaining and, giving a long yawn, settles his head onto the cushion once more as Maurice continues.

But when you face that side of yourself honestly, there is a purification that can occur if you let it, one that helps free you from yourself. Runge doesn't know it, but he's helped me grow tremendously. Through this relationship I've lost some impediments in my life, and I have to assume that I've lost them in my other relationships as well. But this is the one I see it in most.

The effect is transfiguring?

Absolutely. I mean, I'm happier now than I've ever been. It's true. A lot of it is him, maybe most of it is him, but I've been growing up and freeing myself of these shadows. The significance of Runge is that I see how I'm freeing myself through him. I don't see how I'm doing that in any other way because the relationship I share with him is incredibly intense and basic. He shares my room, he shares my bed, he shares my every thought. So much so that it's obvious to me when things change in him for better or for worse, and it's been that way with every animal I've ever had. No doubt I've profited by his being a solid citizen, because if he were a nervous dog we would have had a terrible time. Yet you knew when I got him that he was a tough little bugger. It is his toughness of spirit that has really made me learn. I'll never get over it: I've never intimidated him. Only once or twice when I really got upset at him did he worry, but in general, no. And yet in five years there was only once when he didn't come when he was called.

Would you say that it is the most important relationship you have?

In a very particular sense, yes, I would say so.

Perhaps because you connect with him in a unique way?

I connect with him in a most crucial way that I don't with other people. It has to do with infant intimacy. Since I'm an artist who really thrives on early memory, whose main talent is to mine this thing we've been speaking about and to handle it quite honestly, without softening it or holding it up in a rosy light…that isn't a subject you can discuss with most people. It's not what concerns them. But that's what concerns me! My life, after all, is devoted to being an artist and the best artist I know how, and I have no grandiose concepts of my talent. I have one subject, which is childhood, and I have one intention before I kick the bucket and that's to mine it as much as I can, to really dig down to where the subsoil is. And Runge is my most intimate companion in this project, because I relate to him in this nonverbal way. We journey together.

The doorbell interrupts the conversation. Runge springs from the couch immediately and starts barking as he moves toward the door, while Maurice follows him. A UPS delivery. When Maurice tells him it's okay, Runge stops barking and stands by his owner's side, wagging his tail, as Maurice signs the receipt and thanks the deliveryman. They return, and Runge resumes his watch on the couch.

You were speaking just a moment ago about your work as an artist and the relationship Runge and your other dogs have had with it. When considering your art, one senses the intuitive dimension you bring to it; meanings are thrown in constantly. In a sense, the drawings seem to grow out of your life. What has always struck us about your use of dogs and animals is how they are not decorative objects at all but instruments of meaning. They're always there; you never miss them. Yet it's curious that none of your interpreters has ever picked up on that.

You're right. In my entire career no one has picked up on the significance animals play in my work. They all see it as "Oh, isn't that sweet — he puts his dog in his pictures, just like Hitchcock appeared in a cameo in every one of his movies." That's as much as most people think about what I have done. They have no idea what it means to me. It isn't a conceit that my dogs are there in all my books. Without even being consciously aware of it or trying to draw a particular lesson, I know that dogs are in my books as a reflection of my behavior all the time, of my advance through life. For example, just as Jennie changed graphically, starting to look better as I learned to draw better, I improved as a person as I drew. She was an icon. She had to appear in the books. That's how I registered myself, through my whole relationship with her, with my relationship with the world. So it climaxes in *Some Swell Pup*, that little book where kids get it and say, "Mommy, that's how you treated me," because there is no difference between the nature of a human child and the nature of a puppy. Basically, if you're an indifferent person, a callous person, a sadistic person, you will not differentiate. You'll treat the child just as badly.

Then there is your picture book of the Grimm tale "Dear Mili," where, in the context of a story about a little girl and her mother's passage into the next world, we observe the presence of your dogs throughout the book.

That's right. When people say, "What is that book to you?" I use a word that baffles them, and even me sometimes, but I know it's the correct word, and that is *grace*, pure grace. *Outside Over There* [an earlier picture book] features the same mother, the same atmosphere, the same mood; however, it is full of strife and it ends in strife. *Dear Mili* ends in a solution, and I don't mean death is a solution. It transcends the mere fact of the girl and her mother dying. There's a grace note in it. So it is an amalgamation of things. All my dogs are in it: Runge as a pup, Aggie, Io, and Erda when she was old and near death. So I'm painting this picture of my relationships, and I'm coming to a solution to *Outside Over There* in *Dear Mili*. Where in *Outside Over There* the story ends on a truculent note, where this poor kid gets a letter from her father that dumps this problem on her, in *Dear Mili* something is at peace. Me, that's what's at peace. That book is the rounding off of so much of my life that I can't even gather it all up. And the paradox is that it's such a sad story.

When you look back over these past five years with Runge, how has your perspective on raising dogs changed?

I think of an almost comical thing that happened when I first came to you people: I told you what I had to have. I had to have a dog that would do this, do that. He had to be balanced. But I didn't realize that what I was saying was that the dog was going to have to provide for all the things I didn't have. He had to be the perfectly mature human being that I couldn't be, right? Now, the end of that story is not really the end. Happily I've learned it's me who does all that and, when I do, I get a dog who's like that. The dog can't deal with all of those things. You've got to give them to the dog, and then, if you do it right, you get back all the things you wish for.

Which is precisely what we've been trying to say throughout our book!

The dog becomes your dream come true, the very thing you wanted. But *you* make your dream come true from hard work and application of principles, then you get the dog you hope for. Most of us don't want to accept that responsibility, accept how upsetting it is to raise a puppy and how much effort you have to go through to get what you want. Hard work, self-examination, disappointment, strain, anxiety…all those go into making something happen. And there are no guarantees either. But with Runge, it's like a miracle because he's exactly the dog I hoped to get from you. The paradox is that I had everything to do with that. Before, you were to provide me with a guaranteed puppy, like those little Japanese flowers you put into water and they grow up in two minutes. You were to provide me with a guaranteed German shepherd puppy who would look beautiful, be perfect, and grow up to be Rin Tin Tin in a matter of two years. You promised, that's the guarantee! That's quite a difference, isn't it?

Indeed!

There's one other thing, and it's perhaps the best thing that's happened with Runge. With almost every other dog I've had, the dog was first Philip and Sadie Sendak's baby before it was the dog. Runge is the first dog I've had who finally has been transformed from Philip and Sadie's baby into a dog. He's not me anymore; it's been a long birthing, but he's now a beautiful German shepherd and no longer a cranky kid. He's a dog. He's stopped being me. He's become this gorgeous animal, and the baby, to make an image of it, has disappeared. He's gone; he can come up in books and always in my work, but finally my vision is focused, and I see a dog.

Runge hops off the couch and comes over to Maurice, whining. He butts his nose against Maurice's arm and then paces back and forth several times. It is close to 4:00 in the afternoon and time for his walk. A respectful hint. "Yes, I know, Runge, we'll go out in just a minute." Maurice looks back at us with a smile. "That's just the way he is. He loves the daily routine, the walks, the different timetables. For example, we nap every day. I take a nap at five thirty. And if it gets a little late, he'll look at me like, 'When are we going to nap? It's twenty-five to six, what's the matter with you?' He's so ritualized, it's wonderful."

We follow Runge out the front door, and immediately he sweeps across the lawn with his nose riveted to the ground, zigzagging as if to catalog all the smells. Gradually he zeros in on a scent of particular interest at the base of one of the locust trees. Sniffing it thoroughly for several seconds, Runge licks the bark tentatively with his tongue. Finally he draws his head up and cocks his rear leg high in the air, dousing the trunk proudly with his mark. He then picks up a stick nearby and trots over to the driveway to say good-bye to us.

As we pull out of the driveway and proceed down the main road, the last view we have of Maurice and Runge is the pair crossing into the adjacent field, with Runge leaping into the air for the stick Maurice holds in his hand.

Dux

Whenever we bring a dog into our life, we imagine the potential joy the animal will bring, the companionship, the deeper connection with the natural world that comes from caring for a dog. We don't anticipate being confronted with an emergency situation or a major illness when the animal is young. While we no doubt understand that at some point the dog will pass away (likely sooner than we will), most of us expect this to happen years in the future. We rarely acknowledge that death could occur at any time and that each day we share with our dog is a gift. It is only when we suddenly face a serious health crisis that we come to understand this in a new, more visceral way.

This is precisely the sort of challenge Julia Gates experienced as she watched Dux, a four-year-old German shepherd, progressively become sicker and sicker over the course of several days in November 2009, to the point where she actually began fearing for his life. Julia works at the monastery, assisting Brother John in the breeding program. She had been caring for Dux, one of our breeding studs, for a year and a half, ever since Brother John could no longer keep him due to upcoming hip-replacement surgery. Julia had agreed to take responsibility for Dux for as long as necessary until Brother John was well enough.

To say Julia had gone beyond the call of duty in caring for him would be an understatement. Apart from the ordinary tending and exercise any good owner will provide her dog, Julia had taken Dux through the Canine Good Citizen program and helped him earn certification as a therapy dog so that he could visit Brother John in the hospital. "I just realized what it was going to be like for Brother John during his recovery, which he'd have to spend away from the monastery," Julia says. "Imagine what life without a dog would be like for a man who had lived closely with dogs for forty years. So I went for the training and certification." This allowed Dux to visit Brother John regularly, providing comfort not only for him but for any number of other patients on the floor of the medical facility. After his return from the operation and a long stint in rehab, Brother John boasted to us with great pride how wonderful Dux had been. In particular, Brother John never tired of telling stories of how Dux was a special source of comfort to severely affected patients, such as one man whose leg had been amputated and who was having a very difficult time accepting his new condition. The simple act of petting Dux relaxed the man to the point where he could talk about a wonderful dog he had had years before and about the pet's importance to him. This simple step helped release a flood of emotions necessary for him to truly heal and achieve a certain measure of peace and acceptance. Indeed, Dux had matured into a handsome, friendly German shepherd, an extremely valuable stud dog as well as a multitalented Canine Good Citizen — a wonderful centerpiece of our breeding program.

Now, having endured two sleepless nights with Dux as he periodically dry heaved, Julia was deeply worried: Dux looked terrible, and the vomiting hadn't stopped. It had all started a couple of days earlier when, during the late afternoon, Julia had first noticed Dux in the yard vomiting. *He must have eaten something,* Julia remembers thinking. But when he had several more episodes that evening, she decided to contact our veterinarian, Dr. Tom Wolski, first thing in the morning. He advised her to bring Dux in. Dr. Wolski examined Dux thoroughly and took X-rays, but he didn't find anything suspicious. He thought it might be some sort of virus and prescribed a twenty-four-hour fast, the normal course in such a situation. However, that night Dux was suffering again. The following morning Dr. Suzanne Fariello, another veterinarian on staff, put him on IVs to provide him with fluids, as he was dehydrated. After a day of this, Dux seemed to be doing better. Julia took him home that evening, since the doctor felt he would be more comfortable in his own surroundings. But the script turned out the same: intermittent vomiting and, by morning, an ever sicker Dux. Julia remembers updating both Dr. Fariello and the monastery over the phone: "We really need to do something. This is getting worse, and I'm scared that if we don't act now we're going to lose him." When Dux arrived at the clinic that morning, he indeed looked terrible. Dr. Fariello decided to order another X-ray, and that is when she saw his enlarged spleen dominating the shot — a spleen that had apparently rotated from all the vomiting of the past few days. Dux was suffering from torsion of the spleen, a condition that would quickly turn lethal unless Dr. Fariello operated immediately. At once the doctor began the operation, and when it was finished, the removed spleen — normally the size of cube steak — looked more like a large pork tenderloin. Because of the surgery, Dux was alive and stable, and Julia was able to be with him as he awoke from the anesthesia. The incision ran from the center of his sternum down toward his lower end. Dux would no doubt be in some real pain, so he stayed at the animal hospital for another day to recover under the staff's observation. But the next day he was much better, and with certain restrictions in place that would extend throughout his recovery, he was able to go home.

"Will he still be able to breed?" Julia remembers asking Dr. Fariello, who reassured her that once he recovered Dux could pretty much go back to normal and could still be used at stud. The functions of the spleen would be taken up by other organs. Dux could also resume his normal activities of play and therapy work. The only restriction on him was that he couldn't travel overseas because of his vulnerabilities to nondomestic bugs.

During the next several weeks, Julia and her son, Nate, were responsible for nursing Dux back to full health and keeping him as still as possible, with only short walks on-leash and without any running or jumping. Julia confessed that this was a bit of a challenge, as Dux is an energetic dog with a tendency to play at higher octane levels than Dr. Fariello had recommended. But Dux got through the crucial first days without incident, and because of the time that both Julia and Nate spent with Dux, the bond among them seemed to deepen, something that Brother John was very aware of. Still in the process of recovering from his own hip surgery, Brother John felt that he wasn't yet in a position to care for the dog. He also saw how well Dux was being attended to by Julia and the clear attachment that had formed between Dux and Julia's entire family, so he decided not to take Dux back. "It simply wouldn't have been fair to them. They had invested so much love and energy into caring for Dux, and he had really blossomed in the past couple of years. I felt it was better if they kept Dux with them. I mean, I had him for a time after he came to our breeding program from Germany as a mature pup. He was a joy, a dog I really loved. But, realistically, Julia and her family are in a much better position to give Dux the opportunities to use his therapy certification. And I can't help thinking that they can give him a more active and fulfilling life." Brother John added with a glint in his eye, "I just can't get around now like I used to."

And "getting around" is precisely what Dux has been doing since his recovery. In addition to coming to work with Julia every day, Dux returned to his own "job": visiting children at the local school who have learning disabilities. Before his illness, Dux would spend a weekly session with young students who were learning to read. Teachers found that the presence of the dog helped these students to relax — because the kids didn't have to perform in front of their peers. Nevertheless, the

Dux with a grade-school class.

audience was definitely "live" all the same, and it allowed students to overcome their self-consciousness. Dux would simply lie on the floor of the classroom and look up attentively at the kids as they practiced their reading, one by one, in front of him. This program has been a great success, and Dux's presence has clearly offered real encouragement to the children. In fact, during the time of Dux's convalescence, Julia would run into students from the program in town, and they would ask, "How is Dux? When is he coming back to class, Ms. Gates?"

Dux's help at school even extended in a special way to Julia's son, Nate, who for a time was bashful about participating in the reading program with Dux. Perhaps it was his self-consciousness in front of his own dog, but at first he chose to avoid the session, and Nate's teachers respected his feelings. As Nate became more and more attached to Dux—as he played with him daily after school, and especially after being involved in the process of caring for him during his illness—Julia noticed something important taking place in her son. Nate was becoming more spontaneously affectionate with Dux, which in turn encouraged him to

Dux loves to be read to.

come out of himself and his own shyness, allowing him to be more relaxed with his classmates. Since Dux had become so welcome and popular at school, Nate took pride in the fact that it was his dog who was doing this good work. It freed Nate to talk very naturally about Dux to his classmates, and this helped him deal with his shyness. Even more significant for Julia, Nate finally expressed a desire to participate in the reading program with Dux. Now her son reads with Dux at home, sitting comfortably with the dog at his side. Dux has even become the mascot for Nate's lacrosse team. He is a proud observer at all the games, providing encouragement for the team as they play this very demanding sport.

Some people have a difficult time understanding the lengths good owners will go to in order to ensure the health of their dogs. Many times over the years we've heard comments about how spending a lot of money on a medical condition for the sake of a dog is just not reasonable. It's no mystery that such comments do reflect a real ignorance — ignorance of all that a dog can do to enhance the quality of human life. Dux's story is just one example. He has helped so many in a variety of ways — is there any question that we would do all we could to ensure his health and survival? To see it any other way would reduce the dog to an object solely for the amusement of human beings. It would deny the uniqueness, the individuality, of each particular dog in a manner that would violate his spirit and dishonor our humanity. The more faithfully we care for our dogs, the more we will engage with all of life, and the more we will cultivate an attitude of reverence and respect for life's interconnectedness. That's no small thing.

A New Way of Seeing

To make an end is to make a beginning.
The end is where we start from....
And the end of all our exploring
Will be to arrive where we started
And know the place for the first time.

—T. S. Eliot, *Four Quartets*

There is a story recounted by a seventh-century Christian monk named John Moschus about an old abba [monk] living in an isolated monastery in Palestine with his dog. One day, a monk from another community brings word of an important gathering that will take place at the monastery of Besorum — all the monks of the region are supposed to attend. After receiving the brother graciously, the old abba assures him that he will be present at the meeting and, thanking him, begins to see the man off.

At this point, the story takes a curious turn. As the brother is about to depart, he nervously explains to the abba that he still must journey farther into the wilderness to notify the brothers at the distant monastery of Charembe. The trek will be long, and, since he has never been there before, the brother is afraid of getting lost. He even asks the abba if he would be willing to deliver the message instead, since he knows the way. The old abba smiles and tells him not to worry. Calling over his little dog, he says to the animal, "Go with this brother as far as the monastery of Charembe, so that he may give them his message." Moschus then concludes the story, "And the dog went away with the brother, till he brought him in front of the gate of the monastery."

The story's simplicity lends itself naturally to meditation. First, we feel the connection between the abba and his dog; besides the

Companionship with a dog is a lifelong process that begins as soon as you start to care for your pup. Through conscientious training, loving insight, and affection, your relationship will grow and grow.

noteworthy fact that the abba even has a dog (apparently quite rare in monastic tradition), what stands out is the quality of that relationship, the harmony of understanding between the two. Only insofar as the dog is a companion to the abba is the animal able to guide the other monk.

And what of that monk? What must he have thought as he saw the abba solemnly instructing the dog to take him to Charembe? Moschus is silent about this, leaving us to imaginatively reconstruct the details. But given the particularly unsophisticated attitude toward dogs of Middle Eastern cultures of the time, the possibilities are quite interesting. The monk's initial reaction was probably a mixture of confusion, disbelief, and anxiety. Follow a dog into the wilderness on the simple word of an abba? On one level this would appear to be madness. Nevertheless, despite his misgivings, the monk would have been challenged to obey, since obedience is the heart of monastic living, the cornerstone of a monk's spiritual life. Thus, with the old abba reassuring him, we can easily imagine the monk walking tentatively into the desert, led only by the confident steps of the abba's dog.

And what happens in the desert? More than simply walking to a distant monastery, one would think. The desert becomes the locus of a deeper journey, one taking place in the monk's heart. As he follows the dog farther into the wilderness, he is forced to listen in an altogether new way, one rooted in the recognition of his own poverty. He is wholly dependent on a dog, a creature to whom in ordinary circumstances he would never give a thought, and the experience changes him forever. With the dog leading him steadily through the desert, he becomes increasingly aware of his presumption, his lack of respect, his insensitivity to mystery. The dog is now no longer an object, a thing, but a separate creature responsible for his safety. In a culminating moment of insight, the brother perceives that his view of the dog has been only a reflection of his basic attitude toward life, toward the world around him. The result is that he "sees" the dog — and life — in a completely new way. The dog is different from him, yet even in that difference the animal embodies a dignity all his own — one the brother learns to respect. In such a meditation, as we imagine the monk emerging from the desert at the gate of Charembe, we believe him to be both humbler and wiser, now approaching life from a different perspective.

What of ourselves? In actuality the monk's journey is everyone's journey, though in our frenetic world of activity and distraction we often miss the fact that we are also desert wanderers. Who or what leads us? In this day and age, we are dangerously out of touch with the nonhuman world around us, leaving our hearts dulled and our vision blurred. Nothing impresses us anymore, and we travel farther into a disharmonious cavern of individualism, with ourselves as guides. We arrogantly "process" reality through preconceived notions that are sterile and cold. Our world is stripped of a profound and compelling mystery.

This is blind ignorance. Humankind is in desperate need of recovering its connection with nature, for ultimately this will mean the recovery of ourselves. We become self-aware by tuning in to the world around us — a world filled with the presence of God. Without falling into mawkish sentimentality, we must learn to look at nature as an expression of God's goodness and love, a feast of sight and sound that provokes wonder and amazement. This seems to be what the nature writer Henry Beston was getting at when he wrote in *The Outermost House:*

We need another and a wiser and perhaps a more mystical concept of animals. Remote from universal nature, and living by complicated artifice, man in civilization surveys the creature through the glass of his knowledge and sees thereby a feather magnified and the whole image in distortion. We patronize them for their incompleteness, for their tragic fate of having taken form so far below ourselves. And therein we err, and greatly err. For the animal shall not be measured by man. In a world older and more complete than ours they move finished and complete, gifted with extensions of the senses we have lost or never attained, living by voices we shall never hear. They are not brethren, they are not underlings; they are other nations, caught with ourselves in the net of life and time, fellow prisoners of the splendor and travail of the earth.

To see the world in this manner is to have deep respect for nature's astonishing diversity, to be conscious that it is balanced and related in a mysterious unity. We, too, are interrelated. This does not mean we're being swallowed into some vague, homogeneous cosmic order; rather, we're being challenged to participate consciously in a living communion with God through one another and the whole of creation, attentively listening to the vast symphony of life.

The word *symphony* (from the Greek for "sound together") is significant here. In the tradition of the Christian East, it refers to the idea that all of the individual elements of the created universe, in addition to being interconnected, are ultimately dependent upon God for their existence. To speak metaphorically, these elements are like countless pieces of a vast orchestra that, when played together, produce a harmonious melody of beauty and grace. When we hear the "music" within our hearts, we experience life in a new way, as if seeing the world for the first time. When that happens, the only proper and true response is reverence and respect. This is precisely what the Russian author Fyodor Dostoyevsky emphasizes in *The Brothers Karamazov*, when he has the saintly Starets Zosima exhort his disciples:

Brothers, love God's creation, love every atom of it separately, and love it also as a whole; love every green leaf, every ray of God's light; love the animals and the plants and love every inanimate object. If you come to love all things, you will perceive God's mys-

Healthy and balanced exercise and activity — through work and play — leave pups tired enough to get their needed sleep.

tery inherent in all things; once you have perceived it, you will understand it better and better every day. And finally you will love the whole world with a total, universal love.

For many of us, this love for creation deepens through the relationships we form with our pets, particularly our dogs. By their very makeup and need, dogs draw us out of ourselves: they root us in nature, making us more conscious of the mystery of God inherent in all things. When we take the time and energy necessary to raise our puppies correctly — when we learn to truly listen to them, seeing them as they really are and guiding their development accordingly — a deeper part of ourselves is unlocked. We become more compassionate and less arrogant, more willing to share our lives with another life. And when that happens, we learn the real meaning of happiness.

Evolution and Interpretation of the Puppy Test

Puppy evaluation began in a systematic and objective way with the Fortunate Fields project in Switzerland in the 1920s and '30s. This philanthropic organization developed an elaborate system for evaluating German shepherd dogs for various tasks, most notably for guiding the blind, and then used these results to develop a successful breeding program.

Important advances occurred later, with the research project of John L. Fuller and John Paul Scott in Bar Harbor, Maine. As we have seen, their studies in canine behavior, especially the formulation of "critical periods," have had a profound impact on the way puppies are raised and evaluated. The practical consequences of this work are most clearly seen in Clarence Pfaffenberger's book *The New Knowledge of Dog Behavior*. After drawing heavily on Scott's and Fuller's research and personal advice, Pfaffenberger presented a system for breeding and evaluating puppies that focused on guide dogs, with astounding results: When he began his work in the mid-1940s, only 9 percent of the dogs who started guide-dog training graduated from the program. When he published his findings in the 1960s, 90 percent graduated successfully.

Pfaffenberger stresses the importance of understanding genetics (breeding only dogs of proven working ability and health) as well as implementing early socialization techniques and puppy evaluations. He tested puppy responses to such stimuli as new experiences and encounters with strangers, and evaluated their body sensitivity and overall problem-solving ability. Although the goal of Pfaffenberger's program was the development of consistently sound guide dogs, his work represented a significant breakthrough in breeding as well, by showing that temperament could be reliably evaluated at a very early age; puppy reactions at eight to twelve weeks could predict adult potential.

For the general public, the first workable standardized test for puppies was the Puppy Behavior Test, published by the animal psychologist William E. Campbell in his important and innovative work *Behavior Problems in Dogs*. Though the book was initially designed for veterinarians and other professionals as a source of practical answers to frequently asked behavioral questions, it also included an excellent chapter on puppies that discussed testing and selection, elementary training, and common problems. His puppy test gave breeders and potential owners a consistent and successful way of sizing up puppies that continues to form the basis for more contemporary adaptations.

In our experience, the most successful of these recent evaluations is the Puppy Aptitude Test developed by Jack and Wendy Volhard. This test takes elements from each of its predecessors (Fortunate Fields, Pfaffenberger, and Campbell) and integrates them into one system. The result is a puppy evaluation that reliably measures individual temperament (i.e., dominance versus submission and independence versus social attraction) as well as obedience and working potential. (A detailed explanation of this test — "A Novice Looks at Puppy Aptitude Testing" by Melissa Bartlett — appeared in the March 1979 issue of the *AKC Gazette*.)

The first five sections of the test, an evaluation of temperament, are based entirely upon Campbell's test and reveal a pup's general orientation toward people, measuring his social compatibility and how readily he accepts human leadership.

Puppy Aptitude Test

Date: _____	Age: _____wks	Puppy # _____	M / F	D.O.B.: _____

TEST

SOCIAL ATTRACTION:
The owner or caretaker of the puppy places him in the test area, about four feet from the tester, and then leaves the test area. The tester kneels down and coaxes the puppy to come to him or her by encouragingly and gently clapping hands and calling. The tester must coax the puppy in the opposite direction from where the pup entered the test area. HINT: Lean backward, sitting on your heels, instead of leaning forward toward the puppy. Keep your hands close to your body, encouraging the puppy to come to you instead of trying to reach for the puppy.

FOLLOWING:
The tester stands up and slowly walks away, encouraging the puppy to follow. HINT: Make sure the puppy sees you walking away, and get the pup to focus on you by lightly clapping your hands and using verbal encouragement to coax the puppy to follow you. Do not lean over the puppy.

RESTRAINT:
The tester crouches down and gently rolls the puppy on her back and holds her there for thirty seconds. HINT: Hold the puppy down without applying too much pressure. The object is not to keep the pup on her back but to test her response to being placed in that position.

SOCIAL DOMINANCE:
The tester lets the puppy stand up or sit and gently strokes him from head to back while crouching beside him. The tester sees if the pup will lick his or her face, an indication of a forgiving nature. The pup is stroked continuously until he exhibits a behavior that can be scored. HINT: When you crouch next to the puppy, avoid leaning or hovering over him. Have the puppy at your side with both of you facing in the same direction. TOP-DOG TIPS: During testing, maintain a positive, upbeat, and friendly attitude toward the puppies. Try to get each puppy to interact with you to bring out the best in him. Make the test a pleasant experience for the puppy.

ELEVATION DOMINANCE:
The tester cradles the puppy with both hands, supporting the puppy under her chest, and gently lifts the pup two feet off the ground and holds her there for thirty seconds.

Dam / Sire _____ / _____ Color: Sable / Blk & Tan / Blk & Red / Blk

PURPOSE	SCORE	
Degree of social attraction to people, confidence or dependence.	Came readily, tail up, jumped, bit at hands.	1
	Came readily, tail up, pawed, licked at hands.	2
	Came readily, tail up.	3
	Came readily, tail down.	4
	Came hesitantly, tail down.	5
	Didn't come at all.	6
Willingness to follow a person.	Followed readily, tail up, got underfoot, bit at feet.	1
	Followed readily, tail up, got underfoot.	2
	Followed readily, tail up.	3
	Followed readily, tail down.	4
	Followed hesitantly, tail down.	5
	Didn't follow or went away.	6
Degree of dominant or submissive tendency, and ease of handling in difficult situations.	Struggled fiercely, flailed, bit.	1
	Struggled fiercely, flailed.	2
	Settled, struggled, settled with some eye contact.	3
	Struggled, then settled.	4
	No struggle.	5
	No struggle, straining to avoid eye contact.	6
Degree of acceptance of social dominance by a person.	Jumped, pawed, bit, growled.	1
	Jumped, pawed.	2
	Cuddled up to tester and tried to lick face.	3
	Squirmed, licked at hands.	4
	Rolled over, licked at hands.	5
	Went away and stayed away.	6
Degree of accepting dominance while in position of no control, such as at the veterinarian's or groomer's.	Struggled fiercely, tried to bite.	1
	Struggled fiercely.	2
	Struggled, settled, struggled, settled.	3
	No struggle, relaxed.	4
	No struggle, body stiff.	5
	No struggle, froze.	6

Puppy Aptitude Test (*continued*)

Obedience Aptitude

Date: _____ Age: _____ wks Puppy # _____ M / F D.O.B.: _____

TEST

RETRIEVING:
The tester crouches beside the puppy and attracts his attention with a crumpled piece of paper.
When the puppy shows some interest, the tester throws the paper no more than four feet in front
of the puppy, encouraging him to retrieve the paper.

TOUCH SENSITIVITY:
The tester locates the webbing of one of the puppy's front paws and presses it lightly between his
or her index finger and thumb. The tester gradually increases pressure while counting to ten and
stops when the puppy pulls away or shows signs of discomfort.

SOUND SENSITIVITY:
The puppy is placed in the center of the testing area, and an assistant stationed at the perimeter
makes a sharp noise, such as banging a metal spoon on the bottom of a metal pan.

SIGHT SENSITIVITY:
The puppy is placed in the center of the testing area. The tester ties a string around a bath towel
and jerks it across the floor, two feet away from the puppy.

STABILITY:
An umbrella is opened about five feet from the pup and gently placed on the ground.

Dam / Sire _____ / _____ Color: Sable / Blk & Tan / Blk & Red / Blk

PURPOSE	SCORE	
Degree of willingness to do something for you. Together with Social Attraction and Following, a key indicator for ease or difficulty of training.	Chased object, picked it up, and ran away.	1
	Chased object, stood over it, did not return.	2
	Chased object, picked it up, and returned with it to tester.	3
	Chased object and returned without it to tester.	4
	Started to chase object, lost interest.	5
	Did not chase object.	6
Degree of sensitivity to touch and a key indicator of the type of training equipment required.	8–10 count before response.	1
	6–8 count before response.	2
	5–6 count before response.	3
	3–5 count before response.	4
	2–3 count before response.	5
	1–2 count before response.	6
Degree of sensitivity to sound, such as loud noises or thunderstorms.	Listened, located sound, and ran toward it, barking.	1
	Listened, located sound, and walked slowly toward it.	2
	Listened, located sound, and showed curiosity.	3
	Listened and located sound.	4
	Cringed, backed off, and hid behind tester.	5
	Ignored sound and showed no curiosity.	6
Degree of response to a moving object, such as chasing bicycles, children, or squirrels.	Looked at, attacked, and bit object.	1
	Looked at and put feet on object, put mouth on it.	2
	Looked with curiosity and attempted to investigate, tail up.	3
	Looked with curiosity, tail down.	4
	Ran away and hid behind tester.	5
	Hid behind tester.	6
Degree of startle response to a strange object.	Looked at and ran to the umbrella, mouthing or biting.	1
	Looked at and walked to the umbrella, smelling it cautiously.	2
	Looked and went to investigate.	3
	Sat and looked but didn't move toward the umbrella.	4
	Showed little to no interest.	5
	Ran away from the umbrella.	6

* Developed from the test compiled and first published in the *AKC Gazette*, March 1979.

Interpreting the Scores

- *Mostly 1s* A puppy who consistently scores a 1 in the temperament section of the test is an extremely dominant, aggressive puppy who can be easily provoked to bite. Because of his dominant nature, he will attempt to resist human leadership, thus requiring the most experienced handler. This puppy is a poor choice for most individuals and will do best in a working situation, perhaps as a guard or police dog.

- *Mostly 2s* This pup is dominant and self-assured. He can be provoked to bite; however, he readily accepts firm, consistent, and knowledgeable human leadership. This is not a dog for a tentative, indecisive individual. In the right hands, he has the potential to become a fine working or show dog and could fit into an adult household, provided the owners know what they are doing.

- *Mostly 3s* This pup is outgoing and friendly and will adjust well in situations in which he receives regular training and exercise. He has a flexible temperament and adapts well to different environments, provided he is handled correctly. He may be too much dog for a family with small children or for a sedentary elderly couple.

- *Mostly 4s* A pup who scores a majority of 4s is an easily controlled, adaptable puppy who, due to his submissive nature, will continually look to his master for leadership. This pup is easy to train, reliable with kids, and, though he lacks self-confidence, makes a high-quality family pet. He is usually less outgoing than a pup scoring in the 3s, but his demeanor is gentle and affectionate.

- *Mostly 5s* This is a pup who is extremely submissive and lacking in self-confidence. He bonds very closely with his owner and requires regular companionship and encouragement to bring him out of his shell. If handled incorrectly, this pup will grow up very shy and fearful. For this reason, he will do best in a predictable, structured environment with owners who are patient and not overly demanding, such as with an elderly couple.

- *Mostly 6s* A puppy who scores 6 consistently is independent and uninterested in people. He will mature into a dog who is not demonstrably affectionate and who has a low need for human companionship. In general, properly socialized pups rarely test this way; however, breeds that have been raised for specific tasks (such as basenjis, hounds, and some northern breeds) can exhibit this level of independence, because they require a singularity of purpose that is not compromised by strong attachments to their owners.

The remainder of the puppy test is an evaluation of obedience aptitude and working ability, and provides a general picture of a pup's intelligence, spirit, and willingness to work with a human being. For most owners, a good companion dog will score in the 3 to 4 range in this section of the test. Puppies scoring a combination of 1s and 2s require experienced handlers who can draw out the best in them.

Acknowledgments

This new edition of *The Art of Raising a Puppy* is made possible by the friendship and generosity of many individuals over the past twenty-five years. While we have been breeding and training dogs here at the monastery for well over forty years, any expertise that has come to us is a combination of our own experience and the knowledge and wisdom of a wide variety of dog professionals — breeders, trainers, behaviorists, and veterinarians — who have graciously offered to share their skill and know-how to help us grow. We always will be deeply grateful to Helen Sherlock, Ruth Anderson, Robie Kaman, Wanda Rohloff, and Pat Rosson for the encouragement they provided us in the "early days" prior to the first edition of this book. We also would like to acknowledge Wendy Volhard; Peter Borchelt, PhD; Thomas Wolski, DVM; Donald Lein, DVM; Jeanne Carlson; and many others for their help with the original edition of this book.

In more recent years, our connection with the International Association of Canine Professionals (IACP) has been an invaluable source of inspiration and encouragement for us, and we are honored to belong to that organization. In particular, we would like to thank Martin Deeley, Marc Goldberg, Bob Jervis, Scott MacConachie, Mary Mazzeri, Maryna Ozuna, Aimee Sadler, and Pat Trichter for their assistance in answering specific questions related to this expanded and revised edition. Such willingness to share ideas professionally is one reason that the IACP is such a distinctive organization. Ronald Rompala, PhD, was especially helpful in clarifying for us issues related to canine nutrition, and once again we are grateful to Wendy Volhard for allowing us to use her updated Puppy Aptitude Test.

Here at New Skete, a special thank-you to Janine Lazarus, Julia Gates, and Sarah Todd for the various ways they contributed to this new edition. Finally, we are grateful to our agent and friend, Kate Hartson, for helping us bring this book to completion, and to our editor, Terry Adams, and our copyeditor, Karen Landry, at Little, Brown and Company, who showed such care and discretion in editing the manuscript.

Bibliography

Allen, Durward L. *Wolves of Minong: Isle Royale's Wild Community*. Ann Arbor: University of Michigan Press, 1994.

Aloff, Brenda. *Canine Body Language: A Photographic Guide*. Wenatchee, WA: Dogwise Publishing, 2005.

American Kennel Club. *The Complete Dog Book: 20th Edition*. New York: Ballantine Books, 2006.

Aslett, Don. *Pet Clean-up Made Easy*. Pocatello, ID: Marsh Creek Press, 2005.

Bauman, Diane L. *Beyond Basic Dog Training*. New York: Howell Book House, 2003.

Beck, Alan, and Aaron Katcher. *Between Pets and People: The Importance of Animal Companionship*. West Lafayette, IN: Purdue University Press, 1996.

Benjamin, Carol Lea. *Dog Problems*. New York: Howell Book House, 1989.

———. *Mother Knows Best: The Natural Way to Train Your Dog*. New York: Howell Book House, 1985.

Bergman, Göran. *Why Does Your Dog Do That?* New York: Howell Book House, 1971.

Budiansky, Stephen. *The Truth About Dogs*. New York: Penguin, 2000.

Burnham, Patricia Gail. *Playtraining Your Dog*. New York: St. Martin's Press, 1980.

Buytendijk, F. J. J. *The Mind of the Dog*. New York: Arno Press, 1973.

Campbell, William E. *Behavior Problems in Dogs* (3rd rev. ed.). Wenatchee, WA: Dogwise Publishing, 1999.

Coppinger, Raymond, and Lorna Coppinger. *Dogs: A New Understanding of Canine Origin, Behavior, and Evolution*. Chicago: University of Chicago Press, 2002.

Coren, Stanley. *The Intelligence of Dogs: A Guide to the Thoughts, Emotions, and Inner Lives of Our Canine Companions*. New York: Free Press, 2005.

Cree, John. *Training the German Shepherd Dog* (3rd ed.). Ramsbury, UK: Crowood Press, 2003.

Deeley, Martin. *Working Gundogs: An Introduction to Training and Handling*. Ramsbury, UK: Crowood Press, 2009.

Dodman, Nicholas. *Dogs Behaving Badly: An A-to-Z Guide to Understanding and Curing Behavioral Problems in Dogs*. New York: Bantam, 2000.

Dunbar, Ian. *Before and After Getting Your Puppy.* Novato, CA: New World Library, 2004.

——. *Dog Behavior: An Owner's Guide to a Happy Healthy Pet.* New York: Howell Book House, 1996.

Evans, Job Michael. *The Evans Guide for Counseling Dog Owners.* New York: Howell Book House, 1985.

Fiennes, Richard, and Alice Fiennes. *The Natural History of Dogs.* New York: Bonanza Books, 1968.

Fox, Michael W. *Integrative Development of Brain and Behavior in the Dog.* Chicago: University of Chicago Press, 1971.

——. *The Soul of the Wolf: A Meditation on Wolves and Man.* Springfield, NJ: Burford Books, 1997.

——. *Understanding Your Dog.* New York: Bantam, 1980.

George, Jean Craighead, and Sue Truesdell. *How to Talk to Your Dog.* New York: HarperCollins, 2003.

Hart, Benjamin L., and Lynette A. Hart. *The Perfect Puppy: How to Choose Your Dog by Its Behavior.* New York: W. H. Freeman, 1988.

Hearne, Vicki. *Adam's Task: Calling Animals by Name.* New York: Skyhorse Publishing, 2007.

Holst, Phyllis. *Canine Reproduction: The Breeder's Guide* (2nd ed.). Loveland, CO: Alpine Publications, 1999.

Kilcommons, Brian, and Sarah Wilson. *My Smart Puppy: Fun, Effective, and Easy Puppy Training.* New York: Grand Central Publishing, 2006.

——. *Paws to Consider: Choosing the Right Dog for You and Your Family.* New York: Grand Central Publishing, 1999.

Lopez, Barry Holstun. *Of Wolves and Men.* New York: Charles Scribner's Sons, 1978.

Lorenz, Konrad. *Man Meets Dog.* New York: Routledge, 2002.

McSoley, Ray. *Dog Tales.* New York: Warner Books, 1988.

Mech, L. David. *The Wolf: The Ecology and Behavior of an Endangered Species.* Garden City, NY: Doubleday, 1970.

Mech, L. David, and Luigi Boitani, eds. *Wolves: Behavior, Ecology, and Conservation.* Chicago: University of Chicago Press, 2007.

Millan, Cesar, with Melissa Jo Peltier. *How to Raise the Perfect Dog: Through Puppyhood and Beyond.* New York: Harmony Books, 2009.

Monks of New Skete. *Divine Canine: The Monks' Way to a Happy, Obedient Dog.* New York: Hyperion, 2007.

——. *Dogs & Devotion.* New York: Hyperion, 2009.

——. *How to Be Your Dog's Best Friend* (2nd rev. and upd. ed.). New York: Little, Brown, 2002.

——. *I & Dog.* New York: Yorkville Press, 2003.

Mueller, Scott. *Mueller's Essential Guide to Puppy Development: Teaching Puppy Preschool Classes.* Columbus, OH: Bridgestone Publishing, 2010.

Pfaffenberger, Clarence. *The New Knowledge of Dog Behavior.* Wenatchee, WA: Dogwise Publishing, 2001.

Pinkwater, Jill, and Daniel Pinkwater. *Superpuppy: How to Choose, Raise, and Train the Best Possible Dog for You* (rev. ed.). San Anselmo, CA: Sandpiper Press, 2002.

Randolph, Elizabeth. *How to Help Your Puppy Grow Up to Be a Wonderful Dog.* New York: Fawcett Books, 1995.

Rice, Dan. *The Complete Book of Dog Breeding.* New York: Barron's Educational Series, 1996.

Riddle, Maxwell. *Dogs Through History.* Fairfax, VA: Denlinger's, 1987.

Rutherford, Clarice, and David H. Neil. *How to Raise a Puppy You Can Live With* (4th ed.). Loveland, CO: Alpine Publications, 2005.

Sautter, Frederic J., and John A. Glover. *Behavior, Development, and Training of the Dog.* New York: Arco, 1978.

Scott, John Paul. *Animal Behavior.* Chicago: University of Chicago Press, 1976.

——. *Early Experience and the Organization of Behavior.* New York: Brooks/Cole, 1968.

Scott, John Paul, and John L. Fuller. *Genetics and the Social Behavior of the Dog.* Chicago: University of Chicago Press, 1998.

Sendak, Maurice, and Matthew Margolis. *Some Swell Pup: Or Are You Sure You Want a Dog?* New York: Farrar, Straus and Giroux, 1976.

Siegal, Mordecai. *A Dog for the Kids.* Boston: Little, Brown, 1984.

Smith, M. L. *Eliminate on Command.* Port Washington, WI: Seaworthy Publications, 2003.

Tortora, Daniel F. *The Right Dog for You: Choosing a Breed That Matches Your Personality, Family, and Lifestyle.* New York: Fireside, 1983.

Trumler, Eberhard. *Understanding Your Dog.* London: Faber & Faber, 1973.

Tucker, Michael. *Dog Training Made Easy.* Slough, UK: Foulsham & Co., 1996.

Volhard, Jack, and Wendy Volhard. *The Canine Good Citizen.* New York: Howell Book House, 1997.

——. *The Complete Idiot's Guide to a Well-Trained Dog.* New York: Alpha Books, 1999.

Vollmer, Peter. *SuperPuppy: How to Raise the Best Dog You'll Ever Have!* Escondido, CA: SuperPuppy Press, 1992.

——. *SuperPuppy Goes to Puppy Class: How to Train the Best Dog You'll Ever Have!* Escondido, CA: SuperPuppy Press, 1992.

Walkowicz, Chris. *Choosing a Dog for Dummies.* New York: Wiley Publishing, 2001.

——. *The Perfect Match: A Dog Buyer's Guide.* New York: Howell Book House, 1996.

Index

About the Authors

The Monks of New Skete have lived as a community in Cambridge, New York, for more than three decades. They support themselves by breeding, raising, and training dogs at their monastery. Their widely praised books, including *How to Be Your Dog's Best Friend*, *The Art of Raising a Puppy*, and *Divine Canine*, have together sold more than 1.2 million copies. The Monks of New Skete are also the authors of *In the Spirit of Happiness: Spiritual Wisdom for Living*. For more information, visit www.newskete.com.